STARFINDER

Development Lead • Robert G. McCreary
Authors • John Compton, Jason Keeley, Robert G. McCreary,
    Owen K.C. Stephens, and James L. Sutter
Cover Artist • David Alvarez
Interior Artists • Victor Manuel Leza Moreno, Raph Lomotan,
    Alexander Nanitchkov, Mirco Paganessi, and Pixoloid Studios
    (Aleksandr Dochkin, Gaspar Gombos, David Metzger, Mark Molnar,
    and Ferenc Nothof)
Cartographer • Damien Mammoliti

Starfinder Creative Director • James L. Sutter
Starfinder Creative Design Director • Sarah E. Robinson
Starfinder Creative Lead • Robert G. McCreary
Starfinder Design Lead • Owen K.C. Stephens
Starfinder Developer • Jason Keeley
Starfinder Society Developer • Thurston Hillman

Pathfinder Creative Director • James Jacobs
Creative Design Director • Sarah E. Robinson
Executive Editor • James L. Sutter
Managing Developer • Adam Daigle
Development Coordinator • Amanda Hamon Kunz
Senior Developer • Robert G. McCreary
Organized Play Lead Developer • John Compton
Developers • Crystal Frasier, Mark Moreland, Joe Pasini,
    Owen K.C. Stephens, and Linda Zayas-Palmer
Managing Editor • Judy Bauer
Senior Editor • Christopher Carey
Editors • Jason Keeley, Lyz Liddell, Elisa Mader, Adrian Ng, and
    Lacy Pellazar
Lead Designer • Jason Bulmahn
Senior Designer • Stephen Radney-MacFarland
Designers • Logan Bonner and Mark Seifter
Art Director • Sonja Morris
Senior Graphic Designers • Emily Crowell and Adam Vick
Organized Play Coordinator • Tonya Woldridge

Publisher • Erik Mona
Paizo CEO • Lisa Stevens
Chief Operations Officer • Jeffrey Alvarez
Chief Financial Officer • John Parrish
Director of Sales • Pierce Watters
Sales Associate • Cosmo Eisele
Marketing Director • Jenny Bendel
Outreach Coordinator • Dan Tharp
Director of Licensing • Michael Kenway
Accountant • Christopher Caldwell
Data Entry Clerk • B. Scott Keim
Chief Technical Officer • Vic Wertz
Director of Technology • Dean Ludwig
Senior Software Developer • Gary Teter
Community & Digital Content Director • Chris Lambertz
Webstore Coordinator • Rick Kunz

Customer Service Team • Sharaya Copas, Katina Davis, Sara Marie,
    and Diego Valdez
Warehouse Team • Laura Wilkes Carey, Will Chase, Mika Hawkins,
    Heather Payne, Jeff Strand, and Kevin Underwood
Website Team • Lissa Guillet and Erik Keith

ON THE COVER

The jungles of Castrovel are full of menaces, from carnivorous plants and hungry beasts to more civilized threats such as the Devourer cult leader Tahomen, depicted here by artist David Alvarez.

TEMPLE OF THE TWELVE   2
by John Compton

CASTROVEL   36
by John Compton and James L. Sutter

THE CULT OF THE DEVOURER   46
by Owen K.C. Stephens

ALIEN ARCHIVES   54
by John Compton, Jason Keeley, and Robert G. McCreary

CODEX OF WORLDS: RATHEREN   62
by Jason Keeley

STARSHIP: THAUMTECH CAIRNCARVER   INSIDE COVERS
by John Compton

This book refers to several other Starfinder products, yet these additional supplements are not required to make use of this book. Readers interested in references to Starfinder hardcovers can find the complete rules of these books available online for free at **paizo.com/sfrd**.

paizo®

Paizo Inc.
7120 185th Ave NE, Ste 120
Redmond, WA 98052-0577
paizo.com

TEMPLE OF THE TWELVE

PART 1: QUESTIONS IN QABARAT 3

To understand the strange technology they found on the Drift Rock, the heroes travel to Castrovel, where one of its finest universities holds clues to an ancient and forgotten society—one that identified an advanced alien civilization millennia ago.

PART 2: THE UKULAM EXPEDITION 14

The party sets off across the wild continent of Ukulam in search of ancient elven ruins that may hold the key to the Drift Rock's mysteries. But they must also intercept cultists of the Devourer who have kidnapped the leading expert on the ruins.

PART 3: THE LOST TEMPLE 27

The Cult of the Devourer has broken into an ancient elven temple and stolen its secrets, so the heroes must uncover the lost mysteries for themselves and confront the cult to avert a greater disaster.

ADVANCEMENT TRACK

"Temple of the Twelve" is designed for four characters.

 The PCs begin this adventure at 3rd level.

 The PCs should be 4th level before reaching the Stargazer.

 The PCs should be 5th level by the end of the adventure.

ADVENTURE BACKGROUND

Each of the three major species inhabiting the planet Castrovel has historically laid claim to one of the world's four great continents: the telepathic lashuntas govern Asana, the chitinous formians inhabit the Colonies, and the gate-building elves rule Sovyrian. But Castrovel's fourth continent, Ukulam, has never fallen under the control of any one species for long. Millennia ago, the three great powers came to an informal agreement that Ukulam would belong to none of them. Even during the long-running conflicts between the lashunta city-states and the formians' Everlasting Queendoms, Ukulam has remained largely untamed—honored as a nature preserve dedicated to the planet's beauty.

Despite Ukulam's neutral and unsettled past, dozens of exceptions exist in which a company, city-state, or other entrepreneurial spirit founded a small outpost along a coastline. Only a handful of these remain occupied today, serving as refueling stations, scientific observatories, and small joint military bases. Tales of the ancient societies that may have once ruled Ukulam are more grandiose than aerial surveys have ever confirmed, yet at least one expedition into the continent's wild interior claimed to have discovered a complex culture dedicated to the stars.

Thousands of years ago, while many of their kin emigrated from Sovyrian to settle on Golarion, a smaller group of elves traveled to Ukulam in pursuit of the astronomical wonders visible only from Castrovel's northern hemisphere. The lowland jungles provided the elves ample food and shelter, and there they founded a settlement called Loskialua, but the high mountains of Ukulam's interior provided the most unobstructed view of the sky. Upon the highest summits the elves constructed their greatest observatories, storing their accumulated knowledge in a grand temple complex perched on the slopes of the mighty Alhuenar Spire, one of the tallest peaks in the Singing Range. These elven scholar-priests made extraordinary breakthroughs in astronomy, even capturing eons-old messages echoing from across the galaxy and communing with cosmic demigods.

The elves' greatest obsession, though, was a perfectly circular array of 12 stars that seemed to be more than a random constellation. In fact, they had discovered the megastructure known as the Gate of Twelve Suns, the stellar gateway to the demiplane where the ancient kishalee hid the sivv superweapon called the Stellar Degenerator. So intent were the elves on unlocking this mystery that they patterned their settlement's most prominent structure after these stars and their surrounding constellations, naming it the Temple of the Twelve. The temple complex thrived for several centuries before its sudden abandonment—a mystery

to this day—when the residents built a new magical portal called an *aiudara* (or "elf gate") and departed for another solar system they had discovered.

Within a few lifetimes, the Temple of the Twelve and its eccentric inhabitants, now known to archaeologists as the Oatia culture, had largely faded from popular memory, and the site gradually fell to ruin. It resurfaced only a few decades after the Gap, when a human explorer named Halkueem Zan violated local travel bans to investigate a buried site his scanners had identified from space. When Zan emerged from Ukulam's jungles months later, lashunta authorities arrested him and confiscated his findings, though he retained enough notes to publish a sensationalist travelogue titled "Pyramid People of Ukulam" after he was released weeks later. Precious few have followed up on this work, not only because it was overshadowed by early contact with the Veskarium, but also because of Castrovel's limits on travel to Ukulam. Of late, the kasatha scholar Olmehya Solstarni has dedicated herself to retracing Zan's footsteps, and she has thoroughly annotated and digitized his original findings in preparation for a new expedition to the temple.

Unfortunately, the Cult of the Devourer believes that clues found on the so-called Drift Rock, which recently emerged at Absalom Station, point to the existence of some ancient superweapon that the cult could turn against the Pact Worlds and beyond. The leader of a cult cell on Castrovel, a lashunta mystic named Tahomen, has already connected the clues to Halkueem Zan's findings and arranged the abduction of Dr. Solstarni. With the captive kasatha as its guide, the Cult of the Devourer has already begun its trek to the Temple of the Twelve.

PART 1: QUESTIONS IN QABARAT

By the conclusion of "Incident at Absalom Station," the PCs should have explored the contested Drift Rock in service of the Eoxian ambassador Gevalarsk Nor, learned how the *Acreon's* crew perished fighting akatas, and secured a fully functional ship, the *Sunrise Maiden*, to call their own. They are also likely in possession of Ambassador Nor's package from the *Acreon*, and they may well have discovered that his "cargo" is actually a Corpse Fleet officer named Hebiza Eskolar. In addition, the observer bot that Nor sent with the PCs has transmitted their findings, and the ambassador has made the feed public (after editing it to hide any evidence of Commander Eskolar) to all of Absalom Station. As a result, the station is abuzz with the news of the Drift Rock's ancient origins, and opportunists are already maneuvering to find some way to profit off the discovery.

TEMPLE OF THE TWELVE

PART 1: QUESTIONS IN QABARAT

PART 2: THE UKULAM EXPEDITION

PART 3: THE LOST TEMPLE

CASTROVEL

THE CULT OF THE DEVOURER

ALIEN ARCHIVES

CODEX OF WORLDS

HOSTILE WITNESSES (CR 4)

The adventure begins with the PCs leaving the Drift Rock in their new ship, the *Sunrise Maiden*, to return to Absalom Station. Unfortunately, another ship is lying in wait for them, ready to attack the PCs as soon as they are clear of the asteroid.

Starship Combat: The attacking ship is a scout from the Corpse Fleet, the renegade armada of Eoxian starships that Eox has officially severed ties to (though many suspect that the bone sages still call upon the fleet to perform clandestine and politically insensitive military operations). The Corpse Fleet wishes to keep any knowledge of the *Acreon*'s special "cargo"—Commander Eskolar—a secret, and it has entrusted the task of eliminating any witnesses to the capable crew of the *Iron Rictus*, a Thaumtech Cairncarver.

Shortly after the PCs take off from the Drift Rock, the *Iron Rictus* closes in for combat. The ship's stat block is printed on the inside front cover of this volume. If the PCs already sent Commander Eskolar to Absalom Station (such as on the shuttle *Hippocampus*), the *Iron Rictus* simply tries to destroy the PCs and their ship. If the *Iron Rictus*'s crew believes the PCs have Eskolar aboard the *Sunrise Maiden*, the Corpse Fleet ship aims to disable the PCs' ship, demand the release of the *Acreon*'s "cargo," and then destroy the PCs. If pressed, the *Iron Rictus* seeks to destroy the *Sunrise Maiden* even if Eskolar is on board, knowing that the bone trooper can survive the vacuum of space long enough to be extracted from the wreckage.

When the PCs first boarded the *Sunrise Maiden*, they should have selected crew roles, as described on page 316 of the *Starfinder Core Rulebook*; if not, have them select those roles now. The *Sunrise Maiden*'s statistics appear on the inside front cover of *Starfinder Adventure Path #1*; the only adjustments the PCs need make to the statistics at this time are adjusting the ship's Armor Class and Target Lock based on the chosen pilot's Piloting skill ranks.

This encounter uses the starship combat rules in the *Starfinder Core Rulebook*. A PC can identify the make and model of the *Iron Rictus* with a successful DC 13 Engineering check to identify technology. A PC who succeeds at a DC 15 Culture check recognizes the ship's affiliation with the Corpse Fleet and recalls that the Corpse Fleet is outlawed in the Pact Worlds.

IRON RICTUS	TIER 2

Corpse Fleet Cairncarver (see the inside covers)
HP 40

Development: If the PCs win the starship battle, they can resume their return trip to Absalom Station. The crew of the *Iron Rictus* is trained to keep a low profile while in Pact Worlds space. If the *Iron Rictus* is disabled or destroyed, its elebrian crew activates data safeguards that wipe the ship's computer of any data in short order before destroying themselves to avoid capture. The *Iron Rictus* carries no other evidence of its crew's intentions.

If the *Iron Rictus* disables the PCs' ship, the Corpse Fleet vessel flies past the *Sunrise Maiden* and fires its light particle beam one more time for good measure—unlikely to fully destroy the starship, though it does increase the repair bill. At that point, other starships begin closing in on the scene, and the *Iron Rictus* beats a quick retreat to avoid tangling with bystanders. A ysoki wrecker ship hails the *Sunrise Maiden* shortly afterward, offering to tow the ship back to Absalom Station for the low price of 200 credits.

Story Award: If the PCs successfully defeat the *Iron Rictus*, award them 1,200 XP for the encounter.

RETURN TO ABSALOM STATION

When the PCs arrive back at Absalom Station, they find their fame has preceded them—their images have appeared on countless video screens thanks to Gevalarsk Nor's broadcast, and the PCs find that they have become minor local celebrities—at least while the buzz lasts. Their newfound popularity earns them priority docking from Absalom Traffic Control and temporarily waived docking fees. Once the PCs disembark, a small crowd of onlookers and reporters quickly tracks them down, asking for statements, autographs, and confirmation of conspiracy theories. Partaking in a few short photo opportunities and drinks on the house is fairly harmless, though using the media attention as a platform to make any inflammatory accusations could make enemies of any number of power brokers and gangs on Absalom Station. In any event, the PCs should probably meet with those on Absalom Station responsible for their most recent adventure: Chiskisk and Ambassador Gevalarsk Nor.

THE AMBASSADOR AND THE OFFICER

As the person who hired the PCs to explore the *Acreon* and the Drift Rock, Ambassador **Gevalarsk Nor** (LE male elebrian necrovite) is eager to meet with them, though his disposition depends on what the PCs have done with his "cargo." Once back on Absalom Station, the PCs have only a short window in which to contact someone regarding Commander Eskolar, should they wish to do so. If the PCs notify the Stewards, station security, or another legal authority, a squad of security personnel meets the PCs when they dock to confirm the nature of their captive, take her into custody, take the PCs' statements, and record their contact information. Due to the nature of the prisoner, the security officers request that the PCs avoid publicizing their discovery and allow the Stewards to handle the matter to avoid political fallout. Commander Eskolar goes quietly, though she once more claims diplomatic standing and demands legal representation while being escorted away.

If the PCs contact Ambassador Nor instead, he acknowledges their update and sends a team to quietly convey the *Acreon*'s "cargo" to a safe location; alternatively, the PCs can bring Eskolar to him directly. If the PCs sent Commander Eskolar back to Absalom Station separately, such as on the *Hippocampus*, Nor's agents have already recovered her. Whichever decision the PCs make will have repercussions later in the Adventure Path, so note their actions.

When the PCs meet with Ambassador Nor, he congratulates them on the success of their mission. Even though he recorded the PCs' activities on the *Acreon* and the Drift Rock, Nor would still like to hear the PCs' report firsthand. If the PCs successfully delivered Commander Eskolar to the Eoxian embassy, Nor thanks them and upholds his end of the bargain, paying each of the PCs 500 credits as payment for the task. He adeptly deflects any questions about Eskolar and his interest in the commander, and he absolutely denies any connection, official or unofficial, with the Corpse Fleet. If pressed, the ambassador suggests that securing a renegade officer is an act of interplanetary safety, not some indication that he is in league with the Corpse Fleet.

Nor has a keen mind and can quickly help piece together any of the clues that the PCs unearthed on the Drift Rock but failed to interpret. Most importantly, he can decipher the complex alien computer code the PCs found in the Drift Rock's ancient control room (see page 35 of "Incident at Absalom Station"), allowing the PCs to identify the approximate age of the technology, interpret some of the phrases, and recognize that the Drift Rock represents only a fragment of a much larger structure. The ambassador does not recognize the alien language, however. Nor also suspects that any device that large might have incredible destructive potential; he does not share these suspicions with the PCs, but he does convey that information to his Eoxian contacts after the PCs depart.

If the PCs did not deliver Commander Eskolar, or if they handed her over to the authorities, Ambassador Nor's reception is considerably cooler. He still wants to hear their report, but he does not provide the additional payment to the PCs or offer his help deciphering the secrets of the Drift Rock. He briskly informs the PCs that their business is now concluded and ends the meeting. His displeasure is almost palpable.

Development: Since the PCs were hired to investigate the *Acreon* and Drift Rock as part of Ambassador Nor's mediation between the Hardscrabble Collective and Astral Extractions, they may well be interested in the results of the ambassador's arbitration. In truth, this factional dispute has no bearing on the rest of the campaign—the PCs will soon discover they have more pressing and more dangerous concerns! As a result, it's up to you how the dispute is resolved and when. Neither Astral Extractions nor the Hardscrabble Collective has a role to play in the rest of the Adventure Path.

Story Award: If the PCs deliver Commander Eskolar to Ambassador Nor as agreed, award them 400 XP for completing the job. If they capture Eskolar and turn her over to security, award them 800 XP instead. These rewards are the same as those listed on page 26 of "Incident

at Absalom Station." The PCs can earn this award only once; if they already received experience for dealing with Commander Eskolar in the previous adventure, do not award them XP a second time.

THE STARFINDER SOCIETY

Within the Starfinder Society, **Chiskisk** (N host shirren) is likely the PCs' preferred contact, especially the more they learn about Gevalarsk Nor's relationship (however tenuous) with the Corpse Fleet. Even if the PCs don't contact the shirren, Chiskisk approaches them within an hour of their return to the station, keen to hear what their explorations revealed.

The shirren can telepathically provide the PCs with much of the same information as Nor could above, though they don't have any sense of the immense device's purpose. The nature of the device puzzles Chiskisk, and they encourage the PCs to find out more. After all, this is an excellent opportunity to uncover an extraordinary secret, and the answer might both earn the PCs fame as explorers and unlock hitherto undiscovered technologies that could better the Pact Worlds. What's more, Chiskisk has access to the Starfinder Society's detailed databases, which the shirren uses to search for any prior appearances of the language displayed on the Drift Rock's displays. As the search concludes, Chiskisk energetically scans over the findings, bobbing their head appreciatively at first before their antennae droop dejectedly and they explain their findings.

"There is some good news. The Starfinder Society's linguistic database recognized many of the symbols you found on the Drift Rock, because this is not the first time they've appeared post-Gap. The bad news is that the source is... highly unreliable," Chiskisk notes, as segments of their chitinous body scrape together in agitation. "All that we have about these earlier texts comes from Halkueem Zan nearly three centuries ago, and it seems that no published studies of those texts have appeared since. According to these records, Zan's original findings were donated to the Qabarat University of Xenoarchaeology and Xenoanthropology on Castrovel shortly after his—" The shirren pauses while contemplating how best to phrase the sentence. "—disruptive expeditions.

"Fortunately, the Society has numerous alumni from that university, and I can readily secure you a contact there and forward my personal recommendation to a few faculty members. Perhaps they can show you Zan's notes and even take you to the original site so that you can search for more clues about whatever this Drift Rock once was."

The PCs probably have questions. The following are likely inquiries and Chiskisk's telepathic responses.

Who was Halkueem Zan? "As you know, the Starfinder Society is an organization dedicated to uncovering the secrets of the universe and its past. As in any pursuit, a sensational hero can attract new recruits, and a buffoon can tarnish the

TEMPLE OF THE TWELVE

PART 1: QUESTIONS IN QABARAT

PART 2: THE UKULAM EXPEDITION

PART 3: THE LOST TEMPLE

CASTROVEL

THE CULT OF THE DEVOURER

ALIEN ARCHIVES

CODEX OF WORLDS

whole field. Halkueem Zan was both. He traveled throughout the Pact Worlds making a name for himself as an explorer and archaeologist, but his techniques were utter rubbish. He was a looter with a good press agent, and he published lurid gibberish like 'Pyramid People of Ukulam.' His articles were popular with the public, but for every diligent explorer they inspired, another two were unscrupulous treasure hunters who just wanted to blow things up and call it archaeology."

Was Halkueem Zan a Starfinder? Chiskisk shudders visibly. "No. Zan did most of his work at about the same time the Starfinder Society formed, but I don't believe he was ever associated with us."

What trouble did Halkueem Zan experience on Castrovel? "Different planets have different regulations for explorers. Zan wanted to explore a site on the restricted continent of Ukulam, but when the authorities denied him passage, he went anyway. I believe they confiscated most of his findings, and the whole incident spurred a decade of restrictions on offworld explorers."

What's the university known for? "The Qabarat University of Xenoarchaeology and Xenoanthropology is one of the foremost institutions of higher learning for explorers and galactic ethnographers in the Pact Worlds. In addition to training many great archaeologists, the university maintains a staggering archive of artifacts, recordings, and other findings from throughout the system."

Who are we meeting there? The shirren taps a few keys. "There is a postdoctoral student named Whaloss who has worked with the Society in the past. I'll ask him to greet you when you land in Qabarat."

Chiskisk believes this is a strong lead, and because the PCs have so far been at the forefront of this investigation, the shirren believes it's only proper that they have the right of first refusal to visit the university and learn more. In fact, they would rather the PCs do so, as thanks to the broadcast of the Drift Rock exploration, it's only a matter of time before someone else beats the Society to the prize. If the PCs are uninterested, Chiskisk might try to incentivize them by reminding them of the fame and fortune that can accompany a major find like this. As a last resort, they might offer the PCs 1,000 credits as a stipend for tracking down Zan's old site.

The shirren also sends them a digital copy of "Pyramid People of Ukulam," which is a tawdry travelogue that lauds the author's bravery as much as it describes the culture that built the sites using ample nonacademic language such as "exotic," "savages," and "time immemorial."

Development: If any of the PCs declined to join the Starfinder Society in the previous adventure, give them the opportunity to do so now—their recent investigation of the

Acreon and the Drift Rock is more than enough experience to warrant membership in the Society.

IN SEARCH OF LOST RECORDS

The adventure assumes that the PCs travel to Castrovel aboard their new starship, the *Sunrise Maiden*. Beyond dealing with a few fans of the PCs' recent celebrity on the way to the spaceport, their voyage is speedy and largely uneventful. The journey itself takes 1d6 days using Drift travel.

Castrovel is a vibrant planet of sparkling blue oceans, continents blanketed in vividly green forests, and swirls of clouds. As the *Sunrise Maiden* enters the atmosphere near Qabarat, the city-state's aviation authorities hail the starship, ask for identification, and direct them to one of the landing pads at the city's spaceport, Ship's End. As a matter of course, a guard and a customs official briefly interview the PCs about their business in Qabarat, whether they have local contacts, the expected duration of their stay, and whether they are importing any foreign life-forms—at worst, a PC might be required to endure a short disinfection procedure or register a pet. Carrying personal weapons is not illegal in Qabarat, merely frowned upon. After the customs process, the officers issue the PCs travel papers to keep with them for the duration of their stay.

UNIVERSITY INVESTIGATIONS

The PCs' Castrovelian contact, **Whaloss** (NG male damaya lashunta) is waiting to meet them just outside the spaceport. Even for a damaya, he is tall and thin, almost to the point of seeming gaunt. His clothing is a stylish blend of local silks, though the overall ensemble shows considerable wear, as though he has relied on this nicer outfit for formal meetings for many years. Nonetheless, he positively beams with antennae-twitching excitement to meet the PCs and show them around Qabarat. As an advanced student of xenoarchaeology, he has collaborated with members of the Starfinder Society before and he's eager to hear about the PCs' recent findings.

Meanwhile, Whaloss hails a robo-taxi to carry the group into the heart of Qabarat and to the university. As the taxi wends its way deeper into the city, trees give way to elegant towers of carbon fiber, glass, and steel, each artistically sculpted to create a stunning forest of dazzling skyscrapers. The Qabarat University of Xenoarchaeology and Xenoanthropology is just north of the downtown commercial district and consists of about 10 buildings scattered over a campus of groomed lawns and gardens.

Whaloss does not have the background to decipher the Drift Rock's writing and technology, but he offers to introduce the PCs to Professor Muhali, the head of the linguistic anthropology department. Her office is in the Alsima-Karei Hall, an eight-story building whose lobby is currently home

WHALOSS

to a small pack of journalists insistently trying to convince a receptionist to let them upstairs. Whaloss is unfamiliar with any news that would warrant this level of attention, and if the PCs inquire, a journalist can convey that Dr. Ailabiens 21:2 gave an incendiary lecture that some interpreted as a defense of violent xenophobia; the media is here primarily to secure interviews and comments from ranking academic staff.

Creatures: The receptionist, **Ikimsi** (LN male korasha lashunta), is out of his element dealing with the media. It's all he can do to keep them at bay on the ground floor while paging for support from the university's publicist or deans. Lest the journalists try to piggyback on the PCs' access, Ikimsi is unwilling to let the Starfinders upstairs until he has control of the situation here. The PCs can peacefully wait for a dean to arrive and shepherd the media away, but they can also sweep in to Ikimsi's rescue by tricking the journalists, causing a scene, impersonating security staff, or even leveraging the PCs' recent celebrity by offering to give an interview about the Drift Rock in exchange for the media giving Ikimsi some space. A variety of skill checks might work here, with a base DC of 18 that might be as much as 5 higher or lower depending on the PCs' strategy. Most approaches should require succeeding at a minimum of two different checks, such as a Disguise check to impersonate a university official and an Intimidate check to scare off the media.

Development: Once the journalists are no longer clamoring to get upstairs, Ikimsi is amenable to hearing why the PCs would like to meet with various professors upstairs. He notes that Professor Muhali is currently very busy, but if the PCs helped him deal with the media, Ikimsi rearranges the professor's schedule for the day and creates an official appointment for them; this grants the PCs a +2 circumstance bonus to Bluff and Diplomacy checks to influence Professor Muhali. Ikimsi or Whaloss can lead the PCs to Muhali's office on the fifth floor.

In the event the PCs attempt to force their way upstairs or perform acts of violence, Ikimsi frantically rings for campus security. These guards escort the PCs off campus. The PCs can visit again the next day, though they take a −2 penalty to checks to influence university students and faculty.

Story Award: If the PCs help Ikimsi deal with the journalists and get an appointment with Professor Muhali, award them 600 XP.

PROFESSOR MUHALI'S OFFICE

As the head of the linguistic anthropology department, Professor Muhali has one of the nicer offices in Alsima-Karei Hall. Her door is unlocked, and she willingly accepts visitors introduced by Whaloss or announced by Ikimsi. Read or paraphrase the following when the PCs enter.

This office is clean, roomy, and orderly. A large desk stands imposingly before a broad window that offers a charming view of a nearby park, and a small table in one corner has a quartet of chairs arranged evenly around it. Near the door is a wide examination table covered with broken fragments of stone, many of which bear incomplete words or letters written in a spiraling text. Several tiny fountains throughout the room burble soothingly and shimmer with soft light.

Creature: Professor **Muhali** (LN female damaya lashunta) is fairly stern, having wrestled with offworld authorities to secure excavation permits, cut through red tape, and debunk fraudulent ideas vigorously defended by stubborn fools. She is dark-skinned for a lashunta, with pale green facial markings and purple hair cut in an asymmetrical style. Muhali has spent the past several hours corresponding with colleagues and devising ways in which to resolve the scandal Ailabiens 21:2 started. With the media and university deans breathing down her neck over the incident, Muhali is largely uninterested in working on anything else, even as a favor to the Starfinder Society. She answers some questions—ideally to assuage the PCs' curiosity and convince them to either help her or leave.

Why are there so many journalists around? "One of my colleagues, Ailabiens 21:2, gave a rather incendiary public lecture last night in which he examined a war from nearly a millennium ago and used the cultural fallout from it to rationalize the genocide of the formian species. Even before the lashunta city-states and formian Colonies signed peace accords thirty years ago, such brutal conclusions would have been dismissed. Now he is fomenting hate crimes under the guise of 'pure logic' and anthropology. This is not what the

MUHALI

TEMPLE OF THE TWELVE

PART 1: QUESTIONS IN QABARAT

PART 2: THE UKULAM EXPEDITION

PART 3: THE LOST TEMPLE

CASTROVEL

THE CULT OF THE DEVOURER

ALIEN ARCHIVES

CODEX OF WORLDS

university stands for, but it's what the public now believes. I've placed him on academic leave and restricted his access to university resources until we can clean this up."

Can you help us decipher this Drift Rock writing? "I'm not in any position to assist you or instruct my department to assist you—not until I can resolve the current debacle."

What can you tell us about Halkueem Zan's expedition? "I have neither the time nor the inclination to discuss that showboating amateur's exploits. However, my colleague Doctor Olmehya Solstarni has a strong interest in the ruins of Ukulam." Muhali examines a screen and scrolls through several pages. "According to my records, though, she departed on personal leave two days ago." A PC who succeeds at a DC 15 Sense Motive check can determine that Professor Muhali is somewhat confused by this development. Muhali does not recall approving Dr. Solstarni's absence, which the PCs can convince Muhali to share with a successful DC 19 Diplomacy check. Even then, Muhali is not willing to let the PCs into Dr. Solstarni's locked office at this time.

How can we help? Professor Muhali sighs and delicately massages the bases of her antennae. "You're persistent. Maybe that could come in handy. What the university needs right now is to smooth this over quickly, and Ailabiens 21:2 is not listening to anything I say. He has not quite violated enough protocols to be dismissed; firing him would otherwise be good for optics. I think the media would settle for a public apology. If you can convince him to do that, I should be able to handle the rest."

Development: Professor Muhali is unwilling to assist the PCs unless they help her defuse the current scandal by convincing Ailabiens 21:2 to apologize. Whaloss or Ikimsi can take the PCs to his office and introduce them to the contemplative (see Ailabiens 21:2's Office below).

AILABIENS 21:2's OFFICE

Read or paraphrase the following when the PCs visit the contemplative Ailabiens 21:2.

Dust, debris, and discarded papers litter the floor of this disorganized office. A single chair stands in the corner, and the desk and shelves are crowded with books, scrolls, statuettes, and loose computer hardware.

Creature: The office of the academic **Ailabiens 21:2** (N male contemplative) is a model of disorganized chaos, containing a mishmash of texts and cultural artifacts from across the Pact Worlds and beyond. Because he flies using psychic powers, the contemplative is nonchalant about the filthy floor, which crunches noisily under visitors' feet. With little else to do with his time, Ailabiens 21:2 is willing to entertain visitors, communicating almost exclusively through telepathy while doing so. If necessary, you can use the statistics for a contemplative presented in *Starfinder: First Contact* or *Starfinder Alien Archive* for Ailabiens 21:2.

As is common practice among contemplatives, Ailabiens 21:2 abandoned his childhood name for one based on a favorite quote or intellectual hero—in his case, the second article published by the radically anticonventionalist scholar Ailabiens in the year 21 AG, which contains the famous line, "When the past is unknown, we must make a tradition of challenging so-called tradition." A PC who succeeds at a DC 18 Culture check can recognize the significance of the contemplative's name, and demonstrating this knowledge in conversation grants that PC a +2 circumstance bonus to skill checks to influence him.

Ailabiens 21:2 is an accomplished xenoanthropologist. Although his academic peers cannot doubt the contemplative's knowledge of the subject, his own publications tend to receive mixed reviews due to the utterly sanitary impartiality and lack of empathy with which he approaches his work and subjects. This extends to his interactions with his coworkers and students, whom he boorishly psychoanalyzes to their faces as though he were performing a favor. For his part, Ailabiens 21:2 boasts of his emotional detachment with hypocritical pride, claiming that his objectivity makes him a superior analyst.

Despite his uncouth demeanor, few have read as many articles and files as he has, and he commands an unrivaled mental catalog of the university's collections. He reviewed Halkueem Zan's confiscated notes a decade ago, dismissing it as drivel. Even so, that makes him one of the few who has personally read the explorer's notebooks, few of which are properly digitized. However, thanks to his punishment for his recent lecture, he is unable to help the PCs track down the documents. In the meantime, he can answer the PCs' questions, such as the likely ones below.

What can you tell us about Halkueem Zan's expedition? "I reviewed the entirety of Zan's original notes early in my time here as faculty, and to my considerable knowledge, only Doctor Solstarni has studied them more recently. Zan's methodology was imperfect, catering to an uneducated reader's lexicon, fetishizing the 'exotic,' and conveying a pathological love of his self-image as an adventurer—likely to earn money or as an elaborate mating ritual. As a result, his work is scientifically wanting and his conclusions doubtful. Nevertheless, his notes provide enough detail to hypothetically retrace his steps."

Can you get us Zan's notes? "Normally, I could, but I am currently on probation due to the weak-willed public's inability to process the logical arguments I posited in my recent lecture. Until I am reinstated, I cannot assist you."

How can you be reinstated? "Professor Muhali has suspended me, and barring the unlikely intervention by a dean, only she can undo this. Your convincing her to do so would allow me to help. If you also repair the damage she has dealt, you shall have my undivided attention."

How has she hurt you? "I am on track to attain tenure at this university in several more years—requiring practically

8

twice as long an observation period as a lashunta would, I might add, likely because my assessors are compensating for inferiorities, real or perceived. This incident reflects an egregious stain on my record that challenges my advancement and scholarly recognition here. She must agree to erase this insult from my file. I have spoken with her about the matter, and her judgment is clouded by stress and emotion. If she truly cared about scholarly integrity, she would debate my assertions. Instead she stoops to censorship in violation of the university's free speech principles."

Why was your lecture offensive? "Offense indicates a narrow perspective in the listeners. I analyzed ancient lashunta armies' strategies against their formian neighbors and concluded that the former's conditioned sentimentality inhibited more effectively destructive actions against their long-time enemies. The audience found my conclusion upsetting." Ailabiens 21:2 bobs thoughtfully before adding, "Other species are endlessly fascinating."

Ailabiens 21:2 is utterly confident that he has done no wrong. If a PC attempts to point out why he was offensive and wrong, the contemplative disarms most attacks by discrediting the PC on the grounds of being unfit to render such

AILABIENS 21:2

a conclusion or by stating that the argument is rationally flawed, even pointing out common foibles of the PC's species as support of his mental superiority. He may be convinced that upsetting others was wrong and that it was a bad career move, but he does not accept that his academic conclusions are invalid.

Despite his frustrating insensitivity, the contemplative finds the prospect of making an apology less degrading than enduring his academic suspension. He is willing to make this gesture in a convincing manner so long as the PCs can convince Professor Muhali to make three concessions: cancel Ailabiens 21:2's academic suspension, restore his access to the university's restricted collections, and pardon the whole incident in his tenure review file. Should the PCs take this offer to Muhali, she balks at the contemplative's final demand, but she grudgingly agrees to reinstate his status and library access in exchange for a public apology before the media. Professor Muhali accepts all three concessions if the PCs convince her to do so with a successful DC 19 Diplomacy check. Alternatively, the PCs can take Muhali's two concessions back to the contemplative and try to convince him that they secured him all three demands, which requires a successful DC 24 Bluff check. After all, he won't learn about the deception until his next review months from now.

Treasure: If the PCs convince Ailabiens 21:2 to apologize, Professor Muhali offers the PCs a *mk 1 ring of resistance* as a token of her appreciation; in fact, it's among the items that the contemplative requested in a grant application that fell through thanks to his recent gaffe. If the PCs managed to fulfill all three of the contemplative's requests, Ailabiens 21:2 also gives them his earnings from his recent guest lecture circuit (700 credits) in thanks. If the PCs meet both of these conditions, they earn both rewards.

Development: If the PCs fulfill two or more of his requests, Ailabiens 21:2 is willing to publicly apologize. With his library access restored, he can now assist the PCs. He swiftly checks out Halkueem Zan's original journals—a combination of image files in a long-obsolete format and physical notebooks that wouldn't require battery power during an extended expedition—and sets to converting and digitizing them. The process takes the contemplative approximately 8 hours, after which he can provide the PCs with a fairly complete copy of the reckless explorer's original account. However, Ailabiens 21:2 notes that there appear to be some gaps in the records, either because Zan had been negligent in documenting part of his journey or because someone else has removed some documents. Ailabiens 21:2 annotates the records as best he can in this short amount of time, identifying what he believes are the most relevant parts (see the Halkueem Zan's Notes sidebar on page 10). The PCs can access this digital record on a computer of any tier.

These files enable the PCs to retrace Zan's footsteps from centuries earlier. If the PCs acquire both these records and the notes left behind by Dr. Solstarni (see Dr. Solstarni's Office on page 10), the PCs receive a +2 circumstance bonus to Survival checks to navigate Ukulam's wilderness during Part 2 of this volume.

Once the PCs resolve the dispute between Professor Muhali and Ailabiens 21:2, Muhali agrees to examine the language records the PCs found on the Drift Rock. She soon recognizes them as belonging to a non-Elven language group found in association with the few known elven sites on the continent of Ukulam to the west.

Hoping to draw upon specialized knowledge of her colleague Dr. Solstarni, Muhali attempts to contact Solstarni in her office, at home, and through her personal comm unit. Even Muhali's attempts to contact the professor's friends and family turn up

TEMPLE OF THE TWELVE

PART 1:
QUESTIONS IN QABARAT

PART 2:
THE UKULAM EXPEDITION

PART 3:
THE LOST TEMPLE

CASTROVEL

THE CULT OF THE DEVOURER

ALIEN ARCHIVES

CODEX OF WORLDS

HALKUEEM ZAN'S NOTES

Collectively, Halkueem Zan's records provide a fragmented course that the PCs can follow from the coastal outpost of Turhalu Point on the continent of Ukulam inland to the "accursed pyramid city of Loskialua," which Zan claimed to have discovered. These records—both text and audiologs—contain several key warnings and landmarks described in Zan's judgmental verbiage.

Wildlife: "Castrovel crawls with vermin and beasts of all kinds. Thunder-bellied behemoths clear paths through the jungle while bellowing madly. More vexing, though, are what we've come to call stingbats—some hellish cross of monkey, bat, and scorpion that travel in troops and harass us regularly. I fought one off as it attacked a porter and shot another as it fled, and from then on they targeted me. It's as though they can sense strength, yet resent it."

The Rune Obelisk: "A dramatic spire barely rising above the tree line was the first of our great landmarks. Each side of it was once engraved with untold wisdom, but only the sheltered runes near the base have survived the ages. The plants here grow thicker, as if feeding upon some gifts left by the ancient elves—sacrifices of flesh and blood, no doubt."

The Plague Warden: "This massive stone figure is a reclining elven form covered in weathered boils. I suspect it is an effigy that served ritual purposes, such as absorbing the illness of some great king so he might live forever."

The Forsaken City: "The city in the foothills is a forest of small pyramids overgrown with vines. As with the funerary monuments of lost Osirion, it might be this was not a place of the living but a realm of the dead. Initial excavations uncovered multiple stone tiers of fine architecture—displaying skill truly more advanced than the builders' primitive contemporaries."

The Stairs to Eternity: "From the Forsaken City rises a staggering, weathered staircase carved into the mountain beyond, evoking mystical contemplation in all who would climb it. Beyond stands a great temple whose haunted guardians feasted upon my comrades, forcing us to flee the savage sentinels."

no results, making the lashunta concerned. She informs the PCs that she will report the missing Solstarni to the police, and she lends the PCs a spare key card to Dr. Solstarni's office, asking the PCs to investigate to see if there's any sign of where her colleague might be (see Doctor Solstarni's Office below).

Story Award: If the PCs convince Ailabiens 21:2 to make a public apology and they restore his academic status and library access, award them 600 XP.

Dr. Solstarni's Office

The door to Dr. Solstarni's fourth-floor office is made of a heavy wood composite and is locked electronically (hardness 5, HP 15, break DC 18, Engineering DC 20 to disable). Professor Muhali's key card unlocks the door, and if the PCs have resolved her concerns with Ailabiens 21:2, Muhali accompanies them here.

This office is in disarray, with cabinet doors ajar, several stone artifacts scattered across the floor from open archival drawers, and a traveling bag open and half-packed. The computer on the desk at the far end of the room is dark, but a diode at its base blinks regularly.

Dr. Olmehya Solstarni is an archaeologist specializing in archaeoastronomic validation: the study of how ancient cultures viewed the cosmos and expressed those observations in their architecture, artifacts, and writings. Her office contains an assortment of outdated astronomy tools from sundry planets. This disarray is not typical for the kasatha, as Professor Muhali can relay, and even at a casual glance, it appears that someone was packing quickly and erratically—perhaps even ransacking the room. Suspecting criminal activity, Muhali excuses herself to contact local police to file a missing persons report, but she encourages the PCs to investigate to see what clues they can uncover.

There are three main areas the PCs can investigate to find clues: the university's security cameras, Dr. Solstarni's computer, and Solstarni's office, which contains several physical clues. These three areas of investigation are detailed below.

Cameras: The building has security cameras in its hallways and at the entrances, but there aren't any inside individual offices and classrooms. The receptionist Ikimsi can review the video logs to see that a trio of korasha lashuntas carrying heavy backpacks and wearing uniforms entered the building 2 days ago in the late evening—after all reception personnel had left. They then took the stairs up, but there seems to be no footage of them on other floors or even leaving the building. A PC who succeeds at a DC 13 Culture check can identify the uniforms as those of the Gateway District's Port Authority. With a successful DC 17 Computers or Perception check, a PC can note that there are inconsistencies in the footage on several floors (including the fourth floor, where Dr. Solstarni's office is), suggesting that someone hacked into the building's security cameras and looped footage of empty hallways to hide whatever they were doing.

If the PCs fail the Culture check, the Qabarat detective can make the Port Authority connection at a later time (see Development below).

Computer: Dr. Solstarni's computer is in sleep mode, but interacting with its controls brings up her log-in screen. The computer is tier 2 (DC 21 Computers check to hack) with a 1-hour lockout countermeasure. If a PC successfully hacks into the computer, he can review the computer's recent functions and Dr. Solstarni's correspondence. Her personal calendar notes that she is scheduled for a research sabbatical in approximately 2 months, as approved by her department head, Muhali, and the authorities in Turhalu Point on the east coast of Ukulam. However, one of the recent files on the computer is a letter from Professor Muhali granting Dr. Solstarni leave to depart 2 months early to take advantage of special conditions in the field, signed 2 days ago. Muhali has no recollection of submitting this letter, and a PC who succeeds at a DC 19 Computers check can determine that it's a forged document generated by an off-site computer that spoofed Muhali's identity.

The PCs can also find a series of 15 messages exchanged between Dr. Solstarni and a person named Dr. Eyrub Paqual regarding Solstarni's research into the ancient elven settlements of Ukulam. The exchanges begin fairly cordially as Paqual and Solstarni discussed minor details of interest from the minimal research published about these sites. As the discussion continued, however, Paqual grew more insistent and attempted to cajole the kasatha to meet with him at a cafe called the Five Arches in Qabarat's Gateway District 2 days ago to appraise several artifacts he had recovered. Solstarni refused, citing a busy schedule, though a PC who succeeds at a DC 15 Sense Motive check also notices that the kasatha's message conveys she was feeling increasingly skeptical about Paqual's motives.

If the PCs search for information about Eyrub Paqual on Castrovel's infosphere, they can find a series of articles about elven ruins he has published over the past 6 years. At first blush, he appears to be a moderately well-established academic. However, most of his articles appear in poorly vetted journals or cite him as one of numerous secondary authors—a point a PC can identify with a successful DC 15 Culture, Life Science, Physical Science, or relevant Profession check. Furthermore, with a successful DC 21 Computers check, a PC researching Paqual can detect inconsistencies in his online bios and records, suggesting he might be entirely fictitious.

If the PCs fail to access the computer's files, a systems administrator arrives shortly after the Qabarat detective does (see Development on page 12) and overrides the login, allowing the PCs to view the correspondence (but not necessarily identify the forged letter).

Physical Clues: The PCs can find more information by searching the office. One of the cabinets is ajar and contains Dr. Solstarni's field suit, a set of basic lashunta tempweave fitted for a kasatha, though it has fallen from its hanger where Solstarni hastily attempted to grab it when she heard strangers disabling her door lock. With a successful DC 16 Perception check, a PC can make this connection and also

TEMPLE OF THE TWELVE

PART 1:
QUESTIONS IN QABARAT

PART 2:
THE UKULAM EXPEDITION

PART 3:
THE LOST TEMPLE

CASTROVEL

THE CULT OF THE DEVOURER

ALIEN ARCHIVES

CODEX OF WORLDS

EYRUB PAQUAL'S IDENTITY

As the PCs might guess, "Eyrub Paqual" is merely an alias. What they are unlikely to determine at this early stage is that he is a lashunta named Tahomen who leads a Cult of the Devourer cell on Castrovel. When news first emerged about what the PCs found on the Drift Rock, he pieced together its possible connection to old elven ruins on Ukulam and quickly stepped up his correspondence with Dr. Solstarni. When pleasantries did not work, Tahomen arranged her abduction and quickly transferred her and his subordinates to Ukulam to explore the temple.

As the adventure progresses, Tahomen can either infer that a group of Starfinders will soon embark for the temple or confirm that the PCs are actively following his group. He takes several steps—most of them during Part 2 of this volume—to delay, inconvenience, or outright destroy the PCs and ensure that he can acquire and broadcast key information to his cult contacts elsewhere in the Pact Worlds.

notice the slight dent in the carbon fiber cabinet where someone (Solstarni) collided violently with the furniture in a short fight.

In addition, with a successful DC 13 Perception check, a PC can find a printed version of Eyrub Paqual's invitation to the Five Arches. Solstarni printed this out, intending to pass it by her colleagues to see if they had been likewise contacted. When she heard strangers breaking into her office, she slipped it just behind her cabinet as a breadcrumb to help identify her likely assailants.

Finally, with a successful DC 18 Culture, Perception, or academically relevant Profession check, the PCs can find some printed scans of Halkueem Zan's notebooks marked in red pen. These are copies Dr. Solstarni annotated by hand, though the papers found here represent only a fraction of her work on the texts; her abductors snatched most of those notes when they attacked the office. Even so, these notes include both some duplicates of the stolen research and some unique conclusions that are sufficient to help the PCs chart a course from Turhalu Point to, as Zan described it, the "accursed pyramid city of Loskialua." Dr. Solstarni helpfully writes that this regards what's now known as the Oatia culture, a poorly understood dynasty of elven immigrants to Ukulam.

If the PCs do not find these physical clues, the Qabarat detective (see Development below) finds them and shares the information with the PCs.

Treasure: Dr. Solstarni's basic lashunta tempweave suit is in good condition, and it actually belongs to the university. Fearing that her colleague might be in serious trouble,

INFERNO KNIFE

Not all developments in military technology are successful. Originally designed to be a perfect survival tool, the inferno knife combines the cutting prowess of a survival knife with the virtues of a lighter and road flare. By squeezing one trigger, the user can inject a small stream of fuel from the hilt's reservoir onto the blade's tip, and a secondary trigger can ignite it, creating a small torch to signal others or light campfires. The product's launch was disastrous, and users logged hundreds of complaints about the knives' needless complexity. As a result, inferno knives have flooded the market and become showy weapons for criminals and performers, though timing the blade's ignition in combat remains an unpredictable art.

An inferno knife is a 4th-level basic melee weapon with the analog and operative special properties. It deals 1d4 slashing damage and has the burn 1d6 critical hit effect. It costs 2,100 credits and has light bulk. An inferno knife uses petrol as fuel. It contains enough fuel to remain lit for 1 hour, shedding light in a 20-foot radius. Each successful critical hit reduces the remaining duration by 5 minutes. A single charge of petrol refills the weapon's reservoir.

Professor Muhali agrees to give the armor to the PCs, as long as they intend to help track down the missing Dr. Solstarni.

Development: As the PCs are concluding their search of the office, a Qabarat detective called by Professor Muhali arrives to survey the situation. He takes basic statements from the PCs and does a sweep of the room, uncovering any undiscovered clues as noted above. Based on the evidence, it appears the best course of action is to follow up on the connections to the Five Arches and the Port Authority, and based on the nature of the suspects, the officer suspects they might hide at the first sight of law enforcement. The officer is amenable to providing the PCs short-term deputation to investigate the situation further, but he does so under the conditions that at least two of them wear bugs to provide surveillance and that they allow a pair of officers to shadow them at a considerable distance in case of trouble. Concerned for her colleague, Muhali encourages the PCs to pursue these leads. However, the PCs do not have to investigate either site; so long as they have at least one source of Halkueem Zan's documentation, they can travel directly to Turhalu Point.

If the PCs have both Dr. Solstarni's notes and the documents from Ailabiens 21:2 (see page 9), they receive a +2 circumstance bonus to Survival checks to navigate Ukulam's wilderness during Part 2 of the adventure.

Story Award: If the PCs identify that Dr. Solstarni has been abducted and discover the leads to the Five Arches and the Port Authority, award them 600 XP. For each of the three broad evidence categories in which the PCs found clues, award the party an additional 100 XP. They do not get these additional rewards for any clues that they did not find on their own.

FIVE ARCHES (CR 4)

By investigating Dr. Solstarni's office, the PCs likely learned that an academic named Eyrub Paqual was pressuring the kasatha to meet with him at a cantina called the Five Arches. The establishment is easy enough to find through Castrovel's infosphere, and it's located off the beaten path in the Gateway District near the east end of the city. According to its advertisements, the Five Arches is "a café dedicated to serving the discerning palettes of a dozen worlds." According to online reviews, it's an eclectic dive with wildly variable food and drink quality combined with bizarre food pairings for the daily specials. Overall, the reputation suggests it's not a place that right-thinking individuals frequent willingly.

The Five Arches is readily apparent from the street, thanks to its glaring neon sign suggestive of the numerous portals in the district. A riot of different worlds' souvenirs plasters the interior's walls, and each table, booth, and bench bears the name of one of the Pact Worlds' planets or habitable moons.

The proprietor, **Uilee** (CN female android), runs an efficient business marred only by her insistence on developing new recipes that her muted sense of taste can't properly judge. Even so, she delights in creating "authentic" offworld cuisine that is utterly inconsistent. Fortunately, she makes plenty of income from the various low-key criminals and gang members who know to skip the menu and just order drinks. They all know and honor her unwritten policy to take all fights outside. If the PCs arrive during the day or evening, there are likely about a dozen patrons nursing drinks alone or in pairs. The daily special is an unidentifiable avian cutlet smothered in a fig-like fruit compote and served alongside a mashed bitter tuber from Triaxus.

Creatures: The cocky Twonas En, one of three Qabarat smugglers who helped "Eyrub Paqual" and his companions get to Ukulam, is hanging out here watching for future business leads. The lashunta smuggler takes note of the PCs as they enter and listens in on any conversations they have. If they start referencing Paqual or mention traveling to Ukulam, Twonas En figures the PCs are worth investigating directly, either because they're a threat to his team's operation or because they're potential clients. Depending on the PCs' tact, he might offer his services as a transporter or inquire how they know Paqual. The PCs can also pose as possible clients, requiring a successful DC 16 Bluff check.

If Twonas En smells trouble, he presses a panic button on his belt that signals his friends to converge on the location; a PC can spot his subtle move with a successful DC 18 Perception check. It takes about 2 minutes for the other two Qabarat smugglers to arrive, and in that time Twonas En attempts to sneak out of the café. The PCs can coerce him to call off his buddies with a successful DC 19 Intimidate check, so long as they guarantee his safety in return for answering questions (see Development below).

Whether the PCs leave the Five Arches to fight with Twonas En and his comrades or they trick him into leading the way to the rest of his group, combat is likely—and also probably a welcome change in tempo from the ongoing investigation. If the PCs agreed to cooperate with the police, they can signal the officers to close in on the location with a code phrase agreed on ahead of time, or a PC can quietly request that the officers keep their distance. If the PCs request backup, the officers arrive in 4d4 rounds and quickly defeat the smugglers.

QABARAT SMUGGLERS (3)   CR 1
XP 400 each
Lashunta operative
NE Medium humanoid
   (lashunta)
Init +5; **Perception** +6

DEFENSE   **HP** 14 EACH
EAC 12; **KAC** 13
Fort +1; **Ref** +4; **Will** +4

OFFENSE
Speed 30 ft.
Melee tactical baton +6 (1d4+2 B) or
   [Twonas En only] inferno knife +6
   (1d4+2 S; critical burn 1d6)
Ranged azimuth laser pistol +5
   (1d4+1 F; critical burn 1d6)
Offensive Abilities trick attack +1d8
Lashunta Spell-Like Abilities (CL 1st)
   1/day–*detect thoughts* (DC 12)
   At will–*daze* (DC 11), *psychokinetic hand*

TACTICS
During Combat One of the smugglers
   attempts to harass the majority of the
   PCs while the other two try
   to eliminate isolated targets.
   In an ongoing firefight, they
   take cover where they can and
   attempt to dash toward ranged threats.
Morale If only one of the smugglers is conscious, he
   surrenders. If the smugglers spot local police, they
   attempt to flee rather than fight.

TWONAS EN

STATISTICS
Str +1; **Dex** +4; **Con** +0; **Int** +2; **Wis** +0; **Cha** +1
Skills Bluff +11, Culture +6, Piloting +6, Sleight of Hand +11,
   Stealth +11
Languages Castrovelian, Common; limited telepathy 30 ft.
Gear freebooter armor, azimuth laser pistol with battery
   (20 charges), inferno knife (Twonas En only; see the
   sidebar on page 12), tactical baton, credstick (50 credits)

Development: The smugglers would love to make an example of the PCs, but they're far more interested in staying alive. If defeated, the lashuntas can convey that they helped a male korasha lashunta named Eyrub Paqual secure travel documents for 15 individuals, permitting them to use local portals to reach Turhalu Point. Most of the visas were counterfeit—including three fake IDs for Port Authority employees to help move the group's equipment—though the smugglers had to make only some minor adjustments to the legitimate academic visas that Paqual and his ill kasatha colleague had. They also share that they had doubts about Paqual's identity, suspecting he was using an alias to avoid suspicion; ultimately, his money was good enough that the smugglers didn't mind. Because their role focused more on securing paperwork and conveying the group's equipment through customs without scrutiny, the smugglers are not familiar with the group's exact composition. They do, however, know that Paqual was shipping a considerable number of firearms and heavy gear, most notably a shirren-eye rifle and a sizable comm unit that was disassembled into three bulky pieces. The smugglers also had to secure special permits for transporting fungal spores.

The PCs are welcome to turn the smugglers over to local police. If the PCs don't have their own paperwork allowing them to travel to Turhalu Point, though, the smugglers can secure reliable visas at a cost of 300 credits per PC. This is especially useful if the PCs haven't coordinated closely with Professor Muhali or local authorities.

QABARAT PORT AUTHORITY
Whether the PCs are investigating the clues found in Dr. Solstarni's office or attempting to travel to Ukulam, they'll need to visit Qabarat's Port Authority. Qabarat conducts trade by land, sea, and air, and like many other settlements on Castrovel, it also maintains a number of magical gateways known as *aiudara* or "elf gates." These are not large enough to sustain heavy traffic, so the local port authorities manage use of the gateways to prioritize shipments from those who pay a premium for

TEMPLE
OF THE
TWELVE

PART 1:
QUESTIONS
IN QABARAT

PART 2:
THE UKULAM
EXPEDITION

PART 3:
THE LOST
TEMPLE

CASTROVEL

THE CULT OF
THE DEVOURER

ALIEN
ARCHIVES

CODEX OF
WORLDS

instant transportation. Most of these portals are in Qabarat's Gateway District, a smaller area along the city's eastern side, where use of the portals rarely interferes with the busy harbor and spaceports.

Creature: The PCs can flag down a port worker fairly easily and secure some time with a manager in less than an hour—much faster if the police have called ahead on the PCs' behalf. Gate Controller **Raiyiri** (LN female damaya lashunta) is very professional and finds the idea that uniformed employees of the Port Authority might have broken into the university a disturbing one. She quickly pulls up the assignment logs for the past 3 days and confirms that no employees were sent to the university. Furthermore, she knows that few people travel to Turhalu Point, which is a largely decommissioned military base that now serves as a research station. Based on the PCs' information, there's only one group that fits the description: a team of 15 carrying laboratory equipment, cryogenically frozen organic compounds, and specialty foodstuffs with authorization from the Qabarat University of Xenoarchaeology and Xenoanthropology. According to the records, customs confirmed the contents of all of the crates, though the documentation is too sparse for Raiyiri's liking. She also shows the PCs the passenger data, which indicates that the group (including both Dr. Solstarni and Eyrub Paqual) consisted of a kasatha, a shirren, two humans, and 11 lashuntas.

Raiyiri is suspicious about the group upon reviewing the records, but that doesn't mean she's willing to let a second group of scallywags through. Unless the PCs secure the proper authorization, travel to the continent of Ukulam is not permitted. As she explains, the continent has long been considered off-limits for colonization by any of the planet's three dominant species, with only a few dozen military and scientific outposts established around its extensive coastline. A handful of nongovernmental organizations oversee the sanctity of Ukulam, and they allow only limited travel there for academic and resupply purposes.

Development: The PCs should now have all the clues they need to point them toward Ukulam and Turhalu Point in search of "Eyrub Paqual" and the kidnapped Dr. Solstarni. With the university's support, Professor Muhali extends the PCs a stipend of 2,500 credits for their ongoing assistance in recovering her abducted colleague.

If the PCs are working with the Qabarat police, these findings are bittersweet news. It's a fairly clear trail, but it's also clearly outside the bounds of Qabarat jurisdiction, and the police would be happy to have the PCs' continued assistance. Either the police or the university can secure visas for the PCs authorizing them to travel to Ukulam in pursuit of the criminals.

Story Award: If the PCs investigate the Port Authority and confirm that their quarry has traveled to Turhalu Point, award them 600 XP.

PART 2: THE UKULAM EXPEDITION

Travel to Ukulam requires official authorization, and there is little regular transport between Qabarat and Ukulam. In addition, starship landings on the continent are tightly restricted due to its status as a wilderness preserve, so the PCs can't just hop across the planet in their own ship. However, once the PCs have acquired visas to visit Ukulam, they can use Qabarat's *aiudara* to reach Turhalu Point without losing significant time in transit. The eastern coast of Ukulam is hours ahead of Qabarat, making it a completely different time of day when the PCs arrive.

TURHALU POINT
Read or paraphrase the following when the PCs arrive at Turhalu Point.

The station at Turhalu Point sits at the tip of a broad peninsula covered in rolling plains and expanses of tall, pale-green grasses that shimmer with violet hues in the wind. Short-lived blooms of magenta fungus tower nearly twenty feet over the landscape, though many have begun to wilt and others are marred by bite marks of half a dozen sizes. Trumpeting calls echo across the plains as immense, six-legged creatures with long, swooping necks trek steadily across the grass toward the western jungles. Beyond rises the Singing Range, its peaks barely visible through the haze.

Turhalu Point sits at the tip of a broad peninsula characterized by rolling plains, seasonal blooms of immense fans of magenta fungus, and expanses of tall, pale-green grasses that shimmer with violet hues in the wind. The most recent fungal bloom occurred about a week ago, and the 20-foot-tall fans are starting to wilt, drooping to half that height.

Once one of Qabarat's minor military outposts on Ukulam, Turhalu Point has been decommissioned for more than 20 years. It still maintains a token security force to keep the wildlife at bay, but industrious researchers have converted most of its gun turrets and bunkers into greenhouses and biology labs.

Among the researchers is Dr. **Khair al-Nuaf** (NG male human), one of the ranking scientists and a grant beneficiary of the Qabarat University of Xenoarchaeology and Xenoanthropology. Having received the school's recent call for assistance, he is nearby to greet the PCs when they arrive. He can not only inform the PCs that Paqual's group came and departed into the wilderness a little more than day ago, but also convey what he learned of the other group, which

TEMPLE
OF THE
TWELVE

PART 1:
QUESTIONS
IN QABARAT

PART 2:
THE UKULAM
EXPEDITION

PART 3:
THE LOST
TEMPLE

CASTROVEL

THE CULT OF
THE DEVOURER

ALIEN
ARCHIVES

CODEX OF
WORLDS

consisted largely of armed lashunta mercenaries. Based on what he overheard, they were headed toward some elven ruins to the northwest to perform archaeological survey work with the oversight of Dr. Solstarni, though the kasatha appeared to be groggy and perhaps ill.

The research outpost has numerous maps of the region and survey data from aircraft that have flown over most of the continent, so based on the PCs' anecdotal notes and the maps created by Halkueem Zan centuries ago, Dr. al-Nuaf estimates that the journey to the abandoned city will take about 10 to 12 days of steady travel on foot. He advises the PCs that their route should lead them first through the fairly sparse lowlands around Turhalu Point, into the dense subtropical rain forests to the northwest, and finally into the foothills of the Singing Range.

Treasure: The university has instructed Dr. al-Nuaf to assist the PCs by providing them with additional gear requisitioned from his project's inventory. This includes a scratched-up suit of lashunta ringwear II armor, a carbon steel curve blade, a stickybomb grenade II, 4 doses of tier-1 antitoxin, and 4 doses of sprayflesh. He can also supply 3 weeks' worth of field rations to each PC, up to 100 credits' worth of standard ammunition per PC, and access to the outpost's recharging stations. If necessary, Dr. al-Nuaf can also provide the PCs with consumer backpacks and mass-produced tents.

WILDERNESS TREK

Turhalu Point's security forces are willing to drive the PCs about 10 miles outside the outpost, but from there, they're on their own. Strict guidelines control vehicle traffic in this part of the reserve, so the PCs must proceed on foot.

The Temple of the Twelve lies approximately 120 miles west-northwest of Turhalu Point through a trackless expanse of subtropical forest. Assuming a speed of 30 feet, the PCs can cover about 12 miles each day. The PCs' trek across Ukulam will not be easy; in this region, the days are long, hot, and muggy, with temperatures rising to above 90° F shortly after dawn. As a result, the PCs must endure very hot conditions (*Starfinder Core Rulebook* 402) for about 12 hours each day. The PCs' armor can provide them with environmental protection for 1 day per level of the armor (*Starfinder Core Rulebook* 196), and if used sparingly, this could protect the group for most of their journey to the Temple of the Twelve.

Thanks to the jungle's density, the maximum distance at which the PCs can spot creatures is 2d8×10 feet (90 feet on average), except where noted. This reduced visibility makes navigation difficult, but the PCs should have Halkueem Zan's notes, which provide bearings taken at several key landmarks. Rather than attempt a Survival check each hour, have the PCs attempt either a DC 18 Survival check once per day to use the orienteering task to avoid getting lost or a DC 12 Survival check to perform the follow tracks task. Using orienteering

is generally faster, and each such successful check allows the PCs to make a full day's progress toward the temple. Following tracks takes more time and concentration, and each successful check allows the PCs to travel three-quarters of day's progress. Failing the check for either task causes the PCs to become lost several times over the course of that day, making only half a day's progress. How much time the PCs spend in pursuit not only prolongs their travel beyond their armors' environmental protection but also grants the Cult of the Devourer more time to explore the Temple of the Twelve, prepare traps, and destroy valuable records.

Remember that if the PCs both recovered Dr. Solstarni's notes (see page 12) and received the annotated files from Ailabiens 21:2 (see page 9), they receive a +2 circumstance bonus to these Survival checks.

Keep track of how far the PCs have traveled each day, especially if they get lost. The PCs will face several encounters on their way to the Temple of the Twelve. These are presented below as both events and location-based encounters.

Each encounter includes a suggested time for it to take place, but feel free to adjust the timing as you see fit, especially if the timeline changes based on the PCs' actions.

EVENT 1: TRAMPLING TITANS (CR 3)

It takes the PCs about 2 days to traverse the grasslands surrounding Turhalu Point. The journey is not difficult, but the grasses are in a tall, seasonally dormant state that attracts few grazers to crop the vegetation. As a result, the grass ranges in height from 3 to 8 feet tall, making it difficult to watch for wildlife. Nevertheless, the PCs face few dangers until they reach the edge of the jungle on the third day of travel.

Creatures: Rather than cover their tracks, the Devourer cultists scattered fungal spores for several miles after they entered the jungle, knowing that the fungi produce a subtle scent that attracts large herbivores that would muddle the group's trail. The plan has worked largely as intended. Dozens of huge beasts called yaruks leisurely patrol the area through which the PCs need to travel, knocking aside smaller trees and trampling the cultists' spoor as the immense creatures sniff out the delicious fungus that drew them here. A PC can identify the creatures as yaruks with a successful DC 22 Life Science check (the DC is reduced to 17 for PCs hailing from or native to Castrovel, as they're more familiar with their home world's fauna). If successful, the PCs also realize that yaruks can be extremely dangerous if the animals are threatened.

The yaruks are fairly calm at the moment, so the PCs can weave among them by keeping their distance and not making any threatening moves—much like a variety of other native creatures are doing. The giant herbivores might stamp their feet threateningly if the PCs make a commotion or draw closer than 30 feet, but only actively harming yaruks or provoking them further triggers any dangerous response.

A full stat block for a yaruk is presented on page 61, but this is not a combat encounter, as a direct clash between the PCs and even a single yaruk would likely end poorly for the characters. Instead, this is a more cinematic encounter, as the PCs race to escape the riled beasts as they blare loudly, shake the ground, and topple trees. The yaruks do not make direct attacks so much as cause potentially lethal collateral damage that the PCs must dodge and outrun (see Hazard below).

The PCs can choose to avoid this area altogether, but doing so requires an additional day of travel during which they cannot navigate using Survival to follow tracks.

Hazard: If the PCs pick an ill-advised fight with the yaruks, the beasts bellow angrily to one another and begin trampling in the PCs' general direction. Even if the PCs do their best to avoid spooking the yaruks, they're still in danger from the Cult of the Devourer. Suspecting a rival group might be in pursuit, a shirren Devourer cultist named Salask (see area **B5**) doubled back here to gather intelligence. Spotting an opportunity with so many yaruks nearby, she climbs to a promising vantage point in the understory hundreds of feet away to line up a good shot with her sniper rifle. When the PCs are in the midst of the yaruk moot, she fires at one of the largest animals, which rears up in pain and bellows a distress call to its neighbors. A PC can discern the general direction of the shot with a successful DC 18 Perception check, and exceeding the DC by 5 or more allows the PC to spot the suppressed muzzle flare off in the distance. There's little opportunity to pursue Salask, however. Some of the yaruks bolt from the scene, while others rally to the wounded yaruk's defense to crush or chase away the PCs.

This encounter takes the form of a chase. Rather than use normal combat rounds, the chase occurs over several phases, with each phase representing approximately 1 minute of action. The yaruks act at the beginning of each phase, followed by the PCs' actions (see Yaruk Actions and PC Actions below). The encounter ends once the PCs accrue a number of successes equal to three times the number of PCs (12 successes for a party of four characters). Many of the PC actions detailed below can earn successes if a PC succeeds at a certain skill check, while others can mitigate the rampaging yaruks' damage.

Yaruk Actions: Yaruks are infamously destructive. At the beginning of each phase, roll 1d8 and consult the table below to determine the yaruks' behavior.

D8	EFFECT
1	**Bellow:** A nearby yaruk trumpets loudly at 1d3 randomly selected PCs, each of which takes 2d6 sonic damage and takes a –2 penalty to skill checks during this phase (Fortitude DC 14 negates the penalty and reduces the damage by half).
2	**Body Check:** A yaruk runs alongside a randomly selected PC and buffets him with its body. This attack has a +13 bonus to hit and deals 2d6+6 bludgeoning damage.
3	**Falling Tree:** A yaruk topples a tree that crashes into the PCs' path. A randomly determined PC takes 2d6+6 bludgeoning damage (Reflex DC 14 negates), and all PCs take a –1 penalty to Acrobatics, Athletics, and Survival checks during this phase.
4	**Shower of Splinters:** A yaruk crashes through the branches, sending sharp fragments of wood raining down and dealing 2d6 piercing damage to each PC (Reflex DC 14 half).
5	**Gang Up:** Several yaruks converge on a randomly determined PC. Roll two more times on this table, ignoring results of 5 or higher. The first

result affects only that PC, and if the second result would affect one or more randomly selected PCs, that PC is automatically one of the targets.

6-8	**Sudden Shift:** Whether due to terrain or following the lead of one of the senior animal, the yaruks begin veering in an unexpected direction that requires the PCs to change tactics. During this phase, each PC takes a –4 penalty to any skill check used to perform the same action he used during the previous phase.

PC Actions: During a phase, each PC can perform one of the actions below to distract, dodge, or outthink the yaruks while scrambling for safety. A PC can attempt more than one of these actions during a phase, but doing so imposes a cumulative –3 penalty to each check he attempts during that phase. Failing a check does not harm the PCs, but it does prolong the chase. For some of the PC actions, if a PC succeeds at the check, the PCs earn a "success," which contributes to the PCs escaping the rampaging yaruks (see Development below). A PC can also perform one reaction per phase.

- *Activate an Ability (No Check):* The PC activates a special ability or casts a spell that takes a standard action or

TEMPLE OF THE TWELVE

PART 1: QUESTIONS IN QABARAT

PART 2: THE UKULAM EXPEDITION

PART 3: THE LOST TEMPLE

CASTROVEL

THE CULT OF THE DEVOURER

ALIEN ARCHIVES

CODEX OF WORLDS

RUNE OBELISK

A. RUNE OBELISK
1 square = 5 feet

EVENT 2: DANGEROUS FLORA
1 square = 5 feet

full action. This does not necessarily earn the PCs any successes, though at the GM's discretion, using an ability or spell with limited uses to perform a flashy distraction or eliminate an obstacle might count as a success.

- *Distract (Bluff or Intimidate DC 14):* The PC draws the yaruks' attention away from the PC's companions. With a successful check, the PC takes a –2 penalty to AC and saves against all effects in the Yaruk Actions table during the next phase, and the other PCs receive a +2 circumstance bonus to AC and saves against those effects during that time. Only one PC can use the distract action at a time, and if a second PC performs this action, it negates earlier distract actions. This does not earn the PCs any successes.
- *Hide (Stealth DC 15):* The PC takes cover to avoid being attacked. With a successful check, the PC receives a +2 circumstance bonus to AC and saves against all effects in the Yaruk Actions table until he takes another action. During this time, if one of those effects would randomly target the PC, randomly determine the target again and use the second result. This does not earn the PCs any successes.
- *Navigate (Survival DC 17):* The PC identifies a good path to temporarily escape the yaruks. With a successful check, the PCs earn one success.
- *Scramble (Athletics DC 18):* The PC clambers over obstacles, swings across gaps, and runs ably through the jungle. With a successful check, the PCs earn one success.
- *Spook (Intimidate DC 20):* The PC attempts to scare a yaruk–not necessarily enough to stop it, but enough to

slow it or make it veer off course. The PC can attempt a single ranged attack (EAC 20, KAC 22) as part of this action, and if he hits, he gains a +2 circumstance bonus to the Intimidate check; if his attack deals at least 10 damage, he gains a +4 bonus instead. With a successful check, the PCs earn one success.
- *Squeeze (Acrobatics DC 19):* The PC slips between two large obstacles or nimbly crosses fallen trees as a shortcut, stymieing the yaruks in pursuit. With a successful check, the PCs earn one success.

Development: Once the PCs accrue a number of successes equal to three times the number of PCs, they reach an ancient stone bridge crossing one of the river tributaries that flows through the jungle. The bridge easily supports the PCs, but once they are across, an angry yaruk pursuing them gets only a few steps across before collapsing the old elven architecture. The rest of the moot considers this the end of the chase, and the group gradually disperses after another minute of aggressive posturing. Beyond the bridge stands the landmark identified by Halkueem Zan as the Rune Obelisk (area **A**).

The thundering ruckus from the chase echoes for miles, alerting curious creatures, scaring off many animals, and attracting hungry scavengers that associate angry yaruks with fresh corpses. This serves as the impetus for several later antagonists, such as the kaukarikis (see area **A1**) and the ksarik (see **Event 2**).

Story Award: If the PCs escape the yaruk stampede, award them 800 XP.

A. RUNE OBELISK

The elven Oatia culture created a few lasting architectural works during its occupation of eastern Ukulam, among them the bridge the PCs crossed to escape the yaruks and a grand watchtower that stood vigil near what was then the edge of the jungle. The outpost towered nearly 300 feet, peeking over the trees' emergent layer and topped by an elaborate observation deck. Within a century of the elves' abandonment of the region, however, the observation deck decayed and toppled from its lofty height, leaving behind only the stone post carved with the elves' laws. But after millennia of erosion, even these have faded, barring a few sheltered inscriptions near the base. When Halkueem Zan found this site, he believed it was a mighty monument and dubbed it the Rune Obelisk. The PCs reach this area immediately after escaping the yaruks in **Event 1**. Use the Rune Obelisk map on page 18 for this encounter.

A1. The Approach (CR 5)

The area surrounding the Rune Obelisk is uneven, where soil deposition and plant growth have covered most of the building foundations that surround the site. Even so, the stubborn trees that grow sparsely here have displaced many stones with their roots, leaving carved blocks scattered haphazardly around the area. With a successful DC 10 Perception check, a PC can spot a few such building stones and their purposefully smoothed forms among the mosses. A successful check also allows the PCs to spot clusters of blue-striped orange fruit ripening in the canopy above. With a successful DC 13 Life Science check, a PC can identify these as ralyrian figs, one of the more prolific fruiting trees in Castrovel's northern hemisphere and a staple food for many forest creatures. Wild ralyrian figs are rather tart but safe to eat, and a number of ripe figs have fallen from the branches and landed on the ground.

Creatures: The Rune Obelisk is part of a kaukariki troop's territory, and the past several days have been especially kind to the kaukarikis. Not only are the ralyrian figs in this area ripening, but the Cult of the Devourer also passed through the area, providing the incorrigible creatures considerable entertainment, plunder, and even meat. Also known as "stingbats," the kaukarikis clamber through the forest's understory, sometimes just bobbing their heads while inquisitively watching the PCs. Other times they actively warble their namesake "kau-kar-eeee-keeee" warning calls, throw fruit at the PCs, or even creep close to a PC to touch his leg or snatch a loose trophy before scampering away to the screeching adulation of their comrades. If a PC responds with violence, the kaukarikis scatter for several minutes before returning in greater numbers to scold and prank that PC more aggressively. Even so, the creatures avoid violence until the PCs approach the Rune Obelisk. A PC can identify the kaukarikis as such with a successful DC 11 Life Science check (DC 6 for Castrovel natives).

Earlier this season, a carnivorous plant called a vracinea took residence here, coiling itself around the obelisk and

hiding much of its body with other vines (see area **A2**). The kaukarikis were quick to investigate and harass the trespasser, which promptly lured in and consumed two troop members. The kaukarikis have since kept their distance while observing with excitement that the vracinea tends to toss aside trinkets, bones, and other treasures that are difficult to digest. In the intervening weeks, the two species have come to an unspoken understanding: the kaukarikis goad prey toward the obelisk, and the vracinea largely ignores the troop when the latter descends to recover scraps and trophies.

There are currently 13 kaukarikis in the troop. When the PCs are within a few hundred feet of the obelisk (area **A2**), the kaukarikis escalate their teasing and begin chasing one another through the trees to determine which of them are going to attack the PCs directly. They quickly establish a new pecking order and set aside any captured valuables (see Treasure below) before four of them descend to attack as their peers scream encouragement from the branches.

KAUKARIKIS (4)	CR 1

XP 400 each

HP 18 each (see page 56)

TACTICS

During Combat One of the kaukarikis harasses the largest group of PCs while the others converge on any isolated target. They amble around the battlefield, attempting to poison one target before scampering to the next. In the event that the PCs withdraw toward area **A2** and trigger the encounter there, the kaukarikis attempt to chase any other PCs into range of the vracinea's lure ability but otherwise stand aside to let the vracinea do the work; the PCs should not have to fight both encounters simultaneously.

Morale If only one of the kaukariki combatants is conscious, it flees, but the kaukarikis might retreat earlier if their tactics are utterly stymied.

Treasure: The kaukarikis managed to steal a few items of value from the Devourer cult as it passed by. Before attacking, one of the four kaukarikis hurriedly stows three *mk 2 serums of healing* in a hollow about 20 feet up a tree. A PC can spot this caching behavior with a successful DC 12 Perception check, and climbing the tree to recover the serums requires a successful DC 15 Athletics check.

Development: Once the PCs defeat the first wave of kaukarikis, the others become more skittish and screech angrily from a safe distance. The troop remains in sight, though, endeavoring to pester and goad the PCs in the direction of the obelisk and the waiting vracinea.

A2. The Obelisk (CR 4)

The Rune Obelisk rises above the jungle, just as Halkueem Zan's notes promised. It's an immense pillar of stone,

TEMPLE
OF THE
TWELVE

PART 1:
QUESTIONS
IN QABARAT

PART 2:
THE UKULAM
EXPEDITION

PART 3:
THE LOST
TEMPLE

CASTROVEL

THE CULT OF
THE DEVOURER

ALIEN
ARCHIVES

CODEX OF
WORLDS

approximately fifteen feet wide with an X-shaped cross section that provides climbing plants—including a network of green vines, several brilliant fuchsia bromeliads, and a host of violet flowers—excellent purchase.

The inaccurately named Rune Obelisk was a massive post that supported a now-missing observation deck, which a PC can hypothesize with a successful DC 15 Engineering check and at least 5 minutes of study.

A few Elven letters are visible through the climbing vines, but deciphering anything substantive requires cutting down the clinging plants and either the ability to understand Elven or a successful DC 25 Culture check to decipher writing. What survives of the Elven inscriptions warns visitors that they approach "Loskialua, monastery of starsong, embassy of the spheres, and Temple of the Twelve." Fragmentary notes also include mentions of paying respect, messengers from beyond, an academy, and "interpreters of the beacon."

Creature: A carnivorous plant creature called a vracinea hides among the other plants at the obelisk's base, and a PC who succeeds at a DC 27 Perception check notices that something is hiding there. The ample plant cover grants the vracinea partial cover (+2 to AC, +1 to Reflex saves) until it emerges from hiding. The vracinea's lure ability affects anyone who approaches within 120 feet of it.

VRACINEA   CR 4
XP 1,200
HP 51 (*Starfinder Adventure Path #1* 60)

TACTICS
During Combat The vracinea prefers to let lured PCs approach within striking range before it emerges to bite its prey. If the PCs approach within 40 feet without being affected by the lure, the vracinea emerges to chase down a nearby target.

Morale So long as prey is nearby, the vracinea fights to the death. If repeatedly subjected to ranged attacks without any nearby targets or lured victims, it abandons the obelisk and flees.

Treasure: About 30 feet south of the obelisk lies a torn estex suit I once worn by one of the Devourer cultists who fell prey to the vracinea after being chased here by the kaukarikis. The vracinea tore the suit free and flung it aside, after which the kaukarikis tore at it further before discarding it here. The armor is now worthless, but among the cultist's other gear is a frostbite-class zero rifle and a silvery credstick holding 290 credits. The credstick landed on the ground during the vracinea's attack, and a PC can spot it while approaching the obelisk with a successful DC 15 Perception check. The vracinea gnawed on the rifle for several minutes after eating the cultist before its jaws clamped down on the battery, rupturing it and spraying painful chemicals over the area. It then dropped the scratched rifle into the northeast foliage adjacent to the obelisk.

An approaching PC can spot the rifle and superficial damage to the nearby plants with a successful DC 18 Perception check. After the PCs have resolved the encounters in area **A**, they can find both treasures without difficulty.

Development: If the PCs defeat the vracinea, the remaining kaukarikis howl in fear and clamber about the understory in distress. Barring some exceptional opportunity to attack an isolated target, the impish creatures avoid confronting the PCs directly for the rest of the adventure. They do, however, continue following the PCs, grazing on nearby fruits, and vocalizing to unnerve the travelers—even performing low-risk acts of sabotage like dropping a rock or modest tree branch on a PC's tent in the middle of the night.

EVENT 2: DANGEROUS FLORA (CR 4)
The kaukarikis' antics aside, much of the next day's travel passes without incident as the terrain gradually begins to slope upward. This encounter occurs on the fourth day of travel and continues to the fifth day.

Creatures: Shortly after the PCs break camp on the fourth day, a powerful plant creature known as a ksarik catches their scent and begins trailing them. It's a cautious hunter, but not an especially stealthy one. With a successful DC 13 Perception check, a PC can catch sight of the colorful predator a little more than 100 feet away. The first time it's spotted or attacked, the ksarik gallops away and waits to heal any damage incurred. As the day progresses, it becomes bolder, wriggling its feeding tentacles curiously and even gurgling audibly, which the PCs might confuse for a greeting. Shortly thereafter, it assesses that the PCs are viable hosts for its spores, and it fires a thorn dart at one of them before lumbering away. Twice more that day it returns to take a shot or two at a PC before fleeing.

On the following day, the ksarik appears only once before it heads northwest to check on one of its earlier targets, the Devourer cultist **Ralkawi** (CE female korasha lashunta), who has since grown very ill as the ksarik seedlings inside her germinate. Near the middle of the day, the PCs' path takes them near the cultist, who has reached the bedridden stage on the carrion spores disease track. Unable to move, she has spent hours shouting herself hoarse and imploring the Devourer to grant her death. Unable to do much else, Ralkawi makes only feeble threats if the PCs approach (see Development on page 21 for more information). If needed, you can use the Devourer cultist stat block on page 24 for Ralkawi, though she is little threat to the PCs at this point.

The ksarik intends to use Ralkawi as bait, luring the PCs into a location with fewer trees behind which they can take cover. It has also used its ingested adaptation ability to learn her languages to better understand the PCs and adapt to their strategies. Shortly after they arrive, the ksarik attacks. If the PCs ignore Ralkawi, the ksarik shadows the PCs for a little while longer before attacking in a similarly open space.

Use the Dangerous Flora map on page 18 for the clearing where Ralkawi lies and where the ksarik attacks.

KSARIK CR 4

XP 1,200

HP 52; **RP** 3 (*Starfinder: First Contact* 10)

TACTICS

During Combat As the ksarik closes in and weaves between cover, it uses its ranged attacks to soften a chosen target so that it can use its ingested adaptation ability against the wounded foe. Once in melee, it uses its tentacles to maul foes and borrow their abilities.

Morale The ksarik fights to the death.

RALKAWI

Development: Ralkawi joined the Cult of the Devourer to eliminate a string of bad personal and financial choices that left her bankrupt and alone. She's among the least pious of Tahomen's cult, though, and if the PCs are inclined to lend her assistance, she's willing to accept the help rather than stubbornly die. Given the advanced stage of her carrion spores, though, her chances of survival are slim. She likely dies shortly after the PCs find her—possibly even at the end of the encounter—as wriggling, maggot-like ksarik seedlings painfully burrow their way out of her abdomen. Since Ralkawi still has fragments of the original thorn dart in her leg, it shouldn't take much for the PCs to realize the two conditions are connected, especially if one or more of the PCs have also fallen ill.

Although this adventure assumes that Ralkawi dies or that the PCs kill her, it's possible that she survives thanks to the PCs' kindness and medical care. If so, she can aid the PCs, and might one day forsake her evil patron entirely.

EVENT 3: MOLDSTORM (CR 3)

On the morning of the seventh day of travel, the wind shifts direction, carrying with it a tangy scent. Looking to the foliage-obscured sky, the kaukarikis fall silent before yapping warnings to one another. They dash upward toward bucket-sized flowers 100 feet above and wrap themselves in the petals, practically disappearing from sight. Any PC who succeeds at a DC 15 Perception check notices fluffy pink clouds floating gently above the trees. With a successful DC 17 Life Science or Survival check, a PC can recognize these as signs of the imminent approach of one of Castrovel's notorious moldstorms.

Hazard: Moldstorms are short-lived events in which several types of giant fungi all release their spores at once. In smaller quantities, these spores are harmless, but moldstorms can clog creatures' respiratory systems and even take root in living tissues, breaking down flesh and inhibiting neurological systems.

Enduring a moldstorm without shelter is very dangerous. In the short time the PCs have, they can attempt to build a temporary shelter using the Survival skill to endure severe weather, in which case the PCs can gain a bonus to Fortitude saves to resist the moldstorm. Exceeding this Survival DC by 10 or more allows the PCs to avoid the effects altogether, but hunkering down in any of these ways expends half a day of progress toward the temple city. If any of the PCs have remaining environmental protection capacity in their armor, they can also ignore the harmful effects of this moldstorm by expending 4 hours of protection. If any PCs cannot avoid the moldstorm entirely, they are exposed to the disease sarkoneilia mold.

SARKONEILIA MOLD

Type disease (inhaled); **Save** Fortitude DC 14
Track mental; **Frequency** 1/day
Cure 2 consecutive saves

Development: The moldstorm leaves the landscape coated with fluffy tufts of pinkish spores like a dusting of snow, accumulating in waist-high drifts as the wind blows through the forest. The spores quickly lose their harmful potential after the moldstorm ends. The kaukarikis take this as their cue to stop harassing the PCs and return to their territory.

Story Award: If the PCs manage to endure the moldstorm, award them 800 XP.

EVENT 4: THE MOLD-MADDENED BEAST (CR 5)

The following event occurs at dusk on the seventh day after the moldstorm and thus takes place in dim light (*Starfinder Core Rulebook* 261). Use the map of area **B** on page 22 for this encounter.

Creatures: Most animals can sense a moldstorm coming and take precautions, but some just can't reach shelter in time. A whiskered renkroda fell victim to the latest storm, and spores have begun germinating on its body and burrowing into its soft tissues. It is extraordinarily cross and reckless as a result, and as the PCs are setting up camp or settling down for the night, it crashes toward them, arriving 3 rounds after the PCs first hear it. The renkroda fights to the death.

WHISKERED RENKRODA CR 5

XP 1,600

HP 75 (see page 58)

TEMPLE OF THE TWELVE

PART 1: QUESTIONS IN QABARAT

PART 2: THE UKULAM EXPEDITION

PART 3: THE LOST TEMPLE

CASTROVEL

THE CULT OF THE DEVOURER

ALIEN ARCHIVES

CODEX OF WORLDS

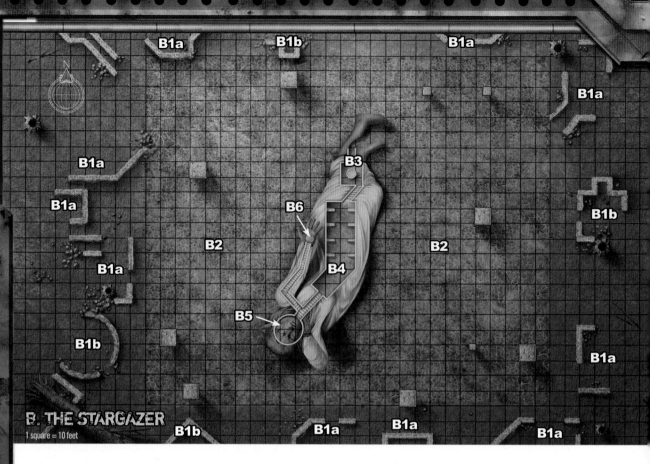

B. THE STARGAZER

1 square = 10 feet

B. THE STARGAZER

The PCs reach this location on day eight. Read or paraphrase the following as they approach.

The trees thin ahead, forming a broad clearing centered on an immense stone statue of a reclining elf whose skin bears dozens of raised markings like painful welts. The figure rests on one partially buried elbow while extending its other hand toward the sky. The elf's simple robe and hair are both sculpted of heavily weathered metal that has corroded entirely in places. Numerous crumbling outbuildings ring the clearing, where only mosses and a few stubborn, stunted trees grow.

Among the Oatia elves' greatest monuments and ritual sites was the Stargazer, an immense statue of an androgynous elf reclining and holding one hand up toward the sky. Elven scholar-priests traveled here to cleanse their bodies, meditate on their stellar observations, and tattoo their greatest discoveries into their skin as a living testament to their astronomic accomplishments. To the explorer Halkueem Zan, the immense statue depicted not an astronomer marveling at the heavens but a sickly elf wasting away from an unknown disease, leading him to dub it the "Plague Warden." In fact, the markings that cover the elven figure's skin do not indicate boils but rather stars, much like the skin of the elven monks that frequented here.

Having confirmed that the PCs are pursuing the Devourer cult, Tahomen dispatched several of his cultists under the direction of the shirren Salask to kill or delay the PCs. The team fell afoul of predators that are drawn to the Stargazer

to exploit the relative lack of cover to snatch up prey. One of the cultists fell to a pair of ksariks that still warily patrol the area (see **Event 5**), and the cult's movement also attracted an aerial ambush predator called a sky fisher, which lazily circles far above on thermals, watching for an opportunity to dive on an unsuspecting meal (see area **B1**).

Salask and two Devourer cultists survived, however, taking shelter inside the giant statue (see areas **B4** and **B5**). Salask considers the Stargazer an easily defendable site that affords her ample vantage points to watch for the PCs and snipe at them from a distance. As the PCs explore the Stargazer, they are likely to come under attack from the shirren sniper. Salask's possible actions are detailed in each encounter location.

Use the map above for this location.

B1. SHATTERED OUTBUILDINGS (CR 5)

Untold ages have reduced these buildings to low walls and buried foundations, with only a few fragmented walls standing more than four feet in height. The more complete structures have trapped millennia of sediment and runoff, forming a spongy floor of silt and moss.

Most of the buildings (marked **B1a**) consist of low walls that grant only partial cover against Salask's attacks, whereas a few buildings (marked **B1b**) have higher walls that grant total cover against her attacks. None of the outbuildings have roofs, so they grant virtually no protection against the sky fisher.

Creatures: Once the PCs break into the clearing, the meandering sky fisher begins gradually descending to within 100 feet of them, activating its aerial camouflage in the process. As the PCs investigate the outbuildings or start crossing into area **B2**, the sky fisher attacks.

The cultist Salask (see area **B5**) also keeps watch, and in the likely event she notices the PCs (with her +8 Perception modifier), she begins sniping at the PCs with her shirren-eye rifle, using its sniper special property as needed. Due to the rifle's low capacity and her desire to remain hidden using the Stealth skill to perform the sniping task, Salask can take a shot only once every 2 rounds. As a result, she tries to make the most of each shot, prioritizing PCs out in the open or those wearing minimal armor.

SKY FISHER   CR 5
XP 1,600
HP 75 (see page 59)

TACTICS
During Combat The sky fisher uses its lasso attacks to restrain several PCs before diving at an entangled target. Against multiple foes, it prefers to bite its chosen target a few times before moving to another enemy and waiting for its poison to disable its first target. Against heavy ranged attacks, it either tries to exploit cover while still attacking a creature in melee or launches itself at the ranged threat.

Morale If reduced to 10 or fewer Hit Points, the sky fisher telepathically broadcasts its desire to flee. If the PCs continue fighting, the sky fisher fights to the death.

Development: Salask continues to fire at the PCs so long as she seems likely to hit. She does not pursue them, though, so the PCs can withdraw back into the jungle to recover lost Stamina Points and plan their attack. If reduced to 25 or fewer Hit Points during this encounter, Salask steps back to consume her *serums of healing* before resuming her attacks. If reduced to 25 or fewer Hit Points again, she withdraws to take up a new sniping position in area **B6**.

In addition, the sounds of combat here or in area **B2** alert the cultists in area **B4**, who prepare for battle.

B2. Scholars' Plaza

This broad expanse forms a plaza of jumbled paving stones shifted by sinkholes and tree roots. Several large pedestals stand half-buried beneath leaves, earth, and detritus throughout the area, though any statues that once stood atop them have since eroded into little more than fragile spikes and weathered cobbles.

The millennia have not been kind to this plaza, turning the whole field into a mess of uneven paving stones that are considered difficult terrain (*Starfinder Core Rulebook* 257).

The pedestals provide cover against Salask's attacks, giving clever PCs several places where they can take cover while waiting for another opportunity to race toward the Stargazer's entrance while the shirren reloads.

Creature: Salask (see area **B5**) employs this open space as a killing ground, shooting anyone who breaks cover. If the PCs try to rush for the entrance to the Stargazer, she stops hiding and prioritizes her rate of fire unless the PCs provide significant return fire.

B3. Cleansing Pool

Corroded pipes hang down from the ceiling above a broad basin in the center of this room. The stone walls are slick with moisture and bear carvings of tattooed elves in states of undress as they wash themselves. The domed ceiling depicts hundreds of stars connected to form scores of constellations.

The Oatia elves considered the Stargazer a sacred space, and cleansing oneself of terrestrial influences was a necessary exercise before traveling deeper inside the monument. A PC can discern the ritual significance of this process with a successful DC 14 Mysticism or DC 19 Culture check (see Development below).

The constellations on the ceiling include both ones commonly taught on Castrovel as well as numerous esoteric designs. With a successful DC 16 Physical Science check, a PC can ascertain that many of the constellations are known to modern scholars but only thanks to advanced telescopes and faster-than-light travel. That the Oatia elves had identified these suggests they had extraordinary astronomical equipment, supernatural techniques for surveying the sky, or some other means of seeing far beyond the Pact Worlds system.

Development: The corroded pipes still channel rainwater to the basin, albeit more messily than in ages past. If a PC spends 1 minute washing at least her hands and head to observe the ritual cleansing, she is immune to the hazards in areas **B4** and **B5**.

B4. Hall of Inscription (CR 3)

The walls in this long gallery depict elves using needles to tattoo one another with constellations, geometric designs, and strange runic patterns. Rows of tall stone benches line either side of the hall. Carved along the ceiling are twelve stylized elven figures, heavily tattooed, adorned in different ways, and marked with starbursts on their foreheads.

As the carvings suggest, this is where the scholar-priests from the Temple of the Twelve received sacred tattoos to mark their discoveries and status within the order. The 12 carved figures on the ceiling were leading scholars at the temple

TEMPLE OF THE TWELVE

PART 1: QUESTIONS IN QABARAT

PART 2: THE UKULAM EXPEDITION

PART 3: THE LOST TEMPLE

CASTROVEL

THE CULT OF THE DEVOURER

ALIEN ARCHIVES

CODEX OF WORLDS

during the Oatia elves' early examinations of the symmetrical constellation that they called the Gate of Twelve Suns, and they were immortalized here, each symbolically representing one of the stars. This practice of living personification fell out of style within a century, though, making these carvings of quasi-saints an outdated relic even during the Stargazer's original occupation. The high stone benches act as low obstacles for cover (*Starfinder Core Rulebook* 254).

Hazard: The Stargazer is a place of cosmic contemplation, and those stained by terrestrial desires cannot properly perceive the galaxy's mysteries. At the start of each round spent in area **B4** or **B5**, any PC who did not perform the cleansing ritual in area **B3** gains either the flat-footed or the off-target condition (equal chance of each) until the beginning of the next round. Salask and the cultists have grudgingly performed the ritual and do not take penalties from this hazard.

Creatures: The two surviving cultists who accompanied Salask rest here, awaiting her signal to depart or attack. If they hear combat, they draw their weapons and take whatever cover is available.

DEVOURER CULTISTS (2)   CR 1
XP 400 each
Lashunta soldier
CE Medium humanoid (lashunta)
Init +2; **Perception** +5

DEFENSE   HP 20 EACH
EAC 12; **KAC** 14
Fort +3; **Ref** +1; **Will** +3

OFFENSE
Speed 25 ft.
Melee *defiant longsword* +7 (1d8+4 S; critical bleed 1d4)
Ranged utility scattergun +5 (blast 1d4+1 P) or shock grenade I +5 (explode [15 ft., 1d8 E, DC 12])
Offensive Abilities entropic wound, fighting styles (hit-and-run)
Lashunta Spell-Like Abilities (CL 1st)
1/day—*detect thoughts* (DC 11)
At will—*daze* (DC 10), *psychokinetic hand*

TACTICS
During Combat The cultists fire their scatterguns before rushing at their foes, thereafter favoring their longswords.
Morale The cultists fight to the death.

STATISTICS
Str +3; **Dex** +2; **Con** +1; **Int** +1; **Wis** +0; **Cha** +1
Skills Intimidate +10, Mysticism +5, Survival +5
Feat Opening Volley
Languages Castrovelian, Common; limited telepathy 30 ft.
Gear lashunta ringwear I, *defiant longsword*, shock grenades I (2), utility scattergun with 25 scattergun shells, field rations (2 weeks), credstick (150 credits)

SPECIAL ABILITIES
Entropic Wound (Su) Devourer cultists can channel a mote of their deity's hatred of life into their attacks. Any melee weapon a Devourer cultist wields gains the additional critical hit effect bleed 1d4. If the weapon already has a critical hit effect, the cultist can choose to apply either the weapon's normal critical hit effect or the entropic wound effect when he scores a critical hit.

B5. REFLECTION ROOM (CR 3)

This domed room has numerous open skylights and windows, creating a steady flow of outside air. A ring of slime mold forms a misshapen circular pattern on the floor.

SALASK

Here, within the Stargazer's head, the elven scholar-priests pondered cosmic revelations and enhanced several of their greatest galaxy-gazing divinations. The floor bears a weathered yet perfectly symmetrical circle of 12 carved stars, replicating the pattern of the Gate of Twelve Suns. Unfortunately, the carvings also collect water and bits of organic matter, promoting the ring of mold. By taking a few minutes to clean the floor, the PCs can uncover the original pattern as well as the surrounding designs—many of which resemble words and letters from the strange writing the PCs found on the Drift Rock!

The apertures through the Stargazer's ears and a smaller one near the back of the head provide clear arcs of fire for Salask (see Creature below).

Hazard: This area is subject to the same vertiginous hazard as area **B4**.

Creature: Salask was once a member of the Stewards, though early in her career her team fell afoul of a terrible aberration while pursuing a criminal on Apostae. Although Salask at first tried to defend her teammates, her desperate defense quickly grew into morbid fascination as she watched from afar as the alien monstrosity rent and consumed her comrades. She became increasingly obsessed with observing carnage, even feeding false intelligence to her replacement teams to lead them into lethal situations that she could watch with delight. By the time the Stewards began to suspect her treachery, Salask had already been inducted into the Cult of the Devourer, whose agents had learned of her macabre interests. Since then, she has served Tahomen as an assassin and guide, eliminating targets while he handles the more delicate planning.

Salask uses this area as her primary sniping position, relocating elsewhere as needed.

SALASK   CR 3
XP 800
Female shirren
CE Medium humanoid (shirren)
Init +4; **Senses** blindsense (vibration) 30 ft.; **Perception** +8

DEFENSE   HP 45
EAC 14; **KAC** 16
Fort +5; **Ref** +5; **Will** +4

OFFENSE
Speed 30 ft.
Melee tactical dueling sword +8 (1d6+4 S)
Ranged tactical shirren-eye rifle +11 (1d10+3 P)
Offensive Abilities expert sniper

TACTICS
During Combat Salask takes considerable pains to avoid melee combat. She fires her shirren-eye rifle slowly and methodically, using Stealth for sniping at foes and taking advantage of her expert sniper ability. If her foes are closing on her location, Salask seeks new hiding places as needed.

Morale Salask fights until reduced to 10 Hit Points, at which point she attempts to flee. If escape seems impossible, she surrenders.

STATISTICS
Str +1; **Dex** +4; **Con** +2; **Int** +0; **Wis** +1; **Cha** –1
Skills Athletics +8, Bluff +8, Culture +8, Diplomacy +8, Stealth +13, Survival +8
Languages Common, Shirren, Vercite; limited telepathy 30 ft.
Other Abilities communalism, trailblazer
Gear kasatha microcord I, tactical dueling sword, tactical shirren-eye rifle with 50 longarm rounds, *mk 1 serums of healing* (2), personal comm unit, field rations (3 weeks), credstick (1,000 credits)

SPECIAL ABILITIES
Expert Sniper (Ex) Salask is adept at remaining hidden while firing at distant targets. When she attempts a Stealth check to snipe, creatures that are at least 50 feet away take a –10 penalty to their Perception checks to spot her. This penalty increases to –20 for creatures that are at least 150 feet away.
Trailblazer (Ex) When determining how far she can move while traveling overland, Salask treats trackless terrain as though she were traversing a trail and treats terrain with a trail as though she were traversing a highway.

Treasure: An elegant wall tapestry threaded with opal beads once hung in this room. It decayed long ago, scattering its beads across the floor. Each bead is worth 80 credits, and a PC can find eight of them without difficulty. With a successful DC 19 Perception check, a PC can find all 15.

Development: If the PCs capture Salask, she is more than willing to share the core tenets of the Devourer's minimalist doctrine of annihilation, but she is reticent to talk about Tahomen's specific plans. All she knows is that Tahomen saw something in the broadcasts from the Drift Rock that he thinks has some connection with the Temple of the Twelve, and he believes there is more to learn from the ancient elven temple city. Because she has busily traveled back and forth to harry the PCs, Salask has not seen the temple; she just knows that Tahomen believes it holds grand secrets that will speed the bloody end of the galaxy.

Although physically compliant as a prisoner, Salask makes a habit of telepathically reminding her captors that in the end, the Devourer will consume all. All the while, she watches for an opportunity to escape. Better yet, she hopes that the PCs will encounter more of her comrades, at which point she waits for a good opportunity to break free while telepathically advising the other cultists of the PCs' strengths and weaknesses.

Salask's comm unit is password protected (DC 20 Computers check to unlock) and has several logged communications with another unit (Tahomen's). These convey updates about her movements through the jungle and ways in which she has harassed the PCs. She also has an extensive number of

TEMPLE OF THE TWELVE

PART 1: QUESTIONS IN QABARAT

PART 2: THE UKULAM EXPEDITION

PART 3: THE LOST TEMPLE

CASTROVEL

THE CULT OF THE DEVOURER

ALIEN ARCHIVES

CODEX OF WORLDS

C. TEMPLE OF THE TWELVE

1 square = 5 feet

C2

C3

C6

C6

C6

C6

C6

C5

C4

C8

C6

C7

C1

N

C9

recorded broadcasts of Eoxian "reality" programming and blood sport, favoring productions by the elebrian celebrity Zo!, including an entire season of the viscerally grotesque *Survival Deathmatch Extreme!*

B6. Observation Deck

A second, much steeper staircase branches off the main stairs from area **B4** to area **B5**, leading to a 60-foot-long series of ladderlike handholds that ascend to the upraised palm of the Stargazer's hand (DC 5 Athletics check to climb). The slightly cupped hand lost its delicate guardrails long ago, but there is still space for several creatures to stand here.

Event 5: Ksarik Raid (CR 6)

This encounter occurs once the PCs have eliminated the cultists occupying the Stargazer. The PCs will likely want to recover Stamina Points and explore the rest of the monument and its environs, but the reprieve doesn't last long.

Creatures: Two ksariks that have been hunting nearby have detected a host of new scents. Curious and hungry, they scout the plaza's perimeter and then approach the Stargazer. Depending on where the PCs are during their downtime, they might spot the approaching predators and attack the beasts at range as they cross the plaza. If heavily injured during their approach, the ksariks climb to a sheltered part of the Stargazer and allow their fast healing to repair the damage before chasing down the PCs.

KSARIKS (2)	CR 4

XP 1,200 each
HP 52 each; RP 3 each (*Starfinder: First Contact* 10)

TACTICS

During Combat The ksariks are cunning enough to take advantage of cover, each using their ranged attacks to soften a chosen target so that they can use their ingested adaptation ability against the wounded foes. Once in melee, they use their tentacles to maul foes and borrow their abilities.

Morale The ksariks fight to the death.

Development: With the ksariks dead, the PCs are free to travel the last several days to the Temple of the Twelve (area **D**).

PART 3: THE LOST TEMPLE

The closer the PCs get to the Temple of the Twelve, the more noticeably steep the trek becomes. By the time they are within a half day's travel from the site, the jungle thins out slightly and the ground rises, giving way to a stretch of verdant, rolling foothills crisscrossed by meandering creeks with sources in the striking peaks of the Singing Range to the north and west.

The PCs soon reach the ruins of what Halkueem Zan called the "Forsaken City," but millennia ago, these ruins were Loskialua, the small elven settlement that sustained the Temple of the Twelve and its astronomers. The citizens built their homes upon tiered platforms, both to create an even surface in the sloping region and because the elves believed that elevation reflected the heavens' blessing. As a result, those ranked higher in society lived atop low pyramids, and in places these connected to form honored acropolises. After the elves abandoned the site long ago, their homes crumbled, windblown soil accumulated, and plants took root, creating a graveyard of pyramids studding the landscape that rise between 2 and 25 feet in height. With hundreds of structures, Loskialua represents a rare archaeological treasure that would require years of dedicated fieldwork to excavate and document. Of greater interest to the PCs, though, is the intact temple and observatory—the Temple of the Twelve—perched hundreds of feet up the side of Alhuenar Spire, one of the Singing Range's highest mountains.

Story Award: If the PCs reach the Temple of the Twelve within 11 days of departing Turhalu Point, award them 1,200 XP. If they reach the temple within 13 days, award them 600 XP instead. If they arrive later, the PCs earn no additional XP.

C. TEMPLE OF THE TWELVE

Read or paraphrase the following as the PCs approach the Temple of the Twelve.

Standing imperiously on a promontory partway up the mountainside is a temple of elegantly sculpted stone with a single domed tower rising from its center. Expanses of the structure's weathered exterior bear scores of tall, glass-paned windows that cause the facade to shimmer in the sunlight. Wide stairs are carved into the rock face, winding back and forth as they ascend to the temple from the ruins below.

When the Oatia elves first settled Loskialua, they built a modest shrine to Desna on the mountain several hundred feet above their town. There they could cleanse themselves and pray to the goddess before ascending higher into the mountains, where the thinner atmosphere provided a clearer view of the stars. As the settlement grew and the astronomers' discoveries proved ever more exciting, the elves carved a staircase into the rock, creating a steep but direct route to the shrine. These buildings catered both to the astronomers, whose primary tools were mathematics and scientific instruments, and to the scholar-priests whose techniques blended divinations with the astronomers' data, who worked together here.

In the latter half of Loskialua's occupation, the elves made contact with an extraordinary alien entity known as Ibra, now

TEMPLE OF THE TWELVE

PART 1: QUESTIONS IN QABARAT

PART 2: THE UKULAM EXPEDITION

PART 3: THE LOST TEMPLE

CASTROVEL

THE CULT OF THE DEVOURER

ALIEN ARCHIVES

CODEX OF WORLDS

known throughout the Pact Worlds as the god of celestial bodies, the cosmos, and the mysteries of the universe. Adopting Ibra's worship long before anyone on Castrovel knew of the god's existence, the Oatia elves built a grander temple around their Desnan shrine. They reconsecrated the building to honor both deities, calling it the Temple of the Twelve after the strange circular constellation they had discovered. Eventually, the astronomers reached the limits of their combined magic and technology. When they realized they could learn no more here, they decommissioned the site, laid enough defenses to ensure their discoveries would not fall into the hands of the incompetent, and departed for a realm beyond the stars.

The greater temple complex once included numerous smaller outbuildings to house the scholar-priests, their equipment, and food. These have largely collapsed over time, being of less durable construction than the temple itself.

All of the inscriptions in the Temple of the Twelve are written in Elven. If the PCs can't read or translate Elven, they can learn little from the temple's records. Furthermore, the temple disrupts communications for several thousand feet around itself, introducing enough static to interfere with data uploads over comm units or computers.

C1. Path of Enlightenment (CR 5)

When the Temple of the Twelve began receiving more pilgrims and required greater upkeep, the elves carved a staircase into the steep slope leading up to the site. They called this the Path of Enlightenment, placing small monuments at each landing carved with cosmic wisdom that have since eroded beyond legibility. The climb is steep—a reflection of Ibra's teachings that the greatest discoveries require hard work to reach. The ascent also hides numerous traps, though the cult disabled most on its way up, whereas others had fallen apart with time. Having no idea of the temple's true purpose, Halkueem Zan called this pathway the "Stairs to Eternity."

Creature: The Devourer cultists failed to notice one trap, which launched a volley of magical darts, leaving one of them at death's door. The group abandoned him and climbed on. The dying lashunta attracted the attention of a young mountain eel, an immense bug-eyed predator that has only recently had to fend for itself. The cultist represented a caloric windfall, and as the PCs approach, the mountain eel is pinning the corpse as it tears off gobbets of flesh to consume. It attacks, both to defend its catch and to secure future meals, but it flees if reduced to 15 Hit Points or fewer.

ADOLESCENT MOUNTAIN EEL   CR 5
XP 1,600

N Large animal (*Starfinder Alien Archive* 78)

Init +7; **Senses** low-light vision; **Perception** +11

DEFENSE   HP 76
EAC 17; **KAC** 19

Fort +9; **Ref** +9; **Will** +4

OFFENSE
Speed 40 ft.

Melee bite +14 (1d6+9 P)

Space 10 ft.; **Reach** 5 ft.

Offensive Abilities paralyzing gaze (60 ft., DC 13)

STATISTICS
Str +4; **Dex** +3; **Con** +2; **Int** −4; **Wis** +0; **Cha** +0

Skills Athletics +16, Stealth +11

SPECIAL ABILITIES
Paralyzing Gaze (Ex) The sight of a mountain eel's strange compound eyes causes the muscles of most living creatures to freeze up. A living creature that has a sense of sight and begins its turn within 60 feet of a mountain eel must succeed at a DC 13 Fortitude save or be paralyzed for 1 round. A creature that succeeds at its save is immune to that mountain eel's paralyzing gaze for 24 hours. Other mountain eels and creatures without a sense of sight are immune to this effect.

Treasure: Most of the dead cultist's gear is demolished, though the PCs can recover a battery (17 charges remaining) and a survival knife.

C2. The Veil (CR 6)

A series of weathered pillars arcs around the entrance of the temple, marking a curving border around a small plaza.

The Oatia elves were versed in using the *aiudara* that linked nearby worlds, but they were incapable of true spaceflight. Unable to experience the cosmos directly, they built a symbolic barrier to protect their temple from contamination by terrestrial interference, much as their astronomers minimized light pollution to properly view the sky. They called this sacred threshold the Veil.

A steep, narrow trail leaves the plaza from the northwest, winding more than a mile up the mountainside to the temple's main observatory and the location of the *aiudara* the elves used to eventually depart Castrovel. This ruined observatory is not detailed in the adventure, but Tahomen and several of his cultists made the ascent to set up their system-wide comm unit and broadcast their discoveries to a Devourer cult base hidden in the Diaspora. By the time the PCs arrive at the temple, the cultists have already concluded the communication and are preparing to descend the mountain (see **Event 6**).

Creature: In addition to their traps, the elves left behind one of their own to guard their legacy and guide those seeking knowledge for its own sake. The elf Panelliar was one of the warrior-monks who honored Ibra by channeling the galaxy's power into divine weapons. He volunteered to stand vigil, performing a series of self-mummification rites that preserved his mind and soul within an undead body. Over his long watch, only a few beings have tried to enter the temple, most notably Halkueem Zan, whom Panelliar forcibly repelled, and

Tahomen and his cult, who used the spell *command undead* to control the guardian. Now under the cult leader's control, Panelliar has been convinced to strike down those who would enter the temple.

As the PCs approach, Panelliar steps forward and motions for them to halt outside the Veil before he solemnly greets them in Elven and orders them to turn back. If the PCs don't understand him, he repeats himself in Celestial, eventually resigning himself to concise hand motions if unable to establish verbal communication. The PCs' likely questions and his answers appear below.

Who are you? "I am Panelliar, Sun Spear of the Inscrutable. It is my duty to guard this place against those who would despoil or misuse my people's discoveries."

What is this place? "Behind me lies the Temple of the Twelve, the last repository of my people's lore in this system. Before me is the Veil, beyond which terrestrial ignorance melts beneath the weight of cosmic enlightenment. This is a sacred space."

How long have you been here? "To measure the passage of time as does the universe, my vigil has been but a moment. By the revolutions of Castrovel, I have been here for millennia."

Have others passed this way? "Centuries ago, a child of Golarion came. He sought the secrets beyond for his own glory, so I turned him away with violence. A band of lashuntas and an unfamiliar alien arrived recently. I recognized them as pawns of the Star-Eater, and although I turned them away, the leader's conviction and magic were strong; I relented." (The "child of Golarion" Panelliar is referring to is the explorer Halkueem Zan, whom he remembers as a shameless charlatan and fool. The leader of the recent arrivals whom the elf encountered is the cult leader Tahomen.)

Where did the lashuntas go? "They entered the temple and studied the secrets within. Some of them later ascended the mountain to commune with the heavens with the portable shrine they carried. The others remain inside." (The "portable shrine" is the cultists' system-wide comm unit, though Panelliar is unfamiliar with modern technology and does not recognize its purpose.)

May we enter? "The speaker for the Star-Eater does not wish to allow you to enter, and by his will, I must insist. You are not welcome here."

Once the PCs have conversed with Panelliar, if they ignore his warnings to leave, he manifests his solar weapon and attacks.

PANELLIAR   CR 6
XP 2,400
Male unique undead elf solarian
N Medium undead
Init +3; **Senses** darkvision
60 ft., low-light vision;
Perception +13

DEFENSE   **HP** 90
EAC 19; **KAC** 19
Fort +8; **Ref** +6; **Will** +7
Immunities undead immunities (see page 54)

OFFENSE
Speed 40 ft.
Melee solar spear +16 (1d8+1d4+11 P; critical wound)
Ranged pulse dart +13 (1d6+8; critical burn 1d6)
Offensive Abilities stellar revelations (black hole [25 ft., pull 15 ft., DC 14], corona [2d6 F, cold resistance 10], pulse dart, supernova [10-ft. radius, 7d6 F, DC 14])

TACTICS
During Combat Panelliar favors photon mode, entering it and activating his corona revelation as soon as combat begins. He prefers melee combat, but he tends to ignore dedicated melee combatants (especially those harmed by his corona) in favor of

PANELLIAR

TEMPLE OF THE TWELVE

PART 1:
QUESTIONS IN QABARAT

PART 2:
THE UKULAM EXPEDITION

PART 3:
THE LOST TEMPLE

CASTROVEL

THE CULT OF THE DEVOURER

ALIEN ARCHIVES

CODEX OF WORLDS

pinning down spellcasters and ranged specialists.

Morale If Panelliar has already parleyed with the PCs, he fights until destroyed. If not, he fights until reduced to 35 Hit Points, at which point he calls a temporary truce to converse and discover what his foes desire. If he cannot convince them to turn away after answering their questions, he rejoins the fight.

STATISTICS

Str +5; **Dex** +3; **Con** −; **Int** +1; **Wis** +1; **Cha** +2

Skills Athletics +13, Mysticism +13, Sense Motive +18

Languages Celestial, Elven

Other Abilities solar manifestation (weapon: solar spear), stellar alignment (see page 54), unliving (see page 54)

Gear ancient elven battle armor (archaic), least gluon crystal

SPECIAL ABILITIES

Pulse Dart (Su) As a standard action, Panelliar can fire a dart of stellar energy as a ranged attack against EAC with a range of 60 feet. The pulse dart deals 1d10+6 fire damage and has the critical hit effect burn 1d6.

Development: If the PCs are somehow able to dispel the *command undead* spell, Panelliar does not fight them, gives them his least gluon crystal in thanks, and will even help the PCs fight the cultists inside the temple. With that done, he wanders the interior for the rest of the adventure, conversing with the PCs if they wish but not helping them further until he concludes the long business of cleansing the site. It is his belief, after all, that those seeking knowledge must do much of the work themselves.

C3. ENTRY HALL

Thanks to sophisticated preservative varnishes and the extensive metalwork crisscrossing them, the ornately carved wooden doors leading into the temple have just barely survived the ages intact. They are unlocked and are only a nominal barrier (hardness 5, HP 5, break DC 10).

From its floor to its curved ceiling thirty feet above, this entry hall is covered in sweeping arcs of constellations marked with delicate lines and numbers at regular intervals.

A series of short climbing pitons stick out of the ground near the center of the room, where embedded floor scythes were placed to slash at the unwelcome. The cult readily disabled the trap, and it presents no danger to the PCs.

The intricate constellations and curves depict how key stars and galaxies migrate across the night sky, though the placement of the constellations doesn't match their actual locations as viewed from Castrovel. A PC who can read Elven and succeeds at a DC 15 Physical Science check can ascertain that while the orientation of the constellations is more artistic, the curved paths are scientifically precise, showing exact dates that the stars appear in the sky and how they migrate throughout a year.

In addition, two unknown constellations are present in the display: a jagged line of six stars and a perfect circle made up of 12 stars. With a successful DC 10 Mysticism check, a PC can identify the first as the unknown constellation commonly depicted in the god Ibra's holy symbol. What's more, the Ibran constellation's curving line records erratic dates and coordinates that defy astronomic explanation. However, a PC who succeeds at a DC 19 Physical Science check realizes that these are not true coordinates but rather encoded instructions for how to bypass the trap in area **C4**. The second constellation represents the Gate of Twelve Suns, though the PCs are likely unable to identify it as such unless they have already studied the ancient elven records in the inner sanctum (area **C8**), in which case, a PC can recognize it with a successful DC 15 Physical Science check.

C4. SOVYRIAN GALLERY (CR 3)

The exterior wall of this gallery contains nearly one hundred tall, narrow windows that allow thin streams of anemic light to pass through their foggy panes. The interior wall depicts the night sky and its stars. Dozens of stylized starburst carvings decorate the floor.

This hall was known as the Sovyrian Gallery because its interior wall depicts the night sky as seen from Sovyrian in the southern hemisphere (recognizable with a successful DC 20 Physical Science check).

Trap: The starburst carvings on the floor are about 2 feet wide and creatures can hop from one to the next with relative ease. They are part of a magical trap that rains destructive energy on trespassers, but it can be bypassed by hopping from one starburst to another to follow a defined path through the area. This path is detailed in the constellation carvings in area **C3**. Once the PCs know the proper pattern, they can travel through the area at half speed without triggering the trap.

STAR STORM TRAP	CR 3

XP 800

Type magical; **Perception** DC 24; **Disable** Mysticism DC 19 (disrupt the magical energy)

Trigger location; **Reset** 1 minute; **Bypass** follow the path of Ibra's constellation through the trapped area (Physical Science DC 19 to decipher; see area **C3**)

Initial Effect a rain of glowing stars cascades from the ceiling, striking all creatures in the secondary area and dealing 5d6 damage, half of which is electricity and half of which is fire; DC 14 Reflex half; multiple targets (all targets in a 25-by-30-foot area); **Secondary Effect** any creature that fails the Reflex save is covered in sparkling motes of light that last for 10 minutes, during which time the creature takes a −10 penalty to Stealth checks and cannot benefit from concealment; Will DC 14 negates

C5. Ukulam Gallery (CR 5)

Three wooden doors line the west wall of this gallery. The curving interior wall depicts the night sky and its stars.

This hall was known as the Ukulam Gallery because its interior wall depicts the night sky as seen from Ukulam in the northern hemisphere (recognizable with a successful DC 20 Physical Science check). A 3-foot-tall octagonal stone platform that once served as an auxiliary altar stands in the middle of the hall, where it now supports a small pile of industrial explosives (see Hazard below).

Creatures: Having extracted everything of importance to the Cult of the Devourer from the temple, Tahomen left two cultists under the leadership of Avissa, the cult's explosives expert, to plant explosive charges and demolish the temple in a blazing tribute to their merciless deity. Once the cultists hear the PCs enter the temple, they prepare for a fight, talking cover wherever they can find it.

AVISSA   CR 3
XP 800
Female korasha lashunta soldier
CE Medium humanoid (lashunta)
Init +2; **Perception** +8

DEFENSE   HP 41
EAC 15; **KAC** 18
Fort +5; **Ref** +3; **Will** +4

OFFENSE
Speed 20 ft.
Melee cestus battleglove +8 (1d4+7 B)
Ranged squad machine gun +11 (1d10+3 P)
Offensive Abilities fighting style (arcane assailant), withering fire
Lashunta Spell-Like Abilities (CL 3rd)
   1/day–detect thoughts (DC 12)
   At will–daze (DC 11), psychokinetic hand

TACTICS
During Combat Avissa fires short bursts at her enemies until she can catch several targets using her machine gun's automatic mode. After depleting her ammo, she reloads or moves into melee range as suits her needs.
Morale Avissa fights to the death. If reduced to 15 Hit Points with little chance of survival, she activates her detonator (see Hazard below).

STATISTICS
Str +4; **Dex** +2; **Con** +1; **Int** +0; **Wis** –1; **Cha** +1
Skills Athletics +8, Engineering +13, Intimidate +8
Languages Castrovelian, Common; limited telepathy 30 ft.
Other Abilities rune of the eldritch knight
Gear squad defiance series, cestus battleglove, squad machine gun (rune of the eldritch knight) with 120 heavy rounds, detonator, field rations (2 weeks)

SPECIAL ABILITIES
Withering Fire (Ex) Any creature damaged by Avissa's machine gun when she operates it using automatic mode must succeed at a DC 12 Will save or be shaken for 1d3 rounds.

DEVOURER CULTISTS (2)   CR 1
XP 400 each
HP 20 each (see page 24)

AVISSA

TEMPLE OF THE TWELVE

PART 1:
QUESTIONS IN QABARAT

PART 2:
THE UKULAM EXPEDITION

PART 3:
THE LOST TEMPLE

CASTROVEL

THE CULT OF THE DEVOURER

ALIEN ARCHIVES

CODEX OF WORLDS

Hazard: The explosive charges on the altar have not yet been set. Without being armed with a detonator, only an electrical charge (such as electricity damage) can trigger them, and a PC can identify the explosives and how to trigger them with a successful DC 14 Engineering check. The charges are far more destructive when properly installed, but if detonated in the open, they function as an incendiary grenade II (Reflex DC 13 half).

The cultists have already installed numerous charges throughout this area—not yet enough to destroy the building, but enough to collapse part of the ceiling. The cultist Avissa (see Creatures on page 31) currently has a detonator programmed to these explosives, which she can draw as a move action and activate with no action. If she does so, parts of the ceiling collapse and rain down on the marked area, dealing 1d12 bludgeoning damage to all creatures in the area (Reflex DC 14 half) and filling the area within the dotted lines on the map with a cloud of dust that grants concealment for 1d3 rounds.

Treasure: The planted explosive charges present little threat once the cultists are defeated. If the PCs desire, they can carefully defuse and extract the explosive charges with 10 minutes of work and a successful DC 20 Engineering check to disable device. There are 10 charges in total, each of which is equivalent to an incendiary grenade I.

C6. Studies

This series of rooms once served as offices and laboratories for the high-ranking astronomers and scholar-priests that operated the temple. The rooms are now a clutter of crumbling furniture that is only a soft kick away from collapsing into dust. The doors are all unlocked and fragile (hardness 5, HP 5) to the point that a creature can topple a door entirely while moving through it by succeeding at a DC 13 Strength check.

C7. The Vantage

The southernmost point in the temple is a high-ceilinged sanctuary with tall, narrow windows filled with foggy, discolored glass. The vantage point juts out over the cliff below, overlooking the stairs carved into the mountainside and the ruined settlement below.

Creature: The archaeologist abducted from the university in Qabarat, Dr. **Olmehya Solstarni Wehir of House Raimar, Echo of Inshirsi's Dream** (NG female kasatha), has been fettered and left to her own devices here as the cultists patrol the temple and plant their explosives. Once Tahomen's expedition reached the Temple of the Twelve and exploited Dr. Solstarni's knowledge of elven lore to bypass several of the defenses, the cult leader had little use for the kasatha. He left her here to contemplate her imminent demise until he returned to demolish the temple with her inside. Rather than dreading her death, she has instead spent her time studying the carvings and inscriptions in this area. If Dr. Solstarni meets the PCs before they confront the cultists in area **C5**, she silently motions to where her captors are hiding. If the PCs have already prevailed, she greets them with relief—especially once she learns the university sent them.

Dr. Solstarni is a soft-spoken archaeoastronomer, specializing in how past cultures viewed, understood, and depicted the cosmos. As a result, learning more about the Temple of the Twelve and its purpose is the discovery of a lifetime that draws her out of her shy habits. With enough supplies, she would happily remain here for months, but she knows the PCs are operating on a tight schedule. She has, after all, listened to most of Tahomen's plans, and she relays what she knows.

SOLSTARNI

"The so-called Eyrub Paqual was a ploy, as I suspected. The man behind my abduction is a lashunta called Tahomen, who leads a significant Cult of the Devourer cell. From what I gather, he learned of ancient texts associated with the explorer Halkueem Zan's travels here and attempted to recruit me to travel here and decipher anything we found. What I've learned is that the Oatia elven culture found the cosmos utterly fascinating, at first worshiping Desna before fixating on several alien entities and celestial features to worship— especially a constellation of twelve stars, which might be strictly symbolic. He knocked me out after I ceased cooperating here, and I suspect he learned something more in the temple's inner sanctum.

Once freed, Dr. Solstarni can keep up with the PCs, though she's not a reliable combatant. If necessary, you can use the statistics for a Devourer cultist with no special abilities. Given Dr. Solstarni's knowledge of elven culture and language, she is of far greater use helping to translate and understand the temple's texts and art.

Story Award: If the PCs find and rescue Dr. Solstarni, award them 1,200 XP.

C8. INNER SANCTUM (CR 4)

Once a freestanding shrine dedicated to Desna, this butterfly-shaped structure became the inner sanctum of the temple to Ibra later built around it. Even an untrained viewer can tell that the construction styles of the two phases are quite distinct. The astronomers of the Temple of the Twelve stored the records of their greatest discoveries here, and the sanctum is filled with physical books and scrolls (see Development below). A spiral staircase to the north climbs to the temple's observatory tower high above the ground floor (area **C9**).

Creatures: As a final line of defense, the elves left behind a pair of lore guardians—magically animated statues capable of fending off intruders. These lore guardians are slow to attack elves, and an apparently elven PC can convince them to stand down with a successful DC 18 Diplomacy check. Tahomen disguised himself as an elf to avoid combat as he perused the texts here.

LORE GUARDIANS (2)	CR 2

XP 600 each
HP 28 each (see page 57)

STATISTICS
Languages Elven (can't speak)
Other Abilities species tradition (elf)

Treasure: Among the ancient texts are several magic items of note: a *spell gem of flight* (2nd level), a *spell gem of remove affliction*, a *spell gem of see invisibility*, and a *staff of mystic healing*.

Development: The true prize here is the Oatia elves' discoveries, and many of the pre-Gap books here are legible, albeit barely intact. Furthermore, Tahomen was sloppy in returning documents to their proper places, allowing the PCs to uncover the same information he did. Most of the texts here are in Elven, though some are in Celestial, Draconic, and an archaic version of Castrovelian that's very difficult for a modern speaker to parse.

If the PCs study the texts here (possibly with Dr. Solstarni's assistance), they learn that the Oatia elves were a philosophical offshoot that spurned their Sovyrian kin and sought a new life of cosmic contemplation on Ukulam, thousands of years before the Gap. Their techniques quickly improved, and through a combination of telescopes and divination magic, the elves discovered a strange constellation of 12 stars that formed a perfect circle in the sky. The more they studied the constellation, the stranger their dreams became, and powerful scholar-priests began recording the odd language they saw and heard.

As the elves' knowledge of and exposure to the galaxy expanded, they parleyed with increasingly bizarre and powerful alien minds, most notably a powerful being known as Ibra—especially noteworthy because the elves' records suggest that Ibra may not have been a deity at the time. Through Ibra's teachings, the elves studied the mysterious circular constellation, learning that it was not a natural feature but the construction of an impossibly ancient and highly advanced species untold light years away. Casting their minds far into the cosmos, the scholar-priests sensed that the ring pulsed with an unnatural energy, which led them to believe it to be a gateway of some kind. The elves called it the Gate of Twelve Suns, and they renamed their temple in honor of it.

Some of the scholar-priests believed that the Gate of Twelve Suns held back some powerful army. Others postulated that it magnified the thoughts and dreams of another galaxy and that it could be the key to untold knowledge. The most popular hypothesis, though, was that the Gate of Twelve Suns represented such power that it could only be (or serve as the portal to) some cosmically powerful superweapon. One of the scholar-priests even posited the existence of a so-called "Stellar Degenerator," which could drain all energy from a star, turning it into a hypothetical stellar remnant called a black dwarf. Unfortunately, there's no definitive note of where the Gate of Twelve Suns is—as if identifying its location was taboo to the elves.

As interpretive disputes broke out among the elves, they agreed that from the confines of Loskialua, they could never confirm their theories, much less attain enlightenment through discovery under the inspired guidance of Ibra. They packed up what they needed, and then they performed a ritual that the texts referred to only as "the Celestial Voyage." The implication is that the elves traveled to another system, though whether they succeeded or failed is uncertain from these records.

Story Award: If the PCs decipher the Oatia elves' discoveries concerning the Gate of Twelve Suns, award them 800 XP.

C9. OBSERVATORY TOWER

The staircase climbs more than 100 feet to a broad observation platform with high guard walls.

Treasure: Most of the instruments that once stood here have corroded into nothing more than rusty stains and scratched glass. One device remains intact, though: an apparatus that measures and records psychic emanations from across the

TEMPLE OF THE TWELVE

PART 1:
QUESTIONS
IN QABARAT

PART 2:
THE UKULAM
EXPEDITION

PART 3:
THE LOST
TEMPLE

CASTROVEL

THE CULT OF
THE DEVOURER

ALIEN
ARCHIVES

CODEX OF
WORLDS

galaxy for later study. The crystal in which these are recorded ran out of storage capacity millennia ago, but the device continued to record and reconfigure the data, compressing it ever more densely over the ages. The inadvertent result is a *mk 1 ability crystal* that positively hums with the psychic hopes and dreams of a million minds from across the galaxy.

EVENT 6: THE DEVOURER DESCENDS (CR 6)

This encounter occurs once the PCs have had time to explore the temple and its records and are preparing to depart.

Creatures: The cult leader Tahomen and two of his surviving cultists descend from the mountain where they have finished broadcasting their findings to the cult's hidden outpost in the Diaspora. Although Salask has described the PCs to him, this is Tahomen's first time seeing his pursuers up close. Having secured and shared data that could very well spell the destruction of the galaxy, Tahomen is utterly smug and fearless. The cult leader engages in some mocking banter as his subordinates set the heavy comm unit components down, and he pulls out and activates a detonator keyed to the explosive charges in area **C5**. If the charges are still in place, an explosion rocks the temple but does not destroy it—a result Tahomen finds disappointing but still a suitable backdrop of destruction before he attacks. If the PCs disabled the charges, nothing happens, and Tahomen throws aside the detonator in disgust before launching his attack.

Tahomen is a mystic with the devastator connection, a new mystic connection presented on page 50 in the "Cult of the Devourer" article.

DEVOURER CULTISTS (2)	CR 1

XP 400 each

HP 20 each (see page 24)

TAHOMEN	CR 5

XP 1,600

Male korasha lashunta mystic

CE Medium humanoid (lashunta)

Init +1; **Perception** +11

DEFENSE   HP 55
EAC 17; **KAC** 18

Fort +6; **Ref** +4; **Will** +8

Resistances cold 5, fire 5

OFFENSE
Speed 30 ft.

Melee survival knife +8 (1d4+7 S)

Ranged liquidator disintegrator pistol +10 (1d10+5 A)

Offensive Abilities blood mark (see page 50), destructive frenzy (see page 50)

Lashunta Spell-Like Abilities (CL 5th)

1/day—*detect thoughts* (DC 16)

At will—*daze* (DC 15), *psychokinetic hand*

Mystic Spell-Like Abilities (CL 5th)

At will—*mindlink*

Mystic Spells Known (CL 5th; ranged +10)

2nd (3/day)—*caustic conversion*, *command undead* (DC 17), *hurl forcedisk*

1st (6/day)—*carnivorous* (see page 51), *mind thrust* (DC 16), *reflecting armor* (DC 16)

0 (at will)—*fatigue* (DC 15), *telekinetic projectile*

Connection devastator (see page 50)

TACTICS
Before Combat Tahomen casts *reflecting armor* before he descends to the temple.

During Combat Tahomen favors ranged attacks with his spells, though he delights in the opportunity to clobber any foes foolish enough to approach him directly.

Morale Having already sent the critical data to his colleagues, Tahomen welcomes the sweet oblivion of dying in battle.

STATISTICS
Str +2; **Dex** +1; **Con** +3; **Int** +0; **Wis** +5; **Cha** +2

Skills Intimidate +16, Mysticism +16, Sense Motive +11

Languages Abyssal, Common, Castrovelian, Elven; limited telepathy 60 ft.

Gear d-suit I (mk 1 thermal capacitor), liquidator disintegrator pistol (see page 52) with 3 batteries (20 charges each), survival knife, *psychic booster*, detonator, personal comm unit, field rations (2 weeks), R2Es (5)

Treasure: The cultists are carrying a system-wide comm unit including a tier-2 computer with firewall and wipe countermeasures (see Development below). The comm unit is disassembled into three bulky pieces, but it is fully functional once reassembled.

Development: With Tahomen defeated, the PCs can inspect the comm unit his team carried here. The system is massive, only capable of being moved by several strong people once it's been broken into smaller components. Even with the comm unit disassembled, a PC can boot up the system's computer and access its unsecured communications log with a successful DC 10 Computers check. Tahomen has dutifully purged his correspondence history leading up to this expedition, but the PCs can still determine that the comm unit logged a call and significant data upload about 3 hours earlier.

To access more information, a PC must succeed at a DC 21 Computers check to hack the comm unit's tier-2 computer. Once the PC has access to the system, he can read Tahomen's recent communications. The correspondence relays many of the same conclusions the PCs learned in area **C8**, but with more sinister certainty: Tahomen posits that the 12-star constellation—the Gate of Twelve Suns—opens to a demiplane that hides an unspeakably powerful superweapon. The cult leader believes that the Drift Rock is a tiny fragment of this "Stellar Degenerator," broken off when a portion of the demiplane was torn away and added to the Drift as a result of Drift travel. Tahomen also recommended that the

TEMPLE
OF THE
TWELVE

PART 1:
QUESTIONS
IN QABARAT

PART 2:
THE UKULAM
EXPEDITION

PART 3:
THE LOST
TEMPLE

CASTROVEL

THE CULT OF
THE DEVOURER

ALIEN
ARCHIVES

CODEX OF
WORLDS

Cult of Devourer apply as many resources as possible to find the Gate of Twelve Suns—and the Stellar Degenerator— before anyone else does. In addition, the PCs can learn the approximate coordinates of the location Tahomen transmitted his messages to: a stretch of several hundred asteroids in the Diaspora.

The computer also contains access to Tahomen's financial account, protected behind a firewall. Hacking this requires a successful DC 23 Computers check, but a wipe countermeasure purges the data after a second failed hacking attempt. The account contains 2,000 credits.

CONCLUDING THE ADVENTURE

Having thwarted Tahomen and his Devourer cult, the PCs can continue exploring the Temple of the Twelve as much as they like. However, the troubling implication that the Gate of Twelve Suns might provide access to a weapon of almost unimaginable power like a Stellar Degenerator—not to mention the fact that the Cult of the Devourer now knows about the weapon and is actively looking for it—should compel the PCs to expedite their return to civilization.

Whether or not the Stellar Degenerator is real, the Cult of the Devourer could use this information as a rallying cry to attract more recruits to the cult and inflict greater atrocities in the name of their uncaring god. At minimum, the news that the Castrovelian Devourer cult was in communication with other cult elements elsewhere in the Pact Worlds should be enough of a threat to encourage the PCs to retrace their steps back to Turhalu Point, and ultimately Qabarat.

If the PCs return to Qabarat with Dr. Solstarni in tow, Professor Muhali is relieved to see her colleague in one piece, and university officials offer each of the PCs admittance and free tuition to the school for up to 3 years in thanks for their service. Alternatively, a PC can choose to accept a "research grant" of 1,000 credits from the university in lieu of a scholarship (and it's up to each PC how they make use of this grant).

The PCs might also want to update Chiskisk about their findings, either by sending the shirren Starfinder a message or by returning to Absalom Station to report to them in person. In any case, with the Cult of the Devourer actively searching for the Gate of Twelve Suns, the Pact Worlds may need the PCs' assistance more than ever, and there is little time to waste. The PCs' efforts to thwart the cult and learn more about the alien superweapon, from the asteroid fields of the Diaspora to the necropolis cities of dead Eox, are the focus of "Splintered Worlds," the next installment of the Dead Suns Adventure Path.

CASTROVEL

NORTHERN STEPS

Western Sea

UKULAM

Loskialua

Stormshield Mountains

Caliria Maze

Turhalu Point

Singing Range

Ralhoma River

Yaro River

Esowath Nexus

IKAL EXPANSE

Qabarat

Waklohar's Expeditions

Station 9

The Seacrown

Broken Minds

Lemenore
Ocean

Shattered Sea

Qarik

THE COLONIES

Queensrock

Strait of Glory

Komena

Gulf of
Legions

Kebenaut

Plains of Ru

Chisk

The Bulwarks

Watchpost Quinai

Nestwall
Mountains

Jaws of the Mother

Towers of
Memory

Lake
Kechavas

Zysyk

Setae Range

Kai-Hebla Ice Sheet

• Jabask

• Laubu Mesa

Glowsilk Jungle

Lemenore Ocean

Tarakeshi River

Ocean of Mists

Lake Nehan

• Candares

ASANA

Sea of Teeth

Floating Shards

Cordona
Clariel's Arm

Woven River

Telasia   Nerundel   • El

Snowsalt Sea

SOVYRIAN

Korinath
Divide

Southwatch

rovas

TEMPLE OF THE TWELVE

PART 1:
QUESTIONS
IN QABARAT

PART 2:
THE UKULAM
EXPEDITION

PART 3:
THE LOST
TEMPLE

● CASTROVEL

THE CULT OF
THE DEVOURER

ALIEN
ARCHIVES

CODEX OF
WORLDS

CASTROVEL IS A HOT, HUMID WORLD WITH A RICH ATMOSPHERE THAT GIVES LIFE TO CONTINENT-SPANNING JUNGLES THAT ARE HOME TO SAURIAN PREDATORS, MOBILE CARNIVOROUS PLANTS, AND DEVASTATING MOLDSTORMS DURING THE PERIODIC MASS FLOWERINGS CALLED "DEATH BLOOMS." WHILE NEARLY EVERY TERRESTRIAL BIOME CAN BE FOUND SOMEWHERE ON CASTROVEL, IT REMAINS BOTH THOROUGHLY WILD AND DENSELY POPULATED, WITH MODERN CITIES AND CUTTING-EDGE INDUSTRIAL COMPLEXES SEPARATED FROM THE RAVAGES OF THE PRIMEVAL WILDERNESS BY ELECTRIFIED FENCES AND AUTOMATED WEAPONS TURRETS.

OVERVIEW

Given its extreme biodiversity, it isn't surprising that Castrovel fostered several major races, each with a unique civilization on its own continent. Most prominent in the Pact Worlds are lashuntas, telepathic humanoids with a cultural emphasis on scholarship and self-improvement from the continent of Asana. The thousands of hives of the ant-like and equally telepathic formians of the Colonies align readily to the directives of their ruling council. This philosophical battle of individualism versus collectivism (combined with telepathy's advantage in communicating such ideas) sparked a millennia-long war that raged between the two races until just 30 years ago. The elves of Sovyrian remain steadfastly aloof from this conflict—and everything else. They focus on their magical pursuits and guard their shores with stone-faced resolve.

Despite the planet's tumultuous history, the three races are not as fractious as they seem. Outposts of all three can be found beyond the borders of their native continents. The planet as a whole welcomes travelers from offworld, even if the elves largely restrict trade with non-elves to offshore ports designed for that purpose. The planetary economy is robust, due to the strength of Asana's corporations and universities combined with the relentless efficiency of formian manufactory hives.

Despite the constant threat of megafauna, Castrovelians take pride in their planet's wilderness, deliberately preserving large swaths of it for ecotourism and research. Castrovel has the largest population of Green Faith followers in the Pact Worlds and includes the Xenowardens as a prominent theopolitical faction. Even before the rise of starships, magical portals called *aiudara* (or "elf gates") facilitated this commitment by connecting major settlements across the planet without the need for expensive and dangerous roads. Today, these arches remain a major public resource as well as a subject of intense speculation, since the secret of their creation has long been lost and many gates are broken or lead to unknown destinations.

The following pages presents Castrovel's four major continents, with notable locations and a settlement stat block for the city on each continent most visited by offworld travelers.

ASANA

The homeland of the lashuntas, Asana is the largest continent on Castrovel. It boasts everything from snowcapped mountains and sweltering jungles to rocky and rain-shadowed deserts. While heavily populated compared to the other continents, it still contains wide expanses of uncontrolled and even unexplored territory, thanks in large part to the distributed nature of lashunta government.

Lashuntas on Asana traditionally organize themselves by city-state, with each state controlling a few smaller settlements and the land and resources immediately around them. Internally, these cities vary wildly, ranging from egalitarian communes to hereditary monarchies, though most favor democratically elected autocrats. Despite the lashuntas' deep love of scholarship and intellectual and magical pursuits, the constant presence of bold predators just beyond their walls—from savage megafauna to intelligent monstrous races—leads every city to maintain a significant military. This spirit of militaristic self-reliance means that attempts to unify multiple city-states rarely last long, though warring between the states is traditionally about shows of force and daring raids rather than outright slaughter, and even enemy cities will often work together when attacked by outside forces. The divided nature of lashunta government can be a double-edged sword for its citizens, however, as big businesses can easily play the competitive city-states off each other, and many lashuntas fear that their society may soon go the way of Akiton's—co-opted by commercial concerns without regard for the residents' welfare.

While Castrovel's fertile environmental conditions make it a breadbasket for the solar system and the constant discovery of useful plants and creatures makes it an attractive base for research firms, Asana's greatest resource is its people. The charismatic, educated, telepathic populace provides a talented and passionate workforce for interplanetary corporations. The relatively long history of Asana's civilization and the constant reclamation of fallen cities by the jungle also means that a great deal of magical knowledge may be simply lying undiscovered in some jungle clearing.

NOTABLE LOCATIONS

Both new and old locales dot Asana. Its coastlines are the regions that are the best mapped and understood, whereas records of the interior are largely confined to myth and broken history.

The Bulwarks: This chain of islands leads across the Strait of Glory to the Colonies, making its shores and causeways the most hotly contested territory in the planet's history. For thousands of years, formians and lashuntas battled constantly over these tiny islands, using them as beachheads to launch invasions onto each other's shores or score political points at home through minor advances. As a result, the islands are shattered, grotesque palimpsests, with modern fortresses built atop the ruins of ancient castles and the husks of warhives, and entire valleys filled with slowly decaying bones and chitin. Some islands are completely uninhabitable today due to radiation or military biotech. Since the truce between the two civilizations, scholars from both sides have begun cautiously combing through the ruins for lost knowledge, while groups like the Xenowardens attempt to rehabilitate the most damaged isles.

Candares: Every year, the spring meltwaters of the Tarakeshi River slowly back up, filling the massive Lake Nehan and turning the districts of Upper Candares into islands, until at last the waters reach the edge of their banks and come blasting down into the narrow valley of Lower Candares from every direction, creating dozens of spectacular waterfalls. The steep walls of this crevasse have traditionally been lined with hydroelectric turbines and seasonal temples maintained by native spider-limbed kaymos, who live in peace with the city's lashunta citizens. In recent years, however, the city has been flooded not just with water but with riches, as technomancers for the Astral Extractions mining company have discovered new magical uses for corpsicum, a rare material produced when water seeps through the kaymos' cliffside burial grounds. The resulting influx of cash has let the corporation buy leaders and votes, and most of the city is happy enough to let crab-like mining robots scale their cliffs. Exasperated and unheeded, the Wallkeepers—traditionalist rebels from both races who see the mining as a desecration of their ancestors—occasionally send the enormous machines falling in flames to the city below.

Jabask: Located deep in the Glowsilk Jungle and accessible only by *aiudara*, arduous overland treks, or daredevil shuttle flights, Jabask is perhaps the most traditional of the major city-states—and the most embattled. Behind its ugly concrete ramparts, locals live in symbiosis with the Somana Tree-Sages, intelligent plant-creatures of extreme magic and confusing mindsets whose branches are tended by furry split-tailed nobosets. The greatest of the Tree-Sages, the Prophet of the Wood, regularly offers eclectic pearls of knowledge, including advanced scientific revelations and disconcertingly accurate predictions gleaned via mystical communion with some greater power called "the Ken." In exchange, the cityfolk protect the Somana from the horde of beasts that prey upon them, most notably the three-eyed fangsaras. This would be easier if not for the frequent moldstorms that sweep the city, eating through seals and circuits, shorting out technology, and forcing citizens to shelter inside thick bunkers. While the jungle's eponymous lights make the city quite beautiful during calm periods, every citizen in Jabask is constantly listening for the sounds of the mold siren or the invasion alarm.

Komena: The major city closest to the Bulwarks, Komena remains heavily militarized despite its extremely defensible position in the Floating Shards. While originally named for the many fjords that cut through the mountains' feet to make it look like the peaks are bobbing on the sea, the Floating Shards have also earned their name another way. Fueled by powerful magic lost during the Gap, ancient lashunta spellcasters lopped off Komena's peak and levitated it to build an ornate, cylinder-shaped city connecting the mountain's base to its crest. In times of war, the entire city slides down into a subterranean cavity. While a number of these so-called Mountainheart Cities once existed, Komena is the last one known to remain. The wreckage of another to the north and records of up to five such fortresses lead many adventurers to brave the peaks in hopes of finding one hidden since antiquity—perhaps even still inhabited.

LAUBU PILOT

TEMPLE OF THE TWELVE

PART 1: QUESTIONS IN QABARAT

PART 2: THE UKULAM EXPEDITION

PART 3: THE LOST TEMPLE

○ CASTROVEL ○

THE CULT OF THE DEVOURER

ALIEN ARCHIVES

CODEX OF WORLDS

Laubu Mesa: This desert city sits atop the geological feature of the same name and has famously never been conquered. In ancient times, the city's minaret-topped Aeries were home to the thakasa riders—cavalry who'd mastered a winged version of the planet's famous reptilian shotalashu mounts—but today these same flight schools train some of the best fighter pilots in the system, specializing in death-defying proximity flying and other atmospheric maneuvers. Technomagical pumps bring water and geothermal energy up through the center of the mesa, making the city self-sufficient in case of siege, and the Scholar's Spiral, which winds down around the pumps, contains workshops and libraries handed down from master to student for millennia—ripe with rumors of lost treasures and encoded knowledge hidden behind secret doors.

Ocean of Mists: An atmospheric mystery, this sea of roiling, multicolored mist somehow supports ships that have only minor gas-based flotation capability yet remains dispersed enough for divers to breathe freely as they descend to walk its shrouded canyon floors. Occupying a huge system of canyons in Asana's center, the ocean hosts many floating mining platforms that harvest the gas for use in antigravity technology. Divers who hunt for salvage on the seafloor are always on the lookout for merfolk-like teshki and the deadly mistcallers, whose magical name-speech can turn an explorer into an expanding cloud of bloody droplets.

Qabarat: The Shining Jewel of the Western Sea, Qabarat is arguably the greatest of the lashunta city-states and the planet's largest spaceport. Where the Yaro River cuts through the sea cliffs at the edge of the Stormshield Mountains, ancient walls of crushed, glittering shells rise up to cradle a modern metropolis nestled among venerable structures dating to the civilization's beginnings. Lady **Morana Kesh** (NG female damaya lashunta envoy) and her chief consort and battle leader, **Grantaeus** (CG male korasha lashunta soldier), rule the city from the Threefold House, the city's capitol. They fight a quiet but desperate battle to maintain traditional governments and keep all of Asana from becoming a corporate free-for-all. Visitors to the city often arrive in the spaceport at Ship's End, passing by soldiers and mercenaries training in the legendary Battle Yards and scholars debating on the steps of the city's numerous great universities, before arriving in the Brightstreets, which form the city's commercial center. The city also has several *aiudara*, held by the government for public use, linking it to other settlements, most notably those in the Farstep Commons.

QABARAT

NG port city
Population 819,000 (70% lashunta, 5% elf, 5% human, 4% shirren, 4% ysoki, 3% half-elf, 9% other)
Government autocracy (Lady of the City)
Qualities academic, cultured, financial center, technologically average
Maximum Item Level 16

THE COLONIES

In sharp contrast to their lashunta neighbors' dozens of competing city-states, the ant-like formians of this continent have only one nation: a single vast country stretching from shore to shore. This state has many names, depending on a particular formian's region and beliefs, such as the Everlasting Queendoms, the Unified Hive, or the Glorious and Undeniable Dominion of All Beneath Moon and Soil. Most outsiders refer to it simply as the Colonies. Millennia ago, the disparate formian hives were at constant war with each other, battling over territory and preventing their civilization as a whole from advancing. To end this strife, several of the largest hives agreed to a conference now called the Meeting of Queens, in which they all agreed to work together in service of the "Overqueen," which was a purely theoretical concept that would allow them to act as a federation while still acceding to their hive-insect need for a single ultimate authority figure. Within years, the wars ended, and the newly unified Colonies were able to look outward and begin expanding their territory, thus inaugurating a new age of war against the lashuntas of Asana.

Life in the Colonies is extremely regimented, as formian society is strictly collectivist and authoritarian. Workers bred and raised for specific jobs complete them without complaint under the oversight of taskmasters and warriors, who in turn bow before their own superiors, all the way up to the queen of a particular settlement. Transgressions against authority are rare. Any behavior outside of the order is ignored to reduce cognitive dissonance, seen as ignorance in need of correction, or else punished as treason by immediate execution. Fortunately, generations of diplomatic missions (often by shirren emissaries) have led most hive queens to the belief that non-formian races fall outside the "natural order," and thus their individualism may be tolerated as long as it ultimately serves the Colonies' best interests.

As a result of this broadened perspective, the Colonies are now a hotbed of economic activity. Corporate employees granted honorary rank within hive society oversee massive manufacturing facilities in which the efficiency of formian workers outpaces all but the best automation. The formians' relatively weak regard for environmental concerns compared to the planet's other major races means that even the long-hostile lashuntas are now transferring more and more of their fabrication jobs to the Colonies. Strip mines follow seams of ore while industrial warrens belch smoke into the sky, and vast agricultural plantations stretch for miles aboveground and below, with photosynthesizing crops on the surface and tunnel upon tunnel of bioengineered fungus farms and chemical-synthesizing bacteria vats below.

Yet for all of this industry, the continent remains strangely pristine. While formian hive-cities sometimes mound up into monolithic, tumorous structures, most run for miles underground, and the consolidation of their cultivation for greater efficiency means that large stretches of wilderness remain intact between settlements. Though the Colonies' borders are fiercely defended, the unification of the hives means there's little need to patrol the continent's interior, and thus entire intelligent species live quietly in the trackless expanses overlooked by formian industry.

NOTABLE LOCATIONS

While the formians have little emotional investment in the names and identities of their territories, naming major settlements and features has made it easier to direct visitors.

Broken Minds: Formian society brooks no disobedience, and those formians who refuse to serve are quickly dispatched. In recent years, however, shirren relief workers have succeeded in convincing several hives to sell their "malfunctioning" citizens rather than kill them. These rebellious individuals are brought to the Broken Minds, a sort of intellectual colony quarantined on the harsh desert coast. There shirren work with these patients to prepare them for independent lives on other continents or planets—and also study them to see whether this spontaneous rebellion might hold the secret to the shirrens' own break with the Swarm in ages past.

Gulf of Legions: This central sea, the hub of intercolony contact on the continent since the beginning of formian civilization, takes its name from the flotillas of warriors who once darkened the waves as they crossed on the backs of massive water-striding yugolars to lay siege to other hives. Since the alliance, the sea has instead become a hotbed of trade, and most of the largest formian hive-cities—notably Chisk the Unyielding, Kebenaut, and Queensrock—are situated on its shores. Only Qarik on the western shore and Zysyk with its half-submerged ocean tunnels rival these metropolises in size.

Jaws of the Mother: This comparatively narrow strait, where the Nestwall Mountains to the north dip into the ocean across from the larger Setae Range to the south, provides the only water access to the Gulf of Legions. Before the era of aircraft and starships, this was one of the most important defensive positions on the continent, and even before the era of the Overqueen, the nearby insect colonies worked together to defend it and repel invaders or break enemy blockades. At its narrowest point, the channel is only 30 miles wide, and it is still regularly patrolled by floating warhives with their squadrons of buzzing fighters and submersibles. To either side of the strait rise the Mandibles, looming, ancient fortresses that house the primary aerospace defense forces for the entire continent.

Queensrock: The hive-city of Queensrock is constructed like an enormous termite mound; its mud-colored exterior is broken by gaping docking bays and entrance tunnels, albeit with the occasional modernist steel-and-glass addition. Set just offshore in the Gulf of Legions, the city stands upon an island of the same name, artificially constructed along with the narrow causeways connecting it to shore. Thousands of formian workers gave their lives to the monumental task of engineering the city and causeways in ages past. Inside, its chambers are a disconcerting mix of traditional formian architecture and spaces designed to make other species feel at home, with limited degrees of success. The hive's leader, **Morgebard of the Thousand Spines** (LN formian queen), is a commanding presence who brought her city to prominence by seeking trade and collaboration with organizations throughout the Pact Worlds. While the queen herself is almost never seen, her elaborately branded Heralds are a constant presence in the city, and Morgebard can peer through their eyes and take possession of their bodies as the need strikes.

The Seacrown: Nominally controlled jointly by Asana and the Colonies, the Seacrown is actually owned by no one—or at least, no one known to the outside world. Believed to be the central peaks of the ancient impact crater that forms the Shattered Sea, the Seacrown is a collection of sharp mountains rising from the vast and trackless waves. While the lower beaches are accessible, each island is wrapped in a cylindrical force field of unknown technology that starts halfway up the slopes and lances straight up, slowly tapering to a close in the upper atmosphere. Within these half-opaque cells, strange monastery-like cities that conform to no known architectural style are inhabited by lashunta-sized blurs that twist the eye and look like moving gaps in the air. Each time Castrovel's moon eclipses the sun, a door opens briefly in one

TEMPLE OF THE TWELVE

PART 1: QUESTIONS IN QABARAT

PART 2: THE UKULAM EXPEDITION

PART 3: THE LOST TEMPLE

CASTROVEL

THE CULT OF THE DEVOURER

ALIEN ARCHIVES

CODEX OF WORLDS

QUEENSROCK

of the force fields. Several modern expeditions have entered in an attempt to make contact with the inhabitants, but so far none have returned, though their gear sometimes reappears on a beach unharmed or is found years later and thousands of miles away.

Towers of Memory: While many of the continent's other intelligent residents—the tri-winged fakoras, the serpentine zenuways, the armored and plains-roaming carinas with their clan-herds and traveling horn lodges—survive by paying heavy tribute to the hives or hiding themselves away in undesirable regions, the inhabitants of the Towers of Memory live bold and unmolested. Rising from the shores of Lake Kechavas, just east of the Plains of Ru, these five towers confound the eye, never quite holding a defined edge. Within them, mysterious creatures called caulborn—extraplanar scholars with two mouths and crests of skin and bone where their eyes should be—collect and catalog memories of select Castrovelians, taking sustenance from the petitioners' psychic energy while they preserve these memories for eternity. No one knows when the first queen approached them, or what she was told, but all of the Colonies enforce a strict taboo against bothering the scholars, and even queens have their memories preserved if a caulborn requests it. In return, the hives are allowed to petition the scholars for information and otherworldly advice, though only those in great need dare approach the glistening towers, for the prices the caulborn demand are often unsettlingly personal.

Watchpost Quinai: Little do the formians know that the Gulf of Legions' most foreboding stretch of coastline hosts Watchpost Quinai, a secret lashunta listening post. From there, highly trained agents funded by an intercity coalition monitor formian movements and occasionally launch raids into the heart of enemy territory. Despite the recent accord between the two civilizations, lushunta leaders have felt no particular inclination to decommission the watchpost or inform the formians of its existence, and mercenaries or patriots with more courage than sense are still sometimes recruited to launch high-paying—and high-casualty—incursions from its secret bunkers.

QUEENSROCK

LN hive warren
Population 1,150,000 (99% formian, 1% other)
Government autocracy (Queen Mother)
Qualities devout, insular
Maximum Item Level 10

SOVYRIAN

Separated from other continents by the icebergs and frost cyclones of the Snowsalt Sea and the vicious psiwhales and ship-breaking komohumes of the Sea of Teeth, the elves of Sovyrian have always held themselves apart from Castrovel's other cultures. The disaster of the Gap hit their long-lived people harder than most other races, and their traditional standoffishness has since grown into xenophobia. Those elves who choose to live among other races are called Forlorn

by their Sovyrian kin, and their fraternization with lesser, untrustworthy cultures is seen as a stain on their legacy. To an elf of Sovyrian, it is an unfortunate necessity to go among other peoples to trade, and any right-minded elf does so as little as possible, returning home or to elven enclaves abroad as soon as the job is done.

Elven isolationism causes some problems. Given the elves' low birth rate and their reticence to sully themselves with outside contact, Sovyrian is constantly in danger of becoming a bit player on the global and galactic stage, prompting the government to promote several workarounds. The first is the Blood Right, a policy that states any half-elf or person with observable elven blood can automatically claim citizenship in Sovyrian. This is crucial to the nation-continent's economy, as these half-elves (as well as the gnomes who are allowed to live among elves as part of ancient tradition) are able to travel and trade with both elves and outsiders without stigma. The second custom, the Masking, allows elves who are uncomfortable interacting with outsiders to wear masks while doing so, thus allowing any dishonor to be transferred to the masks instead of themselves. This practice is particularly popular among diplomats and soldiers, who find that masks also help emphasize their cultural unity and unsettle their opponents.

For all its isolationism, Sovyrian remains sophisticated and worldly. The cultural norm of emphasizing magic and craftsmanship over mass production helps the elves maintain continuity with their ancestors and means that Sovyrian produces some of the most impressive spellcasters in the system. Their people regularly employ magic items rarely seen by outsiders. Though its citizens have embraced modern technology, their designs tend toward the artistic and fantastical, with an emphasis on biotech; even their densest cities can feel like pastoral wonderlands. These magic and artisan technologies, operating in unique and proprietary ways, are Sovyrian's chief exports, and governmental export restrictions create artificial scarcity to ensure that elven goods remain rare and expensive.

The extreme unified front by Sovyrian's residents leads most to assume Sovyrian is a restrictive totalitarian state. In fact, the opposite is true—the Sova, who are the leaders of the High Families of El and serve as Sovyrian's heads of state, focus almost exclusively on preserving the nation's borders and economic security, leaving cities and settlements to govern themselves. As a result, most Sovyrian residents enjoy great freedom, living in traditional harmony with the land or following their passions in small settlements.

NOTABLE LOCATIONS

The elves' freewheeling nature, combined with a decreased population from the nation's heyday, means the continent is home to a surprising number of lost or abandoned ruins long since reclaimed by the continent's evergreen forests. Below are some of the settlements of modern significance.

Cordona: Positioned at the tip of the Clariel's Arm peninsula, this port city is a bustling and pleasant metropolis, overshadowed only somewhat by the massive steel wall—guarded by soldiers and miles of automated defenses—that cuts it off from the rest of the mainland. All visitors seeking access to the continent without a direct invitation are funneled through Cordona, where they can petition at the various corporate enclaves, embassies, and guild offices. The city is one of the largest on the continent, and a study in irony, for while the elves may officially disdain the sea of outsiders and expats living in its boroughs, they also feel the need to impress these same people with their wealth and majesty, and thus the city is a triumph of beautiful architecture and utopian hospitality. So great is the appeal that many elves actually vacation in the city, especially for Revelnight, the citywide masquerade whose charming colored lanterns and ask-no-questions frivolity greatly bolsters the population of half-elves. This is in direct contrast to the rest of the year, when disembodied eyeballs controlled by the city's overseers float magically on every street corner, carefully watching for danger or signs of subversion.

El: The great capital city of the elves has changed little since antiquity. The neighborhood-sized Great Houses of the city's aristocracy, the High Families, still climb the cliff walls to either side of the city's magnificent waterfall, these traditional structures augmented with the latest biotech and magical architectural advances. The Woven River earns its name with the dozens of elegant canals that crisscross the city in looping designs, the resulting island-neighborhoods connected by footbridges older than the Gap. Yet, while many ancient structures still stand, proudly maintained by their owners, the spaces between them are thick with modern skyscrapers—gleaming glass melded with living trees to create a beautiful surrealist forest, between which hovercars and shuttles buzz like insects. With river trade largely abandoned, the wide current is now enjoyed solely by yachts and pleasure barges, and the venerable docks now serve as the city's spaceport, where ships land under the shadow of artistically concealed energy shields and artillery capable of firing on aggressors in orbit, ensuring that no one lands without proper authorization. Just downriver from the docks stand the ruins of the Arch of Refuge, the great gateway that once demarcated a magical portal to Golarion but crumbled—or was destroyed—during the Gap. Today, this site is a shrine where elves can mourn memories lost to the Gap or aid the monastic Adducai, scholar-therapists seeking to restore some of

those lost connections through painstaking research and clever divination.

Nerundel: Situated high in the Korinath Divide, the mountains that separate eastern and western Sovyrian, this city is inhabited by more gnomes than elves, with all the chaos that entails. While its resident university, Nerundel Halls, is a marvel of both eclectic scholarship and perilous cliffside architecture, Nerundel's true claim to fame is the Greengate, a permanent portal to the First World that allows the gnomes to trade freely with the fey. Some fey travel to Nerundel via the Greengate to study at the university. The Greengate also allows enough primal nature magic through to turn the otherwise rugged mountains into a blooming paradise for several miles around Nerundel, and biotech researchers and spellworkers flock to the city for the chance to harness some of the precious energy. The Xenowardens also keep a permanent delegation nearby to study the ancient artifact and ensure it isn't abused.

Southwatch: This city-fortress sits upon Sovyrian's southernmost point, just miles from the frozen cliffs of Aurovas, Castrovel's southern ice cap. Each winter, the narrow ribbon of ocean between the two landmasses freezes, creating a causeway of ice and snow. That's when the soldiers of Southwatch earn their keep, for across this bridge flood the white-furred horrors of Aurovas's windswept wastes: semi-intelligent aurovaks eager to drink the hot blood of the north. For an entire season, Southwatch

EL

TEMPLE OF THE TWELVE

PART 1: QUESTIONS IN QABARAT

PART 2: THE UKULAM EXPEDITION

PART 3: THE LOST TEMPLE

CASTROVEL

THE CULT OF THE DEVOURER

ALIEN ARCHIVES

CODEX OF WORLDS

holds them off, repeatedly blowing up the causeway only to watch it freeze into shape again. Once the weather grows warm, the aurovaks' feeding frenzy ceases and the creatures vanish back into the glacier mountains of Aurovas. For generations, the elves have tried everything to eliminate the aurovaks once and for all, but the creatures burrow deep into the ice and disappear without a trace during the warm season, making even aerial bombardment ineffective. In recent years, however, the horde has not appeared, leading some to assume such a mission has finally succeeded—and others to worry that the aurovaks may have finally learned to plan more complex assaults.

Telasia, the Portal Grove: Records show that in ancient times, Telasia was a magical transit hub, connecting far-flung settlements across the world. Inside each of the town's fortified tree-shaped buildings stood a different *aiudara*, and travelers paid the resident Transarchs for use of the portals. Sometime during the Gap, however, the situation changed. Today, the city is the sole domain of the green dragon Urvosk, who claims the title of High Transarch and ownership of the entire grove. As much as Sovyrian officials would love to reclaim the "lost" city, the dragon's cadre of high-priced lawyers keeps them from getting far, and claims of thermonuclear devices embedded in every building keep them from trying to take it by force. For now, anyone wishing to use the portals must pay off or otherwise convince the capricious dragon, who smugly reminds travelers that no one but he knows where every portal leads and that some of them connect to magically hidden locations completely lost to history. The dragon does, however, have a soft spot for adventurers and sometimes hires them to explore these secret realms on his behalf.

EL

N port city
Population 600,000 (90% elf, 9% half-elf, 1% other)
Government oligarchy (Convocation of High Families)
Qualities academic, cultured, insular, technologically average
Maximum Item Level 20

UKULAM

Whereas each of Castrovel's three great species has a continent to call its own, few records suggest any large-scale colonization of Ukulam ever took place. Instead, its unconquered depths have remained the domain of powerful beasts, deadly plants, and immense fungi that drive a never-ending cycle of evolution, growth, and decay. These inexorable processes ultimately consume settlements, leaving most ruins damaged beyond easy identification.

Despite this, Ukulam is far from untouched by conventional civilization. The constant conflicts between lashuntas and formians played out over the continent's southern half, littering the Ikal Expanse with craters and starship wreckage that were quickly overgrown. Dozens of bases, fortresses, and

way stations dot the coast in a nearly unbroken ring. Since the shirren-brokered treaty 30 years ago, the lashuntas and formians have systematically scaled back their presence here, decommissioning many of the outposts and allowing nature to reclaim them. Both sides nevertheless monitor the continent, maintain peace, and provide aid to travelers from smaller bases and research stations.

Castrovel's dominant species agreed that preserving Ukulam's ecology was in the planet's best interests. Following the peace accords, several nongovernmental organizations such as the Esowath Conservancy formed to maintain the continent's sanctity, with all parties' blessings. These NGOs tightly restrict travel to Ukulam, issuing a limited number of permits each year to a sizable waiting list of academics and tourists. Concerned with the impact of pollution, unrestricted access, and the disruption of the near-constant migratory patterns of Ukulam's countless aerial species, these groups even limit transit over the continent, enforcing these regulations with a force of frontier soldiers supported by a coalition fleet of interceptor starships. For all these organizations' efforts, reports of poaching—driven by a lucrative trade in hides, horns, and more believed to hold supernatural power, pharmaceutical value, or simple prestige—regularly emerge on the planet's infosphere.

NOTABLE LOCATIONS

The following are several significant locations on Ukulam.

Caliria Maze: Ukulam's jungle where two smaller rivers join to form the broad Ralhoma is especially thick. Attempts to map it (even using satellites) have failed, suggesting that either the flora is constantly changing or some supernatural force obscures its true appearance from the outside world. Ukulam boasts numerous species with primal magic, and these adepts often speak of a sacred place called Caliria, whence the planet's heart beats with water and life. In this area, armies composed of numerous species have united to turn back prospectors and explorers, often using legendary Caliria as their battle cry. Rumors run wild as to whether Caliria is a grand woodland city, an unspeakably powerful magical font, or nothing more than a metaphor for Ukulam's primal rage.

Esowath Nexus: An erstwhile formian outpost, this comblike structure has been retrofitted to serve as the Esowath Conservancy's base of operations on Ukulam, while the organization's political offices are in Qabarat and Queensrock. Conservancy rangers travel far into the Ikal Expanse and patrol virtually all of the coastal waters, watching for poachers and turning away misguided travelers. The head of operations, **Ualia** (CG female korasha lashunta mystic), thinks that exposing offworld species to Ukulam's beauty can lend politicians leverage in continuing to protect the land, so she regularly awards travel grants to explorers with good track records to survey the region's geography and wildlife.

Ikal Expanse: Ukulam's southern forest is a virtually unbroken stretch of deciduous trees overshadowed only by titanic mushrooms that sprout and wither within weeks. Ecological studies suggest that this is among the most biologically productive locations on Castrovel, if not in all the Pact Worlds. Similar to the plants and fungi, the fauna here is plentiful and often immense. Most famously, the powerful yaruks topple trees in pursuit of food, inadvertently aerating the forest and creating openings for new growth. Any signs of past civilization have disappeared beneath the leaves, yet explorers still dive into the wilderness with dreams of uncovering some lost treasure.

Northern Steps: The tectonic buckling that formed the Singing Range has also uplifted the land to the north. Known as the Northern Steps, these broad plateaus descend with increasing abruptness the farther north and east one travels, eventually ending in dramatic cliffs shorn smooth by Castrovel's last known glaciation event. Warmed only by the mild current flowing north from the Western Sea, the Northern Steps are fairly chilly, made all the more so by the katabatic winds that blow icy rainstorms from the polar ice sheet. A thick taiga of scaly cacti covers the Steps' northern half, and the shovel-footed purhuams that graze on the plains regularly kick up nodes of meteoric iron and preserved scrimshaw carved from the bones of long-extinct species.

Singing Range: Home to several species of ever-gnawing rock rats, these severe peaks are riddled with alpine burrows that whistle faintly in the wind during the summers, when the snow recedes from the highest summits. Millions of years ago, two smaller continents crashed into each other here, forming this constantly growing mountain range. Flyover surveys have sighted battered ruins in the high mountains; it may be possible that these belonged to a lost species that predates even elven and lashunta history.

Station 9: The formians' eastern fortresses boasted numerous defenses to intercept lashunta attacks before they could reach the Colonies. At the outpost identified only as Station 9, the formians developed carefully cultured countermeasures to defend against a possible biological or chemical attack. During the Gap, an attack devastated the site, which was promptly abandoned, but the living countermeasures persisted, reproduced, and evolved. In recent years, scientists have identified amorphous creatures that move about

Station 9 with purpose and even skirmish with local wildlife. The Esowath Conservancy believes these creatures are an invasive species but dares not risk an air strike, which could scatter the biological material into the atmosphere. With public outcry building, the organization is desperate for a plan—and someone bold enough to execute it.

Waklohar's Expeditions: Some tourists can't help but fetishize the exoticism of Ukulam's wilderness, and the entrepreneurial lashunta **Waklohar** (N male korasha lashunta operative) has one of the few recreational installations on the continent. He organizes short-range adventures into the Ikal Expanse and to nearby islands for wide-eyed "adventurers," leading them to several famous landmarks and guaranteeing an exciting wildlife experience. Although Waklohar is a capable survivalist, his strength lies in his ability to craft spectacle, and it is his stoic business partner, the formian **Xcibiz** (LN independent formian taskmaster soldier), who tirelessly manages the finances and ultimately organizes rescue operations when a hapless safari encounters trouble.

UKULAM SURVIVALIST

TEMPLE OF THE TWELVE

PART 1: QUESTIONS IN QABARAT

PART 2: THE UKULAM EXPEDITION

PART 3: THE LOST TEMPLE

CASTROVEL

THE CULT OF THE DEVOURER

ALIEN ARCHIVES

CODEX OF WORLDS

THE CULT OF THE DEVOURER

The Cult of the Devourer is one of the most feared and reviled organizations in the Pact Worlds, and clear evidence of its ravages can be found on the fringes of inhabited space throughout the galaxy. The cult has been around for eons, though individual cells rarely last more than a few decades, and its devotees wage a nonstop war to destroy all existence in the name of their god, the Devourer. In most cases, the cult can be thought of like a hurricane on a low-tech world—it comes with little warning, damages or destroys everything in its furious path, and then weakens and breaks apart for no apparent reason.

Nevertheless, the Cult of the Devourer is more than just a mere storm. It is a widespread interstellar and interspecies organization plotting the downfall of all civilization as part of a broader plan to end existence itself. Although the cult is made up largely of anarchists, its efforts are surprisingly well coordinated and carefully considered. Only by understanding the underlying motives and rough organization of the cult's various cells, divine agents, and sects can the true threat of the Cult of the Devourer be understood clearly.

CULT ORGANIZATION

There is no central authority that controls the Cult of the Devourer—no specific headquarters, no single acknowledged leader, and no formal hierarchy. A lack of a universal set of rules makes it difficult to even discuss the organization as a whole in any detail—and that's exactly how its members like it. To the cultists, the destruction of everything is a goal that cannot be achieved by creating new rules or societies. The following generalities apply to most groups that consider themselves Devourer cultists, but even these are not hard rules.

CULT CELLS

Lacking any formal hierarchy, each group of Devourer cultists that works together generally refers to itself as a single "cell" of the Devourer cult. A cell can have as few as two to three cultists, or in rare cases it could have as many as a few thousand, though these larger hordes are more often many cells fused together by an extremely powerful leader or a supernatural agent in order to accomplish a particular goal. Most cells tend toward the smaller side, operating alone but potentially maintaining contact with other cells to coordinate larger attacks. Violent disagreements are common, and different cells or even cultists within the same cell regularly turn on one another. When a cell fractures, it often splinters into multiple smaller cells, each of which strives to grow and recruit more members, thus spreading their destructive faith across the cosmos. Cells usually have a secret base of operations, and sometimes depend on mobile bases such as starships or asteroids.

Within these cells, cultists each join a group (or "choir") within the cult in keeping with their own devotion to the Devourer. Those who take a public role obvious to all are known as "wall breakers," while those who operate in secret are referred to as "hidden ones." Most wall breakers are frontline combatants who generally spend their time attacking outposts of civilization or preparing for such assaults. Hidden ones have roles that require them to pass as ordinary citizens, and many lead double lives, keeping their cult membership secret from coworkers and family members.

There are numerous different sects within the worship of the Devourer, though these are defined more by vague similarities in beliefs and operating methods than by any formal orthodoxy. A cell might drift from sect to sect as its membership and goals change over time, but for all their chaotic squabbling, few cells bother to devise and promote their own doctrines.

Each cell normally has a few senior cultists who guide and command other members of the cell. Called "longteeth," these elder cultists are respected and obeyed not due to any formal rank they hold but simply because a Devourer cultist does not achieve seniority within the cult without battle acumen, cunning, and a long track record of destruction. In some cells, the longteeth are mostly hidden ones, entrusted with planning and organizing tasks the wall breakers then carry out. In other cells, the longteeth are drawn from both choirs and divide their duties to fit their skills and inclinations. It's rare for a cell to have primarily wall breaker longteeth, though a few cells dedicated purely to acting as wandering warbands follow their most accomplished warriors. If a cell is too large for the longteeth to directly command all the cultists, intermediaries step in to lead smaller groups of cultists. These intermediaries are most often called "fangs," though cells develop numerous other terms for them. Fangs arise from subgroups within the cell as needed, primarily through leadership and longevity. If fangs live long enough, they become longteeth. If a fang dies, some other cultist attempts to fill the fallen fang's role.

Above all of these are the atrocites, supernatural agents of the Devourer that sometimes spawn, expand, command, or train specific cult groups in order to accomplish some task important to the atrocite's own efforts to bring an end to all existence. While atrocites never devote themselves completely to a single cell, they occasionally combine cells into vast hordes under their nihilistic banners, and the largest and most effective cells may be visited by atrocites on a regular basis.

Though it's impossible to make a comprehensive list of all the various elements that can be found in the branches of the Cult of the Devourer, some of the more common elements are expanded on as follows.

HIDDEN ONE CHOIR

While the general public envisions all Devourer cultists as maddened warriors who destroy, kill, maim, and go on cannibalistic rampages, some are more subtle in their methods. While the cult has no shortage of drug-addicted and psychopathic combatants ready to spread death and terror throughout space, the Cult of the Devourer does not depend entirely on mindless mayhem. On the other side of the spectrum are those Devourer devotees who move unnoticed among their prey, gather information, sabotage defenses, spread rumors, and recruit new members among the disaffected and the sadistic members of society. While hidden ones are as diverse as the ordinary citizens they emulate, a few common types are detailed here.

Maw: Maws are the primary recruiters of the Cult of the Devourer, and they are the only cultists who regularly travel between cult strongholds and civilized society. While other hidden ones often integrate deeply into a society for years at a time, acting as sleeper agents and deep-cover insurgents, maws journey extensively on the lookout for potential cultists. They seek the angry, the downtrodden, the insane, and the suffering, and they use a variety of sophisticated psychological techniques to convert these people to the Devourer's faith. For some prospective cultists, it's only a matter of stoking their existing rage at society, teaching them to find meaning and savage joy in destroying the civilizations that caused them such pain. For others—those who've suffered but who haven't yet turned the corner into destructive nihilism—the key is often regret or grief: the maw teaches that the Devourer's destruction of this reality won't simply end the universe but retroactively erase it, thus ensuring that the incidents that caused their guilt or pain never happened in the first place. Most maws are experts at sliding easily between strategies until they find the right one for an individual, and some utilize drugs or magic to help make their targets receptive; yet, almost all such conversions involve offering new recruits a helping hand and giving them a sense of acceptance and agency in their own lives. These strategies are largely rediscovered by each cell through trial and error, but a few helpful maxims exist, such as "Heal a soul so they may break a thousand."

While not all potential recruits make the leap from disaffected citizens to Devourer cultists, there are always more

TEMPLE
OF THE
TWELVE

PART 1:
QUESTIONS
IN QABARAT

PART 2:
THE UKULAM
EXPEDITION

PART 3:
THE LOST
TEMPLE

CASTROVEL

THE CULT OF
THE DEVOURER

ALIEN
ARCHIVES

CODEX OF
WORLDS

individuals who have suffered terrible tragedies or injustices, have lost their moral path, or just want to see the galaxy burn. The cult sometimes maintains those who don't convert completely as useful contacts, but more often such potential recruits meet with unfortunate accidents before they can have a change of heart and blow the maw's cover. A maw may bring new recruits to a nearby active cell or use several recruits to begin a brand-new cell. An experienced maw is thus also likely to be a longtooth, acting as the senior advisor and planner for a network of cells the maw established or strengthened.

Plague Bringer: Plague bringers seek to infect the society within which they operate and weaken it as much as possible in preparation for an attack by one of the cult's cells. While some accomplish this by spreading actual diseases—even researching ever more effective and weaponized viruses to assist in such efforts—plague bringers undertake any form of sabotage. Many are computer experts who intentionally corrupt planetary infospheres with insidious viruses. However, those technophiles who specialize in scraping private data for blackmail material are more often silent cannibals (see below).

Silent Cannibal: Silent cannibals are spies who gather information for cult cells, living lies as deep in targeted societies as they can manage. Not all are actual cannibals—the term refers to their being members of the society they seek to destroy, thus metaphorically eating their own kind—but some certainly take the label literally, and many are serial killers. While committing murders even once every year or two puts silent cannibals at much greater risk of discovery, the dedication needed for a Devourer cultist to live a quiet life as a spy is more than most can manage without at least an occasional killing to assuage their need for destruction.

WALL BREAKER CHOIR

Wall breakers are far more common than hidden ones, and they make no effort to pass as anything other than devotees of the Devourer. Instead, they embrace bizarre appearances and elaborate self-mutilation to better shock and demoralize their victims, from elaborate piercings and burn scars to having their own bone surgically exposed and wearing the skins of their enemies. (Unlike in the church of Zon-Kuthon, these modifications are not to give them the masochistic thrill of pain, but they exist purely to further their god's nihilistic ends.) While this choir includes all the frontline troops who carry out raids and murderous rampages in the name of their god, it too has a variety of more specific roles.

Composer: Composers are among the rarest of Devourer cultists, and the majority of cells have at most one composer. A composer is a kind of mad genius and doom prophet who endlessly contemplates how to spread maximum destruction. Unlike hidden ones, a composer never operates within the confines of normal society. Composers are obsessed zealots, spending every moment plotting even greater acts of destruction. Those cells with a composer often defer to whatever plan or need the composer expresses and may

undertake minor missions to steal experimental weapons, kidnap scholars with ancient lore, or throw themselves against a planet's defenses just to see the response as the composer determines what information and resources are needed for a major operation. Composers have no official authority and command respect and obedience only so long as other members of the cell remain convinced that their schemes are the best way to rain down destruction.

Of all the Devourer cultists, composers are the ones most likely to attempt to write some sort of treatise or philosophical explanation of their devotion to the Devourer. Thus, despite their small numbers, they are often quite influential, inspiring entire sects of Devourer worship.

Degenerator: Like any group operating on an interstellar scale, the Cult of the Devourer needs engineers, mechanics, medics, quartermasters, and support personnel. Unlike most other groups, however, Devourer cultists are dedicated to the destruction of all things, and thus fixing or creating new things could be seen as heresy by some. Solutions for this dilemma vary, and some of these needed roles can be filled by robots, slaves, or even hidden ones who justify the work as necessary for a plan destined to bring greater destruction. But neither robots nor slaves can be trusted with all the work needed to keep a large military cult cell functional, and hidden ones are often better utilized in their capacity as saboteurs and spies. Thus, such tasks often fall to degenerators.

Degenerators have technical skills but do not see what they do as organization or repair. Instead, they claim to create "degenerate" versions of any equipment, person, or system they work on. It is often degenerators who add spikes and skulls to wall breaker armor, create new weapon fusions that coat cult weapons with rust and runes of death, file the teeth of cultists to sharp points, and make surgical additions to injured cultists subjected to their care. Even if responsible for tracking supplies, a degenerator often seeks to satisfy the group's needs in ways counter to whatever would be societally acceptable, such as including halfling meat in a starship's freezers. In the Cult of the Devourer, this ability to keep guns shooting and soldiers breathing without becoming part of the structure of civilization is seen as a blessed talent for devolution.

Frenzied: The frenzied are what most people think of when the Cult of the Devourer is mentioned. Frenzied exist purely to destroy, kill, and terrorize anything they can reach. Many are mentally unbalanced, as few sane minds could embrace the ultimately self-destructive lifestyle that the frenzied lead, while others either have lost all sense of right and wrong through trauma and years of drug use or have overcome it through religious devotion. It is popular to think of the frenzied (and all wall breakers) as nearly mindless killing machines, and certainly some are. But there are also frenzied gunners, officers, pilots, and tankers, and despite the name and the penchant for extreme stimulants and hallucinogens in battle, some frenzied are calm nihilists who work methodically toward their destructive goals.

ATROCITES

The greatest successes of the Cult of the Devourer can often be traced back to the arrival of one of the atrocites, horrific divine agents of the Devourer who sometimes appear to cells in order to reveal secret knowledge, task them with specific missions, or organize them into apocalyptic crusades. As atrocites are the only authority a typical cult cell answers to without question, these beings are the inevitable answer to the question of how large-scale groups of anarchists can operate in concert to threaten all of civilization.

Like the cults they often spawn, atrocites have few similarities. Most appear in a form akin to those of the cult it's addressing, from common humanoids such as lashuntas, orcs, and vesk to more bizarre entities like the barathus of Bretheda or the twisted masses of cysts and tentacles found among the Dominion of the Black. According to what passes for scripture within the cult, the Devourer creates nothing, not even new shapes, and thus its most powerful agents borrow their forms from other creatures. In place of eyes, an atrocite may have black voids in its empty sockets, and all atrocites' heads are enshrouded in a constant halo of gray haze that sometimes crackles with red energy or offers momentary glimpses of apocalyptic prophecy.

Atrocites are clearly powerful outsiders, but if they have a native plane of existence, no scholar has been able to find it. Many theologians hypothesize that atrocites spend their time drifting through the void of deep space–the environment closest to absolute nothingness–or perhaps in the accretion disks of singularities consuming stars. Some scholars suspect that all atrocites began as mortals, Devourer cultists who engineered acts of destruction so vast, their god granted them a sliver of its own destructive power. Through the ravings and writings of those few who've survived encounters with atrocites, Pact World researchers have determined that the beings can exist perpetually in vacuum, teleport over vast distances, never work together, and prefer building up cult cells to attack and terrorize societies rather than undertaking such efforts directly. Atrocites often speak of themselves planting the seeds of cult victory and then moving on.

DEVOURER SECTS

Some broad, informal sects within the Cult of the Devourer have differing goals and philosophies on how to best serve their uncaring god. While these distinctions have little impact on how other organizations view or deal with cells of the cult, understanding them can be useful in predicting what sorts of attacks a cell may attempt.

Blood Door: Blood Door cells are motivated by the example of the Blood Scourge, a Devourer mystic who led a small fleet of cult ships to attack lone merchant ships, minor colonies, and outposts at the edge of stellar nations' zones of control. The Blood Scourge is believed to have become an atrocite, and while her cell broke up upon her disappearance, its ships formed the cores of dozens of smaller cells. Blood Door cells endlessly seek to increase the number of lives they claim by whatever means possible, and they keep themselves mobile to constantly search for new targets. They see every death they cause as a sacrifice to the Devourer– the act of killing is referred to as forcing the victim "through the Blood Door"–and they believe such offerings increase their god's power so it can more easily destroy the universe. Some Blood Door cultists insist that when enough sacrifices have been made, the slaughter will create a portal through which the Devourer will enter from some other realm to begin its final onslaught.

Feaster: Feaster cells focus on complete, unrecoverable destruction. While this sounds obvious given their faith, the requirement to prioritize utter annihilation actually causes them to act differently from many other sects. For instance, if a cult of this sect is in a position to damage 20 starships or obliterate just one, its members would zealously focus on the one they can destroy utterly, on the premise that while damage can be healed or repaired, there is no recovery from total annihilation. This also makes them extremely dangerous in ground combat, as a Feaster is likely to take the time to slit the throat of an injured enemy to confirm the kill rather than focus on those still attacking him. Their name comes from sect members' tendency to engage in cannibalism, consuming the body of their foes as a form of destruction.

Nightmare: Nightmare cells hide within society and work to spread discontent, fear, and misery. They are inspired by a book known as *The Darkest Night*, a tome outlawed on many worlds that presents the idea that societies are nothing more than a series of interconnected conveniences and will ultimately collapse if those within them can be made to question their safety and value. The goal of such a cell is to destroy the perceived worth of society, eventually causing a complete societal breakdown, though many also use these tactics to foster upheavals such as civil wars. Members of this sect are nearly all hidden ones, with a rare wall breaker recruited for use in suicide missions. Their efforts often take decades to come to fruition.

TEMPLE OF THE TWELVE

PART 1: QUESTIONS IN QABARAT

PART 2: THE UKULAM EXPEDITION

PART 3: THE LOST TEMPLE

CASTROVEL

THE CULT OF THE DEVOURER

ALIEN ARCHIVES

CODEX OF WORLDS

While mystics of the Cult of the Devourer often choose the mindbreaker or star shaman connection (*Starfinder Core Rulebook* 87, 88), when a particularly large or powerful cult attracts an atrocite, these destructive outsiders often teach their mystic followers the ways of the devastator connection and its related spells. Detailed below, this magic allows Devourer cultists to harness and pervert the universe's mysterious powers to precipitate its eventual destruction. The devastator connection is less common outside of Devourer cults, but it can be found among mystics of any deity devoted to destruction, entropy, or even war.

DEVASTATOR CONNECTION

You have embraced a nihilistic view that values nothing and thus sees only nothingness as having value. You are devoted to destroying the existence of all structure and form, from individual lives to the fabric of societies and even reality itself. You're focused on annihilation through any means, and you draw power from the dissolution of lives.

Associated Deities: Azathoth, Damoritosh, The Devourer, Groetus, Lamashtu

Associated Skills: Intimidate and Perception

Spells: 1st—*carnivorous* (see page 51), 2nd—*caustic conversion*, 3rd—*viral destruction* (see page 51), 4th—*enervation*, 5th—*crush skull*, 6th—*gravitational singularity*

BLOOD MARK (SU)   1st Level

⊕ Whenever you kill or destroy a creature or reduce a creature to 0 HP, you immediately gain a blood mark on your skin, which manifests as a swirled, blood-red black hole. A blood mark lasts for a number of rounds equal to your Wisdom modifier (minimum 1). The blood mark is attuned to creatures of the same type as the creature you killed, destroyed, or reduced to 0 HP to gain the blood mark, and it grants you one of the following benefits of your choice: a +1 morale bonus to attacks against creatures of the attuned type, a +1 morale bonus to AC against attacks from creatures of the attuned type, a +1 morale bonus to saving throws against attacks and effects created by creatures of the attuned type, or a +1 morale bonus to damage dealt to creatures of the attuned type. You choose this benefit when you gain the blood mark, and it lasts for as long as the mark lasts. You cannot have more than one blood mark active at a time, and gaining a new blood mark ends any previous blood mark you had active.

DESTRUCTIVE FRENZY (SP)   3rd Level

⊕ You can expend a 1st-level or higher mystic spell slot as a move action to go into a destructive frenzy. This grants you a bonus to attack and damage rolls with basic melee weapons and small arms. The bonus to attacks is equal the level of spell slot expended – 2 (minimum +1 bonus), and the bonus to damage is equal to the level of the spell slot expended. This frenzy lasts for a number of rounds equal to your Wisdom modifier (minimum 1) plus the level of the spell slot expended. You can dismiss your destructive frenzy early as a free action. While your destructive frenzy is active, you can't cast spells or use any other extraordinary, spell-like, or supernatural ability that requires you to spend an action.

DEVASTATING CRITICAL (SU)   6th Level

⊕ When you score a critical hit with an attack, you can spend 1 Resolve Point as a swift action to add the wound critical hit effect to the attack, replacing any other critical hit effect the attack has. If the attack would already have the wound critical hit effect, you can instead spend 1 Resolve Point to add the severe wound critical hit effect to the attack in place of other critical hit effects.

SHATTER DEFENSES (SU)   9th Level

⊕ You can break a target's defenses. Once per day as a standard action, you can reduce the DR, energy resistances, and hardness of a single target by an amount equal to your mystic level (to a minimum of 0) for a number of rounds equal to your mystic level. The target can attempt a Fortitude saving throw to resist this effect (DC = 10 + half your mystic level + your Wisdom modifier). This ability can affect objects.

GREATER BLOOD MARK (SU)   12th Level

⊕ At 12th level, whenever an ally linked by your telepathic bond class feature kills or destroys a creature or reduces a creature to 0 HP, you can grant yourself or one other ally linked by your telepathic bond a greater blood mark. This functions as the blood mark connection ability (see above), but the bonus is +2 and the subject that gains the blood mark decides which of the benefits to gain. You cannot have more than one greater blood mark active at a time, and granting a new greater blood mark ends any previous greater blood mark you had active. A creature cannot benefit from more than one greater blood mark at a time or from a blood mark as well as a greater blood mark, though you can benefit from both your own blood mark and a greater blood mark.

MYSTIC BLOODLUST (EX)   15th Level

⊕ At 15th level, you gain renewed vigor when one of your foes is brought low. When you or an ally linked by your telepathic bond class feature scores a critical hit against a foe, as a reaction you can spend 1 Resolve Point to regain a number of Stamina Points equal to three times your mystic level, plus your Wisdom modifier (up to your maximum number of Stamina Points). Once you have benefited from mystic bloodlust, you can't gain the benefits from this ability again until you rest to recover Stamina.

CIRCLE OF DEVASTATION (SU) `18th Level`

⊛ At 18th level, you can channel your destructive energies into a sphere of devastation around you. As a standard action, you can spend 1 Resolve Point to create a burst of energy in a 30-foot radius around you, dealing 12d10 force damage (Reflex half) to all creatures and objects in the area. Crackling residual energies turn the area into difficult terrain (even empty spaces in the air or vacuum around you) for 1 round per mystic level. You are not affected by this difficult terrain. You can use this ability a number of times per day equal to your Wisdom modifier.

NEW SPELLS

The following spells are most common among Cult of the Devourer mystics, but any mystic can select them.

CARNIVOROUS `1`

School transmutation
Casting Time 1 standard action
Range personal
Duration 1 minute/level
Your mouth expands to twice its normal size, and fills with rows of razor-sharp teeth, giving you

a bite attack. This attack is treated as an attack with a basic melee weapon with the operative special quality for purposes of proficiency and Weapon Specialization and for other abilities that function with basic melee operative weapons. You can make this attack without using any limbs and when pinned.

The attack deals 1d4 piercing damage. At 7th level, the damage increases to 2d4. At 10th level, it increases to 2d8. At 14th level, it increases to 3d8. At 16th level, it increases to 4d8. At 18th level, it increases to 5d8. At 20th level, it increases to 10d8.

VIRAL DESTRUCTION `3`

School necromancy
Casting Time 1 reaction
Range close (25 ft. + 5 ft./2 levels)
Target one newly dead creature; see text
Duration instantaneous; see text
Saving Throw Will negates, see text; **Spell Resistance** yes
You can cast this spell only immediately after a creature in range dies. On its next turn in the initiative order, the corpse stands up (if applicable; this does not require a move action), can take a single move action to move up to its speed, and makes a single attack using the weapons and bonuses it had when alive (though it can't use class features, spell-like abilities, or spells). You can choose the target of the affected creature's attack or allow the target corpse to select a target entirely at random. If the target of this spell was friendly or helpful toward you in life, the spell works automatically; otherwise, the corpse can attempt a Will saving throw to negate this spell, as if the creature were still alive.

After making its attack, the creature that you have targeted with *viral destruction* falls and is dead as normal. However, if this attack kills the affected creature's target or if it knocks it unconscious, that target must succeed at a Will saving throw (using the spell's DC) or be subject to *viral destruction* and make a single attack on its next turn before returning to its normal dead or unconscious state. If the secondary target of *viral destruction* is merely unconscious and becomes conscious again before its next action, that creature is freed from the *viral destruction* effect and the spell ends. Each attack caused by this spell can transfer the *viral destruction* effect to its target if that target is knocked unconscious or killed by the attack, until the spell has affected a number of creatures equal to your mystic level.

TEMPLE OF THE TWELVE

PART 1: QUESTIONS IN QABARAT

PART 2: THE UKULAM EXPEDITION

PART 3: THE LOST TEMPLE

CASTROVEL

THE CULT OF THE DEVOURER

ALIEN ARCHIVES

CODEX OF WORLDS

DEVOURER CULT GEAR

Members of the Cult of the Devourer often take little care of their equipment. They are perfectly happy to grab whatever is available from communal piles of armor or to rip weapons from their foes, fire them until they're empty, or wield them until they shatter, and then toss them aside. However, the Devourer cultists who infiltrate societies more subtly are well aware of the value of terrifying-looking weapons when they are aiming to cow entire populations. These cultists often encourage others to embrace gear options that spread doubt, fear, and terror and therefore extend the insidious fingers of the Devourer's faith.

Some equipment found among Devourer cultists is detailed below.

WEAPONS
Statistics for each of the following weapons can be found on its corresponding weapon table.

DISINTEGRATOR WEAPONS
Available as pistols (small arms), rifles (longarms), and cannons (heavy weapons), these powerful weapons are often referred to by the more scientific term "high-energy proton decouplers," as they produce streams of energized fields that corrode and break down matter much like subatomic acid would. However, since their effects appear to turn metal to slag, plastic to vapor, and flesh to goo, they're commonly known as "disintegrators." Devourer cultists particular revere disintegrators because the weapons slough away their enemies' flesh.

UNCATEGORIZED WEAPONS
The following weapons are not considered part of any other weapon category.

ADVANCED MELEE WEAPONS

ONE-HANDED WEAPONS	LEVEL	PRICE	DAMAGE	CRITICAL	CAPACITY	USAGE	BULK	SPECIAL
UNCATEGORIZED								
Painclaw, ghoulish	3	1,250	1d8 S & P	–	40 charges	1	1	Injection (see text), unwieldy
Painclaw, demonic	11	25,000	2d8 S & P	Bleed 1d6	40 charges	1	1	Injection (see text), unwieldy
Painclaw, draconic	19	560,000	6d8 S & P	Bleed 2d6	40 charges	1	1	Injection (see text), unwieldy

SMALL ARMS

ONE-HANDED WEAPONS	LEVEL	PRICE	DAMAGE	RANGE	CRITICAL	CAPACITY	USAGE	BULK	SPECIAL
DISINTEGRATOR									
Disintegrator pistol, liquidator	6	4,500	1d10 A	15 ft.	–	20 charges	2	L	–
Disintegrator pistol, decimator	11	28,000	1d20 A	20 ft.	–	20 charges	2	L	–
Disintegrator pistol, executioner	16	200,000	2d20 A	25 ft.	Corrode 1d6	40 charges	4	L	–
Disintegrator pistol, eradicator	20	745,000	3d20 A	30 ft.	Corrode 2d6	40 charges	4	L	–

LONGARMS

TWO-HANDED WEAPONS	LEVEL	PRICE	DAMAGE	RANGE	CRITICAL	CAPACITY	USAGE	BULK	SPECIAL
DISINTEGRATOR									
Disintegrator rifle, liquidator	6	4,740	1d20 A	30 ft.	Corrode 1d6	40 charges	4	2	–
Disintegrator rifle, decimator	11	29,000	3d10 A	30 ft.	Corrode 2d6	40 charges	4	2	–
Disintegrator rifle, executioner	16	210,000	5d10 A	30 ft.	Corrode 3d6	80 charges	8	2	–
Disintegrator rifle, eradicator	20	745,000	5d20 A	30 ft.	Corrode 4d6	80 charges	8	2	–

HEAVY WEAPONS

TWO-HANDED WEAPONS	LEVEL	PRICE	DAMAGE	RANGE	CRITICAL	CAPACITY	USAGE	BULK	SPECIAL
DISINTEGRATOR									
Disintegrator cannon, liquidator	6	4,800	1d20 A	40 ft.	Corrode 1d6	40 charges	4	3	Line, unwieldy
Disintegrator cannon, decimator	11	29,500	3d10 A	40 ft.	Corrode 2d6	40 charges	4	3	Line, unwieldy
Disintegrator cannon, executioner	16	220,000	5d10 A	40 ft.	Corrode 3d6	80 charges	8	3	Line, unwieldy
Disintegrator cannon, eradicator	20	765,000	5d20 A	40 ft.	Corrode 4d6	80 charges	8	3	Line, unwieldy

PAINCLAW (DEMONIC, DRACONIC, GHOULISH)

This powered gauntlet has bladed spikes for fingers, which have built-in injectors connected to three reservoirs for storing substances used with the injection weapon special property. A painclaw can carry up to 3 doses of a drug, an injury poison, or a medicinal compound. Rather than trigger the injection on the weapon's first attack, you can choose whether to inject one of these substances upon dealing damage with the painclaw (and even select which material to inject, if the three reservoirs contain different compounds). A painclaw can inject only one substance per attack.

The hand wearing a painclaw can't be used to hold or operate any other weapon or piece of equipment. Donning or removing the painclaw is a full action. A painclaw cannot be disarmed.

WEAPON FUSIONS

Weapon fusion prices are based on weapons' item levels; see the Table 7–13 on page 192 of the *Starfinder Core Rulebook*.

ANNIHILATOR   LEVEL 8

A weapon with the *annihilator* fusion looks corroded, worn, and crudely formed. If a target is slain by an attack with an *annihilator* weapon, the target disintegrates entirely (as though by the *disintegrate* spell).

VICIOUS   LEVEL 5

Vicious weapons have sinister appearances. A *vicious* weapon gains the boost special weapon property, but when you make an attack with the boosted damage, you take damage equal to the additional boost damage. This damage applies even if your attack misses, and it is not reduced by DR, resistance, or any other ability. The boost is 1d4, plus an additional 1d4 for every 6 item levels the weapon has. If the weapon does not use charges or ammunition, boosting it takes a standard action and does not expend any additional charges or ammunition. You cannot boost an attack made with the automatic, blast, explode, or line weapon special property. Weapons that have the boost special weapon property cannot be *vicious*.

ARMOR UPGRADES

Most Devourer cults acquire whatever armor they can through any means necessary.

UPGRADE	LEVEL	PRICE	SLOTS	ARMOR TYPE	BULK
Grim trophies	1	125	1	Any	–
Weapon spikes	Varies	Varies	1	Heavy, powered	Varies

ARMOR UPGRADE DESCRIPTIONS

Specific armor upgrades favored by Devourer cultists are described below.

DISINTEGRATOR GEAR BOOSTS

Soldiers can choose the following gear boost using the gear boost class feature.

Caustic Burns (Ex): When you score a critical hit with a weapon from the disintegrator category, you increase its corrode critical hit effect damage by 1d6. If it does not have a corrode critical hit effect, the weapon gains a 1d6 corrode critical hit effect. You can add this corrode critical hit effect to your disintegrator weapon even if it has another critical hit effect.

GRIM TROPHIES (MAGIC)

Devourer cultists often adorn their armor with magically enhanced trophies representing their most meaningful kills, such as skulls or other bits of bone or exoskeleton taken from slain foes, defiled holy symbols, broken bits of weapons, or bloodied and tattered badges or seals of authority.

While wearing armor with grim trophies, if you successfully cause a foe to be shaken, the foe applies the –2 penalty from that condition to weapon damage rolls in addition to the other rolls it normally applies to.

WEAPON SPIKES

A suit of armor covered in wicked spikes is an iconic piece of devourer cultist gear. You can add a one-handed basic melee weapon of light or negligible bulk to your armor to act as weapon spikes. You pay 125% of the cost of the selected basic melee weapon to add it as an upgrade. You must have a hand free to attack with the weapon spikes (so you can maneuver a foe into a position where the spikes are effective), unless the foe is grappling you or you are grappling the foe (in which case you can attack with the weapon spikes even if you do not have a free hand). You can also make attacks with weapon spikes when pinned, though only against the creature pinning you.

MAGIC ITEM

Atrocites sometimes give favored Devourer cult leaders and hidden ones a *ring of fangs*.

RING OF FANGS   LEVEL 3

MAGIC ITEM (WORN)	PRICE 315	BULK –

When you wear this ring, your teeth become long and sharp, giving you a powerful bite attack. You can choose to have your unarmed attacks deal lethal piercing damage, and if you are 3rd level or higher, you automatically gain a special version of the Weapon Specialization feat that adds double your level to the damage of these unarmed attacks (rather than adding your level).

TEMPLE OF THE TWELVE

PART 1:
QUESTIONS IN QABARAT

PART 2:
THE UKULAM EXPEDITION

PART 3:
THE LOST TEMPLE

CASTROVEL

THE CULT OF THE DEVOURER

ALIEN ARCHIVES

CODEX OF WORLDS

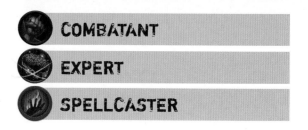

ALIEN ARCHIVES

Castrovel is home to a variety of species, but such strange and dangerous creatures can be found on any world.

UNIVERSAL CREATURE RULES

The following rules apply to many different kinds of creatures.

Construct Immunities (Ex): Constructs are immune to all the same things as undead (see below), as well as necromancy effects.

Stellar Alignment (Su): This creature has stellar and zenith revelations. When using stellar revelations, the creature is always considered attuned. When you roll initiative for the creature, roll 1d3. Once that many rounds have elapsed, the creature is considered fully attuned and gains access to its zenith powers. After it uses a zenith power, it's no longer fully attuned; roll 1d3 again to see how many rounds it will take to recharge.

Undead Immunities (Ex): Undead are immune to bleed, death effects, disease, mind-affecting effects, paralysis, poison, sleep, and stunning. They are also immune to ability damage,

COMBATANT

EXPERT

SPELLCASTER

ability drain, exhaustion, fatigue, negative levels, and nonlethal damage. They are immune to effects that require Fortitude saves (unless the effect also works on objects or is harmless).

Unliving (Ex): A construct or undead has no Constitution modifier and is immediately destroyed when it reaches 0 Hit Points. An unliving creature doesn't recover from damage naturally, but a construct can be repaired with the right tools or magic. An unliving creature with fast healing benefits from that ability. Unliving creatures don't breathe, eat, or sleep. They can't be raised or resurrected.

FERRAN

Ferran mechanic
N Small humanoid (ferran)
Init +0; **Senses** low-light vision; **Perception** +11

DEFENSE   HP 64
EAC 17; **KAC** 18; +2 vs. bull rush and reposition
Fort +6; **Ref** +4; **Will** +8; +4 vs. radiation

OFFENSE
Speed 30 ft.
Melee tactical dueling sword +12 (1d6+7 S)
Ranged frostbite-class zero pistol +10 (1d6+5 C; critical
     staggered [DC 17])
Offensive Abilities momentum, overload (DC 17),
     target tracking

STATISTICS
Str +2; **Dex** +0; **Con** +3; **Int** +5; **Wis** +0; **Cha** +0
Skills Athletics +11, Computers +16, Engineering +16,
     Intimidate +11, Physical Science +16
Languages Common, Ferran
Other Abilities artificial intelligence (exocortex), custom rig
     (datapad), mechanic tricks (energy shield [10 HP, 5 min.],
     neural shunt), remote hack (DC 17), wireless hack
Gear d-suit I, frostbite-class zero pistol with 1 battery,
     tactical dueling sword, datapad

ECOLOGY
Environment any high-gravity (Ratheren)
Organization solitary, pair, or shift (3–5)

SPECIAL ABILITIES
Momentum (Ex) A ferran deals 5 additional damage with
     its first melee attack after it moves at least 10 feet in
     the same round.
Target Tracking (Ex) As a move action, a ferran can
     designate a single foe to track, gaining a +2 bonus to
     attack rolls against that target.

Ferrans are the native inhabitants of Ferrantus-4, a high-
gravity world that disappeared into a massive black
hole several decades ago. The surviving ferrans live
in a sprawling complex on the moon Ratheren (see
page 62), which once orbited their home world but
is now held in place just outside of the black hole's
event horizon. Though the Ratheren moon base
is self-sufficient, ferrans are just another disaster
away from becoming completely wiped out.

Ferrans are short, squat humanoids with
constantly furrowed brows and bald heads. Much of ferran
tradition is rooted in science, and as such, they tend to be
agnostics and atheists. Compared to other species,
the ferran population is relatively small;
they will eventually need to do something
to grow their numbers if they wish to
secure their continuation as a species.

RACIAL TRAITS

Ability Adjustments: +2 Con, +2 Int, −2 Dex
Hit Points: 4

Size and Type: Ferrans are Small humanoids with the
     ferran subtype.
Low-Light Vision: Ferrans can see twice as far as
     humans in conditions of dim light.
Momentum: A ferran deals an additional amount of
     damage equal to its character level with its first
     melee attack after it moves at least 10 feet in the
     same round.
Radiation Resistant: Ferrans receive a +4 racial bonus
     to saving throws against radiation effects.
Sturdy: Ferrans receive a +2 racial bonus to KAC
     against attempts to bull rush or reposition them.

TEMPLE OF THE TWELVE

PART 1:
QUESTIONS
IN QABARAT

PART 2:
THE UKULAM
EXPEDITION

PART 3:
THE LOST
TEMPLE

CASTROVEL

THE CULT OF
THE DEVOURER

ALIEN
ARCHIVES

CODEX OF
WORLDS

KAUKARIKI

N Small magical beast

Init +3; **Senses** darkvision 60 ft., low-light vision;
　Perception +5

DEFENSE　　　　　　　　　　　　　　　　　　　HP 18

EAC 11; **KAC** 13

Fort +5; **Ref** +5; **Will** +1

Defensive Abilities scamper

OFFENSE

Speed 30 ft., climb 30 ft., fly 40 ft. (Ex, clumsy)

Melee sting +9 (1d4+2 P plus kaukariki venom)

STATISTICS

Str +1; **Dex** +3; **Con** +1; **Int** −2; **Wis** +1; **Cha** +0

Skills Acrobatics +10, Athletics +5, Intimidate +5, Stealth +5

ECOLOGY

Environment warm forests (Castrovel)

Organization solitary, pair, or troop (3–18)

SPECIAL ABILITIES

Scamper (Ex) When a kaukariki is hit by an attack of
　opportunity, it can attempt an Acrobatics check as a
　reaction. If the result of the Acrobatics check equals
　or exceeds the result of the attack roll, the attack of
　opportunity misses, and the kaukariki gains a +1 morale
　bonus to attack and damage rolls until the end of its
　next turn.

KAUKARIKI VENOM

Type poison (injury); **Save** Fortitude DC 11

Track Dexterity; **Frequency** 1/round for 6 rounds

Cure 1 save

Kaukarikis are inquisitive pests named after the sound of
their warning vocalizations in the presence of threats;
most who interact with the creatures directly prefer to
call them by the less endearing moniker of "stingbats."
Primarily frugivores, kaukarikis scamper about in
woodland canopies and glide from tree to tree, each
troop migrating widely over its claimed territory
to exploit seasonal food sources. The creatures
readily take advantage of other supplies of food
as needed, including insects,
young leaves, bark, and even
meat on rare occasions. In
fact, particularly large troops—
especially those with a newly
ascendant alpha female—sometimes
organize a hunt to take down modest prey and
share the kill to reinforce social bonds within
the group.

　The creature's eponymous stinger serves both defensive
and offensive purposes. Few predators in the kaukarikis' range
are willing to risk the painful venom, especially because the

pests often rally to one another's defense to mob assailants.
This fearsome reputation seems to embolden kaukarikis,
which infamously incite each other to harass trespassers as
a way of demonstrating bravery and establishing a pecking
order within the troop. For all their venom's power, it isn't
produced directly by the kaukarikis' bodies; many of their
favorite fruits and seeds are toxic, and the creatures' digestive
systems separate and store the poisons within a small venom
sac near the tip of the tail. As a result, kaukarikis fed different
diets might develop venom that damages a different ability
score or lose their poison altogether.

　Kaukariki mating habits often coincide with massive
feasts of fruits, with the male that consumes the most food
being seen as the most desirable mate. The alpha female
chooses first from among the potential mates, followed by
the other females that have the alpha's permission. A female
that attempts to take a mate without permission is often
attacked and driven off by the rest of the troop. Such a
kaukariki is then left to fend for herself, and sometimes she
becomes the alpha of her own troop.

　Kaukarikis are most common on the continent of Ukulam,
though on Asana they have adapted to the dominant
lashunta city-states by adopting new habits better suited
to urban environments. The people of Castrovel err on
the side of deterring and dispersing kaukarikis back into
the wild, though they don't hesitate to take more drastic
action when a local population gets out of
hand. That's even truer in the famed fruit
orchards of southern Asana, where the
kaukarikis can be so disruptive
that local authorities often
incentivize hunting down
the creatures to trim
their numbers.

LORE GUARDIAN

CR 2 | **XP 600**

N Medium construct (magical)

Init +2; **Senses** darkvision 60 ft., low-light vision;
Perception +12

DEFENSE   HP 28

EAC 13; **KAC** 15

Fort +2; **Ref** +2; **Will** +0

Immunities construct immunities; **DR** 2/adamantine; **SR** 13

OFFENSE

Speed 30 ft.

Melee tactical spear +10
(1d6+6 P) or
slam +10 (1d4+6 B)

Ranged tactical spear +8 (1d6+6 P)

Offensive Abilities eldritch
attacks, transposing strike

STATISTICS

Str +4; **Dex** +2; **Con** —; **Int** —; **Wis** +0;
Cha −5

Languages see species tradition
(can't speak)

Other Abilities mindless, species
tradition, unliving

Gear tactical spear

ECOLOGY

Environment any

Organization solitary or
congregation (2–8)

SPECIAL ABILITIES

Eldritch Attacks (Su) A lore guardian's
slam attack and attacks it makes
with analog weapons are treated
as magic for the purpose of
overcoming DR and damaging
incorporeal creatures.

Species Tradition (Ex) A lore guardian
mimics the anatomy and mannerisms
of the culture that created it. A lore
guardian counts as both a construct
and a member of its parent species
for any effect related to its type
and subtype (such as for the
bane weapon fusion). It also
understands but cannot speak one
of its parent species' languages.

Transposing Strike (Su) Once per day
after making a ranged attack
with an analog weapon,
a lore guardian can
activate a special
teleportation effect
as a swift action.

This either teleports the ranged weapon back into the
construct's hands or teleports the construct to the
weapon's location (maximum 100 feet). When using the
latter option, the lore guardian appears with the weapon
in its hands adjacent to the target of its ranged attack
(if it hit) or in a randomly determined nearby space (if it
missed; see Missing with a Thrown Weapon on page 245
of the *Starfinder Core Rulebook*).

Although technological constructs are especially popular
in the modern era, many ancient cultures created magical
automatons in their own images. Known as lore guardians,
these sentries are fairly common in abandoned ruins from
bygone eras, where they tirelessly chase off would-be looters.

Unlike golems, lore guardians have only limited magical
resistances, and they are animated strictly by
magic, not by bound spirits or outsiders.

Lore guardians are echoes of their parent
cultures, and they are often psychically imbued
with those societies' basic traditions. They
infrequently move about their assigned
areas, mindlessly aping their creators'
behaviors and rituals. Even after millennia,
lore guardians recognize their creators'
species, and a creature of such a species can
often approach the constructs peacefully. A
successful DC 18 Diplomacy check is often
sufficient to calm most lore guardians
susceptible to negotiation (though
the GM can decide whether this is
possible for a particular lore guardian).

VARIANT LORE GUARDIANS

Most lore guardians are made of stone,
but different materials are equally
suitable. The following are typical variants,
though versions made of stronger materials
are possible and often have
a higher CR.

Common Metal: The
construct's DR increases
to 4/adamantine, but the
construct's spell resistance
doesn't apply to spells that
deal electricity damage.

Wood: The construct's
base speed increases to
40 feet, and its Reflex
save bonus increases to
+4, but it loses its DR.

TEMPLE
OF THE
TWELVE

PART 1:
QUESTIONS
IN QABARAT

PART 2:
THE UKULAM
EXPEDITION

PART 3:
THE LOST
TEMPLE

CASTROVEL

THE CULT OF
THE DEVOURER

ALIEN
ARCHIVES

CODEX OF
WORLDS

RENKRODA, WHISKERED

CR 5 **XP 1,600**

N Large animal
Init +2; **Senses** low-light vision; **Perception** +11

DEFENSE
HP 75
EAC 17; **KAC** 19
Fort +9; **Ref** +9; **Will** +4

OFFENSE
Speed 50 ft.
Melee bite +14 (1d6+10 P) or
tail +11 (1d8+10 B)
Space 10 ft.; **Reach** 10 ft.
Offensive Abilities roar, upending charge

STATISTICS
Str +5; **Dex** +2; **Con** +3; **Int** –4; **Wis** +1; **Cha** +0
Skills Athletics +16, Stealth +11, Survival +11

ECOLOGY
Environment temperate or warm forests (Castrovel)
Organization solitary or gang (2–5)

SPECIAL ABILITIES
Roar (Ex) As a standard action, a whiskered renkroda can bellow ferociously, causing all enemies within 60 feet to become shaken for 1d4+1 rounds (Will DC 13 negates). If the renkroda hits an opponent with its tail attack, it can activate this ability as a move action before the end of its next turn. After a whiskered renkroda roars, it must wait 1d6 rounds before it can do so again. This is a mind-affecting, sense-dependent fear effect.

Upending Charge (Ex) A whiskered renkroda takes no penalty to its attack roll when using the charge action. If it hits, it can immediately initiate a trip combat maneuver (this takes no action).

Renkrodas make up an extensive category of large reptilian hypercarnivores that are distinguished by their long necks, decorative spines, and deadly sprints. They range across broad swaths of the continents of Asana and Ukulam on Castrovel, and due to their size and place near the top of the food chain, they are often solitary and aggressively territorial. Their terrifying bellows—signaling the creatures' efforts to maintain boundaries between one another and warn scavengers away from fresh kills—are one of the iconic sounds of northern Castrovel's wilderness.

The whiskered renkroda is among the smaller varieties of renkroda, adapted to move easily through heavily forested areas and distinguished by the additional antennae that grow from its chin, which help it detect prey hiding in dense foliage. Like others of its kind, a whiskered renkroda has a four-chambered heart and a throat that can expand up to twice its normal diameter, allowing the creature to gulp air quickly and circulate blood effectively while in pursuit of prey. A typical hunting whiskered renkroda uses trees for cover as it stalks its victims or waits for a target to approach and then makes a sudden charge to snag its victim or knock it down. Because many of Castrovel's herbivores boast deadly defenses, the smaller renkrodas are fairly discerning when selecting prey. Some whiskered renkrodas can be initially timid around unfamiliar humanoids, not knowing whether they are too dangerous or more trouble than they're worth. The hungrier the animals grow, though, the more likely they are to attack, especially during lean times when other prey is limited.

Unlike young males of many other species of renkrodas, whiskered adolescent males sometimes form small gangs for mutual protection against mature adults and even larger predators. They wander widely across forested territory, moving to another location when food grows scarce. As an alpha member of the gang emerges, the rest of the group typically scatters, ceding that territory to the dominant male. In order to broadcast its superiority, this triumphant renkroda often engages in reckless attacks throughout its new home and destroys its surroundings, frequently roaring, scratching at nearby trees and rocks, and marking with its scent to claim its territory.

SKY FISHER

N Huge aberration

Init +5; **Senses** darkvision 60 ft.; **Perception** +16

DEFENSE
HP 75

EAC 17; **KAC** 18

Fort +7; **Ref** +7; **Will** +6

Defensive Abilities aerial camouflage

OFFENSE

Speed 15 ft., fly 50 ft. (Ex, good)

Melee bite +14 (1d6+7 P plus fisher poison) or tentacle +11 (1d8+7 B)

Ranged lasso +14 (1d4+7 B nonlethal plus entangled)

Space 15 ft.; **Reach** 5 ft. (15 ft. with tentacle)

Offensive Abilities lasso

STATISTICS

Str +2; **Dex** +4; **Con** +3; **Int** −1; **Wis** +0; **Cha** −1

Skills Acrobatics +11, Stealth +11

Languages Castrovelian (can't speak); telepathy 60 ft.

ECOLOGY

Environment any sky (Castrovel)

Organization solitary

SPECIAL ABILITIES

Aerial Camouflage (Su) As a swift action, a sky fisher can cause its body to become transparent. While airborne and using this ability, the sky fisher gains the staggered condition, but it also gains a +10 racial bonus to Stealth checks and can attempt Stealth checks without cover or concealment.

Lasso (Ex) A sky fisher is capable of spinning and casting gooey filaments that target KAC and have a range increment of 50 feet (maximum 250 feet). A target struck by one of these filaments takes the listed amount of nonlethal bludgeoning damage and gains the entangled condition for 1 minute. While entangled, the target can't move farther from the sky fisher than where it began its turn. As a move action, a sky fisher can attempt a combat maneuver check with a +8 bonus to reposition the target, though only to move the target closer; a sky fisher can lift a Medium or smaller target into the air in this way. A creature can end the entangled condition early with a successful DC 23 Acrobatics check to escape or by dealing at least 10 fire or slashing damage to the filament, severing it (the filament has the same AC as the sky fisher). A sky fisher can detach or remove slack in a filament as a swift action and can maintain up to three filaments at a time.

FISHER POISON

Type poison (injury); **Save** Fortitude DC 13

Track Strength; **Frequency** 1/round for 6 rounds

Cure 1 save

Sky fishers are aerial ambush predators notorious for casting sticky, anesthetizing filaments with which they reel in their quarry. A sky fisher's blood contains hemocyanin, which gives the creature a bluish tone. However, it can deoxygenate its blood to turn its body colorless, making the sky fisher sluggish but rendering it mostly translucent as it watches for prey.

The aberrations have remarkably complex brains that allow them to analyze patterns and even learn speech, which they observe by using their rounded bodies to magnify sounds emanating from the ground below. This predatory intelligence makes sky fishers a major threat to Castrovelian cities, most of which employ automated defenses to scare off the creatures.

Though they spend the entirety of their adult lives in the air, sky fishers lay their eggs in saltwater. Their amphibious young spend 7–8 months in the seas before clambering onto nearby rocks—losing the ability to breathe underwater—and then catching the seasonal winds to become airborne.

TEMPLE OF THE TWELVE

PART 1:
QUESTIONS IN QABARAT

PART 2:
THE UKULAM EXPEDITION

PART 3:
THE LOST TEMPLE

CASTROVEL

THE CULT OF THE DEVOURER

ALIEN ARCHIVES

CODEX OF WORLDS

WOIOKO

CR 4 — XP 1,200

Floatborn woioko envoy
LN Medium humanoid (woioko)
Init +3; **Senses** low-light vision; **Perception** +10

DEFENSE   HP 45
EAC 17; **KAC** 17
Fort +3; **Ref** +5; **Will** +7
Defensive Abilities slippery mind

OFFENSE
Speed 30 ft., swim 30 ft.
Melee tactical spear +8 (1d6+5 P)
Ranged *trailblazer tactical semi-auto pistol* +10 (1d6+4 P)

STATISTICS
Str +1; **Dex** +3; **Con** +0; **Int** +1; **Wis** +1; **Cha** +5
Skills Athletics +15 (+23 when swimming), Culture +10, Diplomacy +15, Piloting +10, Sense Motive +15
Languages Common, Woiokan
Other Abilities envoy improvisations (get 'em, inspiring boost [13 SP], quick inspiring boost [9 SP]), hold breath
Gear woiokan bodyglove (functions as basic lashunta tempweave), tactical spear, *trailblazer tactical semi-auto pistol* with 90 small arm rounds

ECOLOGY
Environment any oceans (Heicoron IV)
Organization solitary, pair, or delegation (3–12)

SPECIAL ABILITIES
Hold Breath (Ex) A Floatborn woioko can hold her breath for 10 minutes before she risks drowning.

Slippery Mind (Ex) The first time a woioko fails her saving throw against an enchantment spell or effect, she can attempt a second saving throw 1 round later.

Inhabitants of the ocean planet Heicoron IV (*Starfinder Adventure Path #1* 62), woiokos are humanoids who have smooth, eellike skin. They evolved from underwater-dwelling ancestors, but more recently they split into two subspecies when rising sea levels destroyed their terrestrial civilization. The air-breathing Floatborn remained above the waves and now reside in vast floating arcologies divided into dozens of autonomous nations. The Deepborn genetically modified themselves to breathe water as well as air and returned to their primeval homes deep in the ocean, where short-lived domains constantly vie for dominance. The two subspecies have little contact with one another, each remaining in its preferred environment.

RACIAL TRAITS

Ability Adjustments: See Subspecies.
Hit Points: 4

Size and Type: Woiokos are Medium humanoids with the woioko subtype. Deepborn woiokos also gain the aquatic subtype.

Amphibious: Deepborn woiokos can breathe underwater (thanks to the aquatic subtype), but they can also breathe air and survive on land.

Hold Breath: See above.

Low-Light Vision: All woiokos can see in dim light as if it were normal light.

Multinational: To navigate the ever-shifting waters of alliances and enmities between the scattered Floatborn nations and arcologies, Floatborn woiokos must be skilled at dealing with those from different backgrounds; they receive a +2 racial bonus to Culture and Diplomacy checks.

Natural Swimmer: All woiokos are at home in the water and have a swim speed of 30 feet.

Subspecies: Woiokos belong to one of two subspecies: Deepborn or Floatborn. All woiokos start with +2 Charisma and –2 Constitution at character creation. Additionally, Deepborn woiokos are athletic and powerful (+2 Strength), while Floatborn woiokos are lithe and more graceful (+2 Dexterity).

YARUK

CR 8 **XP 4,800**

N Gargantuan animal

Init +0; **Senses** blindsense (scent), low-light vision; **Perception** +21

DEFENSE   **HP** 130

EAC 20; **KAC** 22

Fort +12; **Ref** +10; **Will** +7

DR 5/–; **Resistances** sonic 10

OFFENSE

Speed 40 ft.

Melee slam +20 (3d4+14 B) or

   tail slap +17 (2d6+14 B)

Space 20 ft.; **Reach** 15 ft. (20 ft. with tail slap)

Offensive Abilities bulldoze, trample, trumpet

STATISTICS

Str +6; **Dex** +0; **Con** +4; **Int** –4; **Wis** +2; **Cha** +1

Skills Athletics +16, Survival +16

ECOLOGY

Environment temperate plains and forests (Castrovel)

Organization solitary or moot (2–12)

SPECIAL ABILITIES

Bulldoze (Ex) When a yaruk uses its trample ability, it ignores difficult terrain created by plants. Each inanimate obstacle in its path takes twice the yaruk's trample damage (inanimate plants take quadruple damage), and if this would reduce the obstacle to half its Hit Points or fewer, the yaruk can move through the obstacle as though it were difficult terrain.

Trample (Ex) As a full action, a yaruk can move up to its speed and through the space of any creatures that are at least one size smaller than itself. The yaruk does not need to make an attack roll; each creature whose space it moves through takes 3d4+14 bludgeoning damage. A target of a trample can attempt a DC 16 Reflex save to take half damage; if it does, it can't make an attack of opportunity against the yaruk due to the yaruk's movement. A yaruk can deal trample damage to the same creature only once per round.

Trumpet (Ex) A yaruk's vocalizations are audible up to 3 miles away in typical outdoor conditions. As a standard action once per 1d6 rounds, a yaruk can blare loudly in a 60-foot cone, dealing 2d8+8 sonic damage and inflicting both the deafened condition and the off-target condition for 1d4 rounds (a successful DC 16 Fortitude save halves the damage and negates these conditions).

Yaruks are immense herbivores that can readily crop tree leaves, even using their sturdy forelimbs to partly climb trunks to reach even higher. Yaruks are infamously destructive in their ongoing migrations, toppling whatever isn't convenient to walk around. This has hidden benefits, though. Not only does this create natural pathways and game trails that other species exploit, but it also clears swaths through thick canopies, allowing for new growth.

While most yaruks are solitary, they regularly call to their neighbors with deafening bellows magnified by their hollow crests. The yaruks then form temporary gatherings, called moots, and wander together for up to a week afterward before the individual yaruks gradually disperse.

TEMPLE
OF THE
TWELVE

PART 1:
QUESTIONS
IN QABARAT

PART 2:
THE UKULAM
EXPEDITION

PART 3:
THE LOST
TEMPLE

CASTROVEL

THE CULT OF
THE DEVOURER

ALIEN
ARCHIVES

CODEX OF
WORLDS

RATHEREN

Moon Base of Desperate Survivors

Diameter: ×1/3
Mass: ×1/4
Gravity: Special
Location: The Vast
Atmosphere: Thin
Day: 25 hours; **Year:** 300 days

Centuries ago, as the ferrans (see page 55)—the inhabitants of the planet Ferrantus-4—developed advanced technology and began to look toward the stars, they saw their race's ultimate fate: a region of nearby space so dark that it could only be a black hole. Luckily, the Ferrantus system was just far enough away to be spared the worst effects of the black hole's gravitation and radiation, but the study of the stellar phenomenon, which the ferrans came to call "the Maw," ignited the curiosity of many of the planet's scientists. Astrophysics became a popular field of study, launching a scientific revolution. Eventually, the ferrans achieved limited space flight, traveling to their moon Ratheren to build a self-sustaining research station to better study the Maw.

Decades later, the ferrans discovered that a rogue black hole-like entity was on a collision course with the Maw. Knowing that such a conglomeration of energy would result in the formation of a quasar—and render their system uninhabitable—the ferrans were faced with a multipronged crisis.

To combat the despair that arose from the future's cold truths, faiths sprang up seemingly overnight. The most popular religion declared that the ferrans were destined to merge with the Maw and that they would be safe only once they embraced this fate. The most zealous followers even thought that the catastrophe would transform them into a more advanced state of being.

Those ferrans who approached the crisis with the rationality of science worked feverishly to find some way to save their people. They came close to cracking technological interstellar travel long before the Drift made it commonplace, but in the end, they were too late. The world leader of Ferrantus-4, who firmly believed that the Maw meant their salvation rather than their destruction, enacted an insane plan to launch the planet into the black hole using a combination of industrial force fields and teleportation magic. The fanatic succeeded, but there wasn't enough time to retrieve the moon-based researchers before Ferrantus-4 disappeared with a burst of energy that pushed Ratheren outside of the quasar's gravitational pull. Many of the remaining ferrans believed that their kin had committed an act of mass suicide, but as a few die-hard optimists studied the Maw, they picked up strange signals—signals that shouldn't have been able to pass the event horizon.

Today, most of the ferrans of Ratheren spend their time eking out an existence on their moon base and attempting to discover whether the rest of their people are still alive within the Maw. A few, however, find this pursuit foolish and wish to turn their efforts toward finding a new place to live.

Before the ferrans colonized it, Ratheren was a moon made mostly of dark stone. It has very little atmosphere, almost no natural life, and deep crevasses crisscrossing its surface. Its gravity is irregular, with a gravitational field ranging from about as strong as that of lost Golarion to twice as strong. The Ratheren base now encompasses almost a quarter of the moon—a sprawling metropolis of squat buildings connected by enclosed walkways. Hydroponic gardens provide food and oxygen for the residents, and purifiers recycle liquid waste and clean the water that's collected from the moon's dwindling polar cap. The facilities obtain geothermal power from turbines deep within Ratheren's fissures. Day and night are artificially controlled to simulate Ferrantus-4's original cycle, even though many generations of ferrans were born and lived their lives on the moon without ever knowing the lost planet of their origin.

NEXT MONTH

SPLINTERED WORLDS

By Amanda Hamon Kunz

Tracking the Cult of the Devourer, the heroes travel to the Diaspora, but they must survive the dangers of the asteroid field to find the cult's hidden command post. Exploring the secret base, the heroes find it abandoned by the cult, but they also uncover evidence that the Corpse Fleet was there first. Following this lead, the heroes continue on to Eox, where they must face both the undead inhabitants of the planet and clandestine agents of the officially disavowed Corpse Fleet to learn that the Devourer cult is headed for a distant star system in search of clues to the location of an alien superweapon.

EOX

By Owen K.C. Stephens

Although it was once a verdant world, Eox is now a dead planet, its atmosphere stripped away and its ecosystem ravaged in the fallout of an interplanetary war. The planet's powerful spellcaster leaders turned themselves into undead in order to survive, and these bone sages still rule Eox to this day. Explore many of Eox's notable locations, from the Necropoleis populated by various undead creatures to a vast subterranean city where the living fight for their survival for the amusement of viewers across the galaxy.

THE CORPSE FLEET

By Thurston Hillman

Though Eox is a peaceful member of the Pact Worlds, some of its more militant residents were exiled for questioning the decision to join that alliance. Now known as the Corpse Fleet, this undead armada flies through the depths of space, gathering strength until it can wipe out every living thing in the Pact Worlds.

SUBSCRIBE TO STARFINDER ADVENTURE PATH

The Dead Suns Adventure Path continues! Don't miss out on a single exciting volume—head over to **paizo.com/starfinder** and subscribe today to have Starfinder Roleplaying Game, Starfinder Adventure Path, and Starfinder Accessories products delivered to your door!

TEMPLE OF THE TWELVE

PART 1: QUESTIONS IN QABARAT

PART 2: THE UKULAM EXPEDITION

PART 3: THE LOST TEMPLE

CASTROVEL

THE CULT OF THE DEVOURER

ALIEN ARCHIVES

CODEX OF WORLDS

THE INVASION BEGINS!

STARFINDER®

ALIEN ARCHIVE

Battle or befriend more than 80 bizarre life-forms in this 160-page, hardcover creature collection for the Starfinder Roleplaying Game! Every new world and space station comes with its own dangers, from strange new cultures to robotic killing machines to alien predators ready to devour unwary spacefarers. Inside this book, you'll find rules and ecologies for creatures from across the known multiverse, plus alien equipment and more. Best of all, a robust system for creating your own creatures ensures that your parties will never be without weird new aliens to interact with. Racial rules for many of these new organisms even let *you* be the alien, making the *Alien Archive* not just a collection of creatures to kill but a fascinating menu of creatures to *be*! Want to play a hyperevolved floating brain? A mighty dragonkin? A silicon-based crystalline slug? Explore the limits of your galaxy and your game with the *Starfinder Alien Archive*!

AVAILABLE OCTOBER 2017!

STARFINDER

Development Leads • Jason Keeley and Chris Sims
Authors • Owen K.C. Stephens, with John Compton,
Jason Keeley, and Larry Wilhelm
Cover Artist • David Alvarez
Interior Artists • Oh Wang Jing, Mark Molnar,
Mirco Paganessi, Mary Jane Pajaron, Matias Tapia, and
Ben Wootten
Cartographer • Damien Mammoliti

Creative Directors • James Jacobs, Robert G. McCreary, and
Sarah E. Robinson
Director of Game Design • Jason Bulmahn
Managing Developer • Adam Daigle
Development Coordinator • Amanda Hamon Kunz
Organized Play Lead Developer • John Compton
Developers • Eleanor Ferron, Crystal Frasier, Jason Keeley,
Luis Loza, Ron Lundeen, Joe Pasini, Michael Sayre,
Chris Sims, and Linda Zayas-Palmer
Starfinder Design Lead • Owen K.C. Stephens
Starfinder Society Developer • Thurston Hillman
Senior Designer • Stephen Radney-MacFarland
Designers • Logan Bonner and Mark Seifter
Managing Editor • Judy Bauer
Senior Editor • Christopher Carey
Editors • James Case, Leo Glass, Lyz Liddell, Adrian Ng,
Lacy Pellazar, and Jason Tondro
Art Director • Sonja Morris
Senior Graphic Designers • Emily Crowell and Adam Vick
Franchise Manager • Mark Moreland
Project Manager • Gabriel Waluconis

Publisher • Erik Mona
Paizo CEO • Lisa Stevens
Chief Operations Officer • Jeffrey Alvarez
Chief Financial Officer • John Parrish
Chief Technical Officer • Vic Wertz
Director of Sales • Pierce Watters
Sales Associate • Cosmo Eisele
Vice President of Marketing & Licensing • Jim Butler
Marketing Manager • Dan Tharp
Licensing Manager • Glenn Elliott
Public Relations Manager • Aaron Shanks
Organized Play Manager • Tonya Woldridge
Accountant • Christopher Caldwell
Data Entry Clerk • B. Scott Keim
Director of Technology • Dean Ludwig
Web Production Manager • Chris Lambertz
Senior Software Developer • Gary Teter
Webstore Coordinator • Rick Kunz

Customer Service Team • Sharaya Copas, Katina Davis,
Sara Marie, and Diego Valdez
Warehouse Team • Laura Wilkes Carey, Will Chase,
Mika Hawkins, Heather Payne, Jeff Strand, and
Kevin Underwood
Website Team • Brian Bauman, Robert Brandenburg,
Whitney Chatterjee, Lissa Guillet, Erik Keith, and
Andrew White

ON THE COVER

Leading the Corpse Fleet armada that's attempting
to take control of the Stellar Degenerator, Admiral
Serovox is a powerful, terrifying necrovite illustrated
by artist David Alvarez.

EMPIRE OF BONES   2
by Owen K.C. Stephens

CONTINUING THE CAMPAIGN   38
by John Compton

SHIPS OF THE LINE   44
by Owen K.C. Stephens

SHIPS OF THE CORPSE FLEET   48
by Jason Keeley

ALIEN ARCHIVES   54
by Owen K.C. Stephens and Larry Wilhelm

CODEX OF WORLDS: SHIMRINSARA   62
by Larry Wilhelm

STARSHIP: BLACKWIND ANNIHILATOR   INSIDE COVERS
by Owen K.C. Stephens

This book refers to several other Starfinder products, including the *Alien Archive* by using the
abbreviation AA, yet these additional supplements are not required to make use of this book. Readers
interested in references to Starfinder hardcovers can find the complete rules of these books available
online for free at **paizo.com/sfrd**.

Paizo Inc.
7120 185th Ave NE, Ste 120
Redmond, WA 98052-0577

paizo.com

EMPIRE OF BONES

PART 1: CLOSE TO THE BONE 3

As the Stellar Degenerator is revealed, a massive Corpse Fleet armada arrives! The heroes must sneak onto the fleet's flagship, the *Empire of Bones*, to enact an audacious plan to destroy both the ultranought and the superweapon.

PART 2: MASS GRAVES 7

Once on board the *Empire of Bones*, the heroes can discover a map of the ultranought and a way to elude the ship's security.

PART 3: IN THE MARROW 20

To reach the bridge, the PCs race through the massive of the *Empire of Bones* in a grav-train while hunted by undead.

PART 4: DEAD TO RIGHTS 28

The heroes face off against the admiral of the entire armada in an effort to take command of the ultranought and pilot it onto a collision course with the Stellar Degenerator—hopefully escaping the ensuing destruction!

ADVANCEMENT TRACK

"Empire of Bones" is designed for four characters.

11 The PCs begin this adventure at 11th level.

12 The PCs should be 12th level before they reach the command section.

13 The PCs should be 13th level by the end of the adventure.

ADVENTURE BACKGROUND

The Corpse Fleet was formed when a large portion of the Eoxian navy went rogue after the signing of the Absalom Pact several centuries ago. Since then, those undead have gathered their strength and searched for a way to both destroy all living things within the Pact Worlds system and reclaim what they consider their home world. Fate dropped such an opportunity into their laps when a derelict mining ship called the *Acreon* appeared outside of Absalom Station, towing a strange rock found in the Drift. The Corpse Fleet was already interested in the *Acreon*, as it secretly carried a double agent attempting to return to Eox (see *Starfinder Adventure Path #1: Incident at Absalom Station*), so the undead navy's officers were quite interested when a group of Starfinders—the PCs—became famous for broadcasting their exploration of the asteroid. Undying Admiral Shathrava placed one of his best necrovites, Admiral Serovox, in charge of keeping an eye on these developments in case they yielded fruit.

Serovox was curious to see the Starfinders travel to Castrovel and clash with the Cult of the Devourer (see *Starfinder Adventure Path #2: Temple of the Twelve*), whose agents were following scraps of truth in an ancient doomsday prophecy. As the cultists transmitted the information they discovered to their comrades, Serovox saw a chance to outmaneuver the PCs. The admiral sent a force to the cultists' Diaspora base, but it arrived too late to stop the followers of the Star-Eater from disappearing into the Vast. However, the undead agents were able to discover where the cultists went and why: they had traveled to a distant uncharted star system called Nejeor on the trail of an ancient superweapon called the Stellar Degenerator.

This was more than the Corpse Fleet could have hoped for. As Serovox contacted their superior, the agents—under the command of jiang-shi vampire Captain Zeera Vesh—retreated to their secret hiding place on Eox. Unfortunately, the group of Starfinders tracked down Captain Vesh and her agents, wiped them out, and obtained the Cult of the Devourer's information for themselves (see *Starfinder Adventure Path #3: Splintered Worlds*). As is standard procedure for hidden Corpse Fleet enclaves on Eox, the captain's files held no mention of Admiral Serovox or their ultimate plans. The admiral chose not to retaliate against the Starfinders, instead directing other agents to place a tracking device on the PCs' starship before it left Eox. Serovox also sent a single, speedy Corpse Fleet craft to do the same to the Cult of the Devourer vessel as it reached the Nejeor system. Although the Corpse Fleet craft and its pilot were destroyed in the process, it was successful in its mission. Serovox decided to remain in the shadows and let the two groups uncover the Stellar Degenerator and weaken each other in the process—which they appear to have done admirably.

Admiral Serovox's plan is about to come to fruition. If the admiral can gain control of the ancient superweapon, it will mean a terrible death for all living creatures of the Pact Worlds.

PART 1: CLOSE TO THE BONE

By the end of the previous adventure, "The Thirteenth Gate," the PCs have defeated the sect of the Cult of the Devourer known as the Desperate Hunger, placing the Stellar Degenerator out of the cult's reach—but they haven't won yet. No sooner did they open the demiplane containing the superweapon than a Corpse Fleet armada appeared to lay claim to the Gate of Twelve Suns.

The arrival of the armada headed by the *Empire of Bones* has brought the ancient kishalee defenses of the Nejeor system back to life. While smaller ships such as the PCs' vessel lack sufficiently powerful energy signatures for the megastructure to register them as threats, the Corpse Fleet flagship and its accompanying escorts aren't so lucky. Previously undetected capital weapons have emerged from beneath the surface of the Gate of Twelve Suns' controller moons, and the system is now filled with laser fire and destructive pulses of gravity from the cosmic strings at the center of each. The Corpse Fleet armada is currently occupied with trying to destroy those defenses without otherwise damaging the controller moons, so it can safely enter the demiplane to claim the Stellar Degenerator.

A DARING PLAN

From their position within the control center on Gate 1's controller moon, the PCs can get an idea of the chaos that awaits them outside. The many displays around them flash with multiple warnings, detailing a massive contingent of hostile ships that emit unusual energy signatures. A PC who succeeds at a DC 20 Computers or Culture check recognizes that these vessels are Eoxian in design—strange amalgamations of magic and technology that appear to be made out of bone and are open to the void of space. There are dozens of them in various shapes and sizes, but all are built for war, indicating that they are from the rogue navy known as the Corpse Fleet. In addition, they are accompanied by a flagship that is at least 6 miles long, possibly larger than any starship the PCs have ever seen! Additional information about this type of ship, a Supercolossal ultranought, can be found in Ships of the Line starting on page 45.

It should be obvious to the heroes that they are heavily outgunned (though a PC can deduce as much with a

EMPIRE
OF
BONES

PART 1:
CLOSE TO
THE BONE

PART 2:
MASS GRAVES

PART 3:
IN THE MARROW

PART 4:
DEAD TO RIGHTS

CONTINUING THE
ADVENTURE

SHIPS OF
THE LINE

SHIPS OF THE
CORPSE FLEET

ALIEN
ARCHIVES

CODEX OF
WORLDS

successful DC 10 Wisdom check if necessary). However, the nearby computers also indicate the activation of a number of automated defenses placed all around the Nejeor system, which are keeping the Corpse Fleet at bay for the time being. A PC who succeeds at a DC 20 Computers check or DC 15 Profession (soldier) check realizes that the Corpse Fleet might be distracted enough by this barrage that the PCs aren't completely doomed.

While it is possible to stealthily escape the fray long enough to enter the Drift and escape, that would leave the Stellar Degenerator in the hands of the Corpse Fleet, who would have no compunctions against using the superweapon on the Pact Worlds' sun and beyond. Hopefully, the PCs remember the promise to destroy the Stellar Degenerator that they made to the artificial intelligence Osteth in the previous adventure and won't try to flee.

However, there is a way for the PCs to kill two birds with one stone. By infiltrating and seizing control of the flagship, the *Empire of Bones*, they can steer it into the portal to collide with the Stellar Degenerator and destroy both. If the PCs don't come up with this plan on their own, a PC who succeeds at a DC 24 Computers check or DC 18 Profession (soldier) check while studying the displays realizes this opportunity.

Even if the PCs' immediate reaction is to hide, seek a better tactical position, or try to come up with another plan, they will have to go back to their starship sooner or later if they are ever going to leave the controller moon. Corpse Fleet troops are waiting for them there, and they may even assault the controller moon's control center (see **Event 1** below).

THE STELLAR DEGENERATOR

Now that the superweapon's demiplane is opened, the PCs might want to get a look at the thing they have been chasing after all this time. They can't see it by stepping outside and looking up at the sky, but they can pull up a digital display of the superweapon on the control center's computers.

Over a dozen miles long, the Stellar Degenerator is an enormous conical vessel with a series of ridges running along its circumference in a continuous spiral. Though it appears to have been carved from a single titanic block of stone, various antennae, capital weapons, and control structures jut from its exterior. A dish-like device—an energy collector—protrudes from the vessel's tip. Its engines and weapons are dormant, but the Stellar Degenerator nevertheless emanates a powerful energy signature. Even though it is still on the other side of a planar portal, the superweapon practically hums with destructive potential.

The PCs may want to search for the location on the Stellar Degenerator from which the Drift Rock was removed. A PC can find the damaged spot with a successful DC 30 Computers or Perception check while using the control center's computers: a chunk about 300 feet wide has been neatly carved from one of the aftward ridges, amid a handful of hatches that look like docking bays.

EVENT 1: DEATH COMES CALLING (CR 13)

Thanks to the tracking device placed aboard the PCs' starship, Serovox is aware of where they have landed. While the rest of the armada is dispersing around the Gate of Twelve Suns to deal with its defense, the admiral sent a Blackwind Sepulcher (*Starfinder Core Rulebook* 307) and a squad of undead marines to the controller moon. These troops have orders to find the PCs, kill them, and return their bodies to the *Empire of Bones*.

If the PCs have discovered and destroyed the tracking device, routine scans still inform the Corpse Fleet armada that a starship landed on the controller moon. In this case, the marines' orders are still to track down the vessel's owners, destroy them, and bring their corpses back for undead fodder.

Most likely, the PCs left their starship on the landing pad half a mile from the control center (see Gate 1 on page 11 of *Starfinder Adventure Path #5: The Thirteenth Gate*). The Sepulcher has cleared a separate landing spot in the jungle a few hundred feet away using laser fire, and the marines have disembarked.

This event can take place anywhere you see fit. If the PCs take a long time scanning the skies from within the control center, the marines eventually find the control center and storm in. The PCs might spot the ship landing as they traverse the jungle and decide to ambush the Corpse Fleet troops. The marines could attempt to create an ambush of their own just at the edges of the clearing that contain the landing pad. Alter the staging details as you require to suit your campaign and the temperament of your players.

Creatures: The eight corpsefolk who arrived on the Sepulcher aren't concerned with exploring the entirety of the controller moon, only carrying out their orders, which are to kill any living creatures they come across.

CORPSEFOLK MARINES (8)	CR 7

XP 3,200 each
Corpsefolk soldier (see page 56)
NE Medium undead
Init +9; **Senses** darkvision 60 ft.; **Perception** +14

DEFENSE   **HP 126 EACH**
EAC 19; **KAC** 22
Fort +9; **Ref** +7; **Will** +8
DR 5/magic; **Immunities** undead immunities

OFFENSE
Speed 20 ft.
Melee LFD pulse gauntlet +14 (2d6+9 B & So; critical knockdown)
Ranged dual acid dart rifle +17 (2d8+8 A & P; critical corrode 2d4) or
   flash grenade II +14 (explode [10 ft., blinded 1d4 rounds, DC 15])
Offensive Abilities fighting styles (sharpshoot), focus fire, sniper's aim

TACTICS

During Combat These marines are experienced combatants who take cover if possible, use flash grenades early on to blind foes, and focus their attacks on any foe who seems particularly vulnerable or more effective than the others.

Morale These marines are dedicated to the cause of the Corpse Fleet and fight until they are destroyed.

STATISTICS

Str +2; **Dex** +5; **Con** —; **Int** +0; **Wis** +4; **Cha** +0

Skills Athletics +19, Intimidate +14, Piloting +14

Other Abilities unliving

Languages Common, Eoxian

Gear elite defiance series, dual acid dart rifle with 48 darts, LFD pulse gauntlet with 2 batteries (20 charges each), flash grenades II (2)

Development: Serovox is expecting to hear back from the corpsefolk marines every few hours and sends down reinforcements if they don't report in. Once the PCs defeat the corpsefolk marines, they have only a short period of time before more Blackwind Sepulchers (each filled with increasing numbers of Corpse Fleet marines) begin landing on the controller moon.

If the PCs didn't spot it while landing, they can find the marines' Sepulcher by scouring the nearby jungle for 30 minutes, or in half that time if a PC succeeds at a DC 32 Perception check. There is one cybernetic zombie (*Starfinder Alien Archive* 114) on board the Blackwind Sepulcher, wired into the controls. Thanks to a mechanism known as a command bolt, the zombie can't take actions unless it receives orders with the proper command code from the *Empire of Bones*. The other crew members must contact their commander to receive permission to lift off. The zombie makes no effort to defend itself (and the PCs shouldn't receive XP for defeating it if they destroy it).

The PCs may want to take the Blackwind Sepulcher for themselves after dealing with the corpsefolk marines and the controlled cybernetic zombie. The vessel's computer system is secured, but it can be hacked with a series of checks. A PC must succeed at a DC 29 Computers check to unlock each crew role; if the vessel is subsequently powered down, those roles become inaccessible until the PCs succeed at additional checks to unlock them again. With a successful DC 49 Computers check, the character gains root access to the Blackwind Sepulcher's computers, allowing the PCs to use all crew roles without restriction. If the cybernetic zombie is still intact, a successful casting of *control undead* or a similar spell can force it to turn over control to the PCs, which has the same effect as gaining root access.

While in space on board the Sepulcher, the PCs must use the environmental protections provided by their armor, as the Corpse Fleet vessel has no pressurized atmosphere, unlike starships built for living crews.

EVENT 2: NOT LONG FOR THIS WORLD (CR 13)

As soon as the PCs use a starship to lift off from the controller moon, the conflict between the Corpse Fleet armada and the automated defenses of the Gate of Twelve Suns becomes obvious. Read or paraphrase the following.

The surrounding space is constantly illuminated by flaring beams of energy that lash out from the system's controller moons, and gouts of incandescent flame pulled from the suns by gravitational pulses. The ancient weapons are wildly inaccurate and fire haphazardly, often fading out before reaching their targets or detonating in apparently empty space, but even so, the Corpse Fleet armada is beginning to

CORPSEFOLK MARINE

EMPIRE OF BONES

PART 1: CLOSE TO THE BONE

PART 2: MASS GRAVES

PART 3: IN THE MARROW

PART 4: DEAD TO RIGHTS

CONTINUING THE ADVENTURE

SHIPS OF THE LINE

SHIPS OF THE CORPSE FLEET

ALIEN ARCHIVES

CODEX OF WORLDS

show signs of extensive damage. The largest of the Corpse Fleet vessels is enormous—bigger than many space stations. It is surrounded by explosions and debris, both from its own hull and from the escort ships that were destroyed protecting it, forming a cloud that blocks most efforts to get a clear image of its exact shape. However, blasts from the massive ship's powerful weapons clearly mark it as the most effective member of the armada.

In order to deal with the threat of the ancient kishalee weapons spread around the Gate of Twelve Suns, Serovox has dispatched the armada's ships across the entire megastructure. With so many smaller vessels and the drifting debris interfering with the *Empire of Bones*'s sensor ranges, the PCs can attempt to quickly scan it with a Computers check using their shipboard sensors without drawing direct attention; the result of this check determines how much of the following information about the *Empire of Bones* the PCs learn. Only one PC can attempt a single check before the starship combat starts (see below), after which they have to deal with the ultranought's countermeasures, using the normal rules for the scan science officer action.

Result Information

20+	This massive vessel is the *Empire of Bones*, and it is bigger than even a Colossal starship. It is practically bristling with capital weapons. Like most Corpse Fleet starships, it doesn't contain any atmosphere.
25+	The many explosions of the ongoing battle are partially clouding the *Empire of Bones*'s sensors, and many of its weapons are trained on the ancient kishalee defenses. It might be possible to slip in closer to the vessel and board it without those on board noticing. A Medium or smaller starship that landed on the *Empire of Bones*'s hull could remain undetected for an extended period of time.
30+	The *Empire of Bones* has several hangar bays along its length, one of which is currently launching a small squadron of fighters. This leaves a wide-open entryway protected by a minor force field that keeps out small space debris. A Small or smaller starship can be landed in that bay. Alternatively, a person could slip into the bay via a space walk along the flagship's exterior.

Starship Combat: Once they have launched from the controller moon, the PCs are 30 hexes from the *Empire of Bones* (you can use *Starfinder Flip-Mat: Basic Starfield* to track this distance). The only other ships currently near the *Empire of Bones* are four Crypt Wardens spaced roughly evenly in the space between the PCs and the *Empire of Bones* (with one directly between the PCs' ship and the ultranought). It's important to note the PCs don't have to destroy all the Crypt

Wardens, just get past them intact enough to either land on the *Empire of Bones*'s outer hull (then take a space walk to enter the ship through its open hangar bay) or fly their vessel into the hangar directly.

If the PCs are using their own starship, this is a straightforward starship battle. The *Empire of Bones* neither participates in the combat nor moves from its initial hex (though its stat block appears on the inside front cover if needed), as Serovox is totally unconcerned about the risk the PCs pose to the flagship and the ultranought is busy dealing with the system's ancient defenses. However, the four Crypt Wardens try their best to obliterate the PCs.

If the PCs instead commandeered the Blackwind Sepulcher and piloted it off the controller moon, they should ideally be relying on subterfuge rather than firepower, as that vessel is of a much lower tier than their own starship. There is a high chance that the four Crypt Wardens could easily destroy the Sepulcher if they all attacked at once. Without the proper codes and countersigns to communicate with other Corpse Fleet ships, the PCs must use the new crew actions presented below (applicable only in this single, unique circumstance) to convince the ships between them and the *Empire of Bones* to allow them to pass rather than attack. Flying a Sepulcher at its speed across the 30 hexes takes 4 turns. As the PCs do this, the four Crypt Wardens patrol the intervening space, moving at their normal speeds. At the end of each helm phase, the PCs must answer a "challenge" communication from a different Crypt Warden. The character in the captain role can take the garbled communication action to respond without arousing suspicion (or the player in the pilot role can attempt a similar action, though at a significant disadvantage), while the players in other roles can take special actions to assist.

Regardless of which ship they use or whether the PCs trigger starship combat, if they manage to fly to a hex adjacent to the *Empire of Bones* and no other vessels are within 3 hexes at the end of the helm phase, the armada assumes the PCs' starship was destroyed, since the idea of invading the *Empire of Bones* is too unorthodox and bold for any of the undead to have considered it as a possibility. The PCs can then either land on the hull exterior or enter the hangar as described in the beginning of Part 2.

CAPTAIN ACTION: GARBLED COMMUNICATION

You can transmit an intentionally garbled communication that appears to be a legitimate Corpse Fleet identification. With a successful DC 25 Bluff check, you convincingly answer the Crypt Warden who has just issued a challenge to you. If you fail this check, the Crypt Warden moves within 10 hexes of your ship and attempts to scan it during the next helm phase; if the Crypt Warden succeeds, your science officer must successfully dampen the life signs aboard your ship during this helm phase (see below) or the Crypt Warden attacks. If you fail this Bluff check by 5 or more, the Crypt Warden attacks.

ENGINEER ACTION: FAKE GLITCH

You can fake a glitch in one of your systems, such as communications or sensors, to prevent the nearby Corpse Fleet ships from insisting on direct communication. If you succeed at a DC 20 Engineering check, you grant a +2 circumstance bonus to the Bluff check attempted for the garbled communication action until the next engineering phase.

GUNNER ACTION: COVER FIRE

You can use the Blackwind Sepulcher's weapons to provide cover fire for other Corpse Fleet ships, appearing to attempt to protect them from the Gate of Twelve Suns' defenses. If you succeed at a gunnery check against AC 25, your captain can roll the Bluff check of her next garbled communication action twice and use the better result. Alternatively, if a Crypt Warden is attacking you, with a successful check you convince that ship to cease hostilities and issue a new challenge. In this case, the captain must succeed at a garbled communication action with a –5 penalty to the Bluff check before the next gunnery phase or the Crypt Warden renews its hostilities. The Crypt Wardens can be tricked into ceasing their hostilities only once. The benefits of multiple gunners taking this action don't stack, but one gunner can grant the captain a reroll while another gunner can trick the Crypt Wardens into ceasing hostilities.

PILOT ACTION: FLY CASUAL

You emulate the flight pattern of the armada's ships, neither exposing your ship to too much scrutiny nor showing any sign of attempting to avoid it. If you succeed at a DC 24 Piloting check, you grant a +4 circumstance bonus to the Bluff check for the garbled communication action until the start of the next helm phase. Alternatively, you can attempt a DC 30 Piloting check in place of the garbled communication captain's action, with the same possible results.

SCIENCE OFFICER ACTION: DAMPEN LIFE SIGNS

If you succeed at a DC 24 Computers check, you can dampen the life signs of yourself and any other living creatures aboard your ship. This prevents successful scans from Corpse Fleet ships from detecting life signs on a ship that should either have an all-undead crew or should have called in with a prisoner count. If a Corpse Fleet ship successfully scans your ship and detects life signs, it immediately attacks.

CRYPT WARDENS (4)	TIER 7

Starfinder Adventure Path #3: Splintered Worlds 51
HP 170 each

Development: Assuming the PCs reach the *Empire of Bones* quietly, hid their approach using the surrounding battle, or destroyed the Crypt Wardens, they can enter area **A1** (see the map on page 10) with no resistance. If their ship is reduced to 0 Hull Points, the Corpse Fleet assumes the PCs have been killed,

STARSHIP COMBAT AGAINST THE FLAGSHIP

It's possible the players may decide they want to engage in direct combat with the *Empire of Bones* or try to take over another ship (such as an Omenbringer, though none are currently nearby) and use it to directly attack the ultranought. Any such plan is likely to fail given the massive firepower of the *Empire of Bones*, which would be immediately turned on the PCs if they attacked it directly. Efforts to solve the threat of the Corpse Fleet armada through means other than boarding the *Empire of Bones* and taking control of it are beyond the scope of this adventure.

and a Barrow Dirgesinger (see page 50) is sent out to recover their corpses and bring them aboard the *Empire of Bones* to be turned into loyal undead. In such a case, the PCs have a chance to ambush the crew of the Dirgesinger (eight corpsefolk marines; see page 4), hijack the recovery freighter, land it in area **A1** with no further trouble, and continue their mission.

Story Award: If the PCs reach the *Empire of Bones*, either through straightforward starship combat or by tricking and eluding the Crypt Wardens, award them 25,600 XP.

PART 2: MASS GRAVES

Whether they land a ship directly in the open fighter bay or, more likely, attach a ship to the hull and use the environmental protections of their armor to reach the bay on foot, the PCs enter the *Empire of Bones* in an area known as "hangar country." This is part of the primary launch and recovery decks (see the map on the inside back cover), one of the regions of the ship that primarily serves to launch, recover, repair, and store smaller starships.

If the PCs are going to take control of the *Empire of Bones*, they must find information about the layout of the ship and how to get to its bridge. For security reasons, the only place in hangar country where such information is available is the local security post (area **A8**). The maps of hangar country the PCs can access from most computers in the area don't detail every room; some rooms (areas **A5**, **A6**, **A7**, and **A8**) are marked simply as "secure sites" with a note that access to such sites requires approval from the section security officer, Commander Malakar. See page 17 for more details about the area's chief of security.

By checking these secure sites (areas **A5**, **A6**, **A7**, and **A8**), the PCs can eventually find the security post, but the computers there contain countermeasures that are likely too powerful for the PCs to hack without some kind of advantage. Each of the secure sites includes an emergency security key (see the sidebar on page 15) that aids in attempts to access the computer at the security post. With enough emergency security keys, as well as the body of the officer in charge of hangar country's security, the PCs should be able to access a map of the starship's interior and plot a path from their location to the command section.

Additionally, the PCs might be able to take advantage of Malakar's own plans for advancement, which are entirely unrelated to the Corpse Fleet's effort to acquire the Stellar Degenerator or the PCs' desire to stop them. Malakar hates the captain of the *Empire of Bones*, a vesk mohrg (see page 59) named Ghurd Nashal. Nashal fought for the Veskarium during its clashes with the Pact Worlds and in the Silent War that followed, and he was responsible for destroying thousands of the undead defending Eox. Though Nashal's transformation into a mohrg has made him a loyal member of the Corpse Fleet, Malakar still considers him an enemy of Eox and is jealous of his rapid rise through the ranks. She has been slowly formulating a plan to overthrow Captain Nashal and offer herself to Admiral Serovox as a more reliable replacement. Her plans result in her not reporting the PCs when she first becomes aware of their presence, and her existing breaches into the ship's security systems may prove useful to the PCs (see What is Project Tombstone? on page 19).

FEATURES OF THE EMPIRE OF BONES

Unless otherwise stated, all of the locations within the *Empire of Bones* have the following traits.

Atmosphere and Gravity: The entirety of the ship is devoid of atmosphere. Members of the undead crew don't need to breathe and therefore see no point in wasting time or resources keeping the ship filled with oxygen. The comm units used by the crew transmit broadcasts that directly vibrate their flesh or bone, and the environmental protections of their armor keep them from being damaged by the cold or lack of pressure. However, the *Empire of Bones* has normal gravity, maintained by technomagical devices in the ship's engineering decks. The grav-trains that run the length and breadth of the ultranought sometimes defy this gravity, thanks to fields produced by their tracks.

Lighting: Dull red illumination strips run along the ceilings and floors of most corridors and chambers of the ship, resulting in dim light throughout all areas.

Security: A concealed security camera (Perception DC 35 to notice, Engineering DC 25 to disable) is located in every corner of every room and hallway across most of the *Empire of Bones*. The general description of each area features a description of who monitors these security feeds, as well

as their responses to intruders and any other security precautions in place.

EVENT 3: SECURITY PATROL (CR 11)

In addition to the undead crew, the *Empire of Bones* has several patrols of sentry-class security robots that can be directed from local security stations or given commands from the cybercontrol room (area **C2**) in the command section of the ship. When the PCs first arrive on the ship, there is a single patrol of four sentry-class robots in hangar country. You can have the party encounter the patrol anytime the PCs stay too long in an area after making a lot of noise (such as a fight), or you can use the robots to encourage the PCs into action if the pace of the game slows too much. If the original patrol is destroyed, a new patrol arrives within an hour; it first checks the location of the previous patrol's last report and then (unless it receives other orders) moves methodically through the remainder of hangar country, seeking out intruders.

Creatures: These sentry-class security robots are based on models of other security robots employed throughout the Pact Worlds, but with macabre Corpse Fleet modifications. Each robot's head looks like a metallic humanoid skull, and its plastic exterior has been shaped to appear skeletal.

SENTRY-CLASS SECURITY ROBOTS (4)   CR 7

XP 3,200 each

N Medium construct (technological)

Init +5; **Senses** darkvision 60 ft., low-light vision; **Perception** +19

DEFENSE   **HP** 105 EACH

EAC 19; **KAC** 21

Fort +7; **Ref** +7; **Will** +4

Defensive Abilities integrated weapons; **Immunities** construct immunities

Weaknesses vulnerable to critical hits, vulnerable to electricity

OFFENSE

Speed 40 ft.

Melee slam +15 (2d6+11 B; critical knockdown)

Ranged integrated static arc rifle +18 (1d12+7 E; critical arc 1d6)

TACTICS

During Combat Sentry-class robots are programmed to avoid melee combat if they can. Instead, they normally take cover and spread their attacks among as many foes as they can target. If melee combat is unavoidable, a single robot attempts to be the primary melee target and fights defensively in hopes of lasting long enough for its allies to take out one or more ranged attackers.

Morale Sentry-class robots fight until destroyed.

STATISTICS

Str +4; **Dex** +5; **Con** —; **Int** +2; **Wis** +1; **Cha** +0

Skills Acrobatics +14, Athletics +14

Languages Eoxian

Other Abilities unliving

Gear static arc rifle with 2 high-capacity batteries (40 charges each), personal comm unit

SPECIAL ABILITIES

Integrated Weapons (Ex) A security robot's ranged weapon is integrated into its frame and can't be disarmed.

Overload Attack (Ex) Once per day as a swift action, a sentry-class security robot can overcharge its integrated static arc rifle. This gives the robot's next ranged attack with the rifle a +2 circumstance bonus to the attack roll and a bonus to damage equal to its CR (7 for most sentry-class security robots). On a critical hit, the overcharged attack's arc critical hit effect deals an additional 1d6 electricity damage.

A. HANGAR COUNTRY

When the PCs arrive, hangar country is mostly devoid of crew, as all the fighters normally kept in the hangar bay are out on long-range patrol to protect the Corpse Fleet armada. The highest-ranking officer in the area is the section security chief, Commander Malakar, but the commander has little to do with the area's day-to-day affairs. Those are mostly handled by cybernetic zombies, which receive orders directly from cybercontrol (area **C2**) in the ship's command section.

Attempts to scan the *Empire of Bones* using the sensors of a starship in the hangar bay or to pick up internal communications using a comm unit or similar device fail, though either effort does detect weak signals from a distress beacon broadcasting within the ultranought; this signal isn't strong enough to be received from the outside of the *Empire of Bones*. With a successful DC 18 Computers check, a PC can use a comm unit to track the distress beacon to area **A6**.

Use the Hangar Country map on page 10 for this area. Unless otherwise stated, all of the locations within hangar country have the following traits.

Ceilings, Doors, and Walls: The ceilings are 20 feet high, and the doors are thick steel doors (hardness 30, HP 125, break DC 35). The walls are standard starship interior walls (hardness 30, HP 1,440 per 10-foot-by-10-foot section, break DC 45).

Security: Malakar monitors hangar country's security cameras from area **A8**; she uses her Computers skill to oppose any Stealth checks the PCs might attempt to avoid being noticed anywhere within line of sight of a camera. However, she doesn't trigger any alarms if she notices the PCs, instead observing them and trusting in her own ability to deal with them if necessary. In addition, security robots patrol the area (see **Event 3**).

A1. Hangar Bay (CR 11)

Dull red lights illuminate this massive chamber. A heavy crane arm dangles from tracks on the ceiling, and empty racks for small fighter ships line the fore and aft walls. A nearly invisible force field covers the gaping hole in the starboard end of the room, while two large doors exit to the port. In addition, there is a large window to the port looking into an enclosed room. The floor holds a dozen iris hatches, each fifteen feet in diameter. Most of the hatches are closed, but one toward the fore end of the bay is open.

This is one of the *Empire of Bones*'s hangar bays, though all the Barrow Boneshard starships normally housed on the wall-mounted racks here are out fighting the battle against the Gate of Twelve Suns' defenses. The bay also houses 12 threnody-class assault aircraft within the iris hatches on the floor. These airborne vehicles can launch from or return to the hangar bay when the *Empire of Bones* skirts the upper atmosphere of a planet. The aircraft are normally used to support ground troops from other Corpse Fleet vessels on planetary raids.

The crane is used to lift starships from the wall racks to prepare them for launch and to return them after missions. It is controlled from area **A2**, and it can be used as a large makeshift weapon (see page 11).

The room marked **A1a** is a ready room containing a row of narrow chairs running its length. Each chair is only 2 feet wide, and they are crammed tightly together, as the undead neither twitch nor adjust themselves while waiting, and they never tire. Cybernetic zombie pilots and corpsefolk marines typically sit here prior to being deployed in aircraft and fighters. Cables dangle from the ceiling above each chair, with a few small lights and a computer display next to each cable, intended to be hooked up to each soldier to relay messages and orders to their comm units prior to departure; this is a one-way communication only. The display above each seat shows the status of the undead creature hooked up to it, and since the room is currently unused (nearly all the pilots but marines have recently been deployed), the readouts are all blank.

Creature: When the PCs first enter the hangar bay, a platform within the one open hatch in the floor bears a threnody-class assault aircraft piloted by a corpsefolk marine assigned to perform routine maintenance on the vehicles. The marine is startled by the PCs' appearance and immediately attacks. While the marine can't use the aircraft's maneuverability or speed to good effect within the hangar bay, the vehicle is still heavily armed and armored. Despite being designed for use in an atmosphere, the aircraft can function in the vacuum of the hangar bay.

CORPSEFOLK MARINE	CR 7

XP 3,200

HP 126 (see page 4)

TACTICS

During Combat The marine focuses the aircraft's strafing guns on any character who seems to be attempting a retreat. If the aircraft is destroyed, the marine continues to fight using his acid dart rifle, keeping behind the cover of the wreck if possible.

Morale The marine fights until destroyed.

EMPIRE OF BONES

PART 1: CLOSE TO THE BONE

PART 2: MASS GRAVES

PART 3: IN THE MARROW

PART 4: DEAD TO RIGHTS

CONTINUING THE ADVENTURE

SHIPS OF THE LINE

SHIPS OF THE CORPSE FLEET

ALIEN ARCHIVES

CODEX OF WORLDS

A. HANGAR COUNTRY

1 square = 5 feet

FORE

A1

A2

A1A

A4

A3

A5

A6

A8

A7

THRENODY-CLASS ASSAULT FIGHTER — LEVEL 1

PRICE 62,000

Large air vehicle (5 ft. wide, 10 ft. long, 6 ft. high)
Speed 60 ft., full 1,100 ft., 130 mph (hover)
EAC 24; **KAC** 26; **Cover** total cover
HP 150 (75); **Hardness** 10
Attack (Collision) 10d10 B (DC 18)
Attack heavy reaction cannon (3d10 P)
Modifiers +2 Piloting, –2 attack (–4 at full speed)
Systems autocontrol, planetary comm unit

Development: Since the command crew of the *Empire of Bones* are currently too busy trying to destroy the ancient defenses of the Gate of Twelve Suns, no one immediately reacts to any warnings or alarms set off by the PCs fighting the assault aircraft and its pilot. However, Malakar is fully aware of the PCs' presence, and 10 to 15 minutes after the fight, she directs the patrol of security robots (see **Event 3**) to investigate the disturbance in the hangar bay. Malakar is less interested in capturing or killing the PCs than she is in assessing their capabilities.

Story Award: If the PCs survive the attacks of the threnody-class assault aircraft (either by destroying it or killing its pilot), grant them an additional 9,600 XP.

A2. Flight Control Room (CR 12)

This long, narrow room is crowded with controls, monitors, and readouts that cover the walls and even the ceiling. Colored lights blink and flash adjacent to numerous switches and keypads. The starboard wall has a single, long window that looks out onto the hangar bay, and doors exit to the fore and aft.

This is the flight control room associated with the nearby hangar bay. There are eight stations here, usually overseen by cybernetic zombies that are wired directly to the command center, but it is not fully staffed at the moment (see Creatures below).

The many controls in this room function as a single tier 4 computer with a security I upgrade module. This system is used to track vehicles that have been launched from this hangar bay, send them information from the *Empire of Bones*'s sensors or orders from its command staff, store maintenance records, and so on. A quick glance at the displays shows that the eight Barrow Boneshards that launched from this bay are currently skirmishing their way across the Gate of Twelve Suns.

A PC can access the controls with a successful DC 30 Computers check to hack the system, but the consoles here are designed to track the fighters stored in this bay, and they don't have access to local security or provide maps of the interior of the *Empire of Bones*. Once the PCs access

the computer's basic functions, however, the PCs can see a message has been logged regarding their intrusion into the hangar bay, but as of yet, there's no ship-wide alert to their presence. The PCs can also download a local map of hangar country to their own datapads, but much of the map (areas **A5**, **A6**, **A7**, and **A8**) shows no information beyond describing these areas as "secure sites." Any effort to learn what the secure sites are, get a broader map of the interior of the *Empire of Bones*, or learn about any personnel other than the undead pilots currently out on patrol results in an error message that such information is not available on this system, and that such requests must be presented to the section security officer at the section security post.

A PC who succeeds at a DC 15 Culture check or appropriate Profession check (such as Profession [mercenary]) can determine that the section security post is most likely to be one of the secure sites listed on the map, and that the other secure sites are likely areas with valuable or fragile equipment or personnel but aren't directly necessary for the cybernetic zombies to perform their fighter-monitoring duties. Such a check also reveals that not having a full map of the *Empire of Bones* on minor computer systems is a security precaution. This arrangement is fairly common in strict military groups and paranoid mercenary organizations. Since the rank-and-file crew members don't need the full details of every section of the ship, such information is available only on a need-to-know basis. Any senior officer or security officer at a security post is likely to have access to more complete ship records.

The crane in the hangar bay (area **A1**) is controlled from this area, and the windows give a good view of the bay. The controls for the crane are unsecured, meaning anyone can use it without first having to hack the computers here. As a full action, a character can use the crane to make an attack against a single target within the hangar bay. Though the crane physically smashes its target, the fact that it is being controlled remotely necessitates a ranged attack roll to use properly. Characters using the crane to attack must be proficient with either advanced melee weapons or powered armor to avoid taking a –4 penalty to the attack roll. The crane deals 8d6 bludgeoning damage on a successful attack, though Weapon Specialization doesn't apply to this damage. In addition, the crane has the knockdown critical hit effect and grants a +4 circumstance bonus when used to attempt a grapple combat maneuver.

Creatures: Two cybernetic zombies (*Starfinder Alien Archive* 114) are physically wired into the control panels here. They normally operate the crane and handle communications to arrange for starships and vehicles to enter and leave the hangar bay, but their actions are controlled by orders from cybercontrol (area **C2**). As the *Empire of Bones*'s senior officers are currently busy, the zombies take no actions on their own, even if attacked, unless they are disconnected from their control panels. This occurs automatically if a zombie is moved more than 5 feet from its original position, and there

EMPIRE OF BONES

PART 1: CLOSE TO THE BONE

PART 2: MASS GRAVES

PART 3: IN THE MARROW

PART 4: DEAD TO RIGHTS

CONTINUING THE ADVENTURE

SHIPS OF THE LINE

SHIPS OF THE CORPSE FLEET

ALIEN ARCHIVES

CODEX OF WORLDS

is a 25% chance that a kinetic attack that damages a zombie disconnects it. A disconnected cybernetic zombie attacks any non-undead in the room.

A PC who succeeds at a DC 28 Medicine or Physical Science check determines that the cybernetic zombies are wired to receive commands through the cables from the consoles in the control panels (and are incapable of any actions without receiving a properly coded command). A PC who then succeeds at a DC 28 Computers, Engineering, or Mysticism check can determine that the process of issuing such commands is as much magical as it is technological, and, as no commands are currently being given, there's no way to hack or emulate the signals without either more examples of the system (see area **A7**) or several days spent tearing apart the panels and analyzing their components.

Trap: The doors into the flight control room have sensors built into the frames that check for the presence of life energy. One round after the sensors detect a living creature passing through one of the doors, a death-ray projector bathes everything within the areas marked on the map with lethal necromantic rays. Of course, since the entirety of the *Empire of Bones*'s crew consists of undead, the trap doesn't deal any damage to them even if they set it off accidentally.

DEATH RAY TRAP   CR 12
XP 19,200

Type hybrid; **Perception** DC 38; **Disable** Engineering DC 33 (disconnect ray projector) or Mysticism DC 33 (remove necromantic focus)
Trigger location; **Reset** 5 minutes
Effect death ray (9d8 negative energy [death effect], affects only living creatures); Fortitude DC 21 half; multiple targets (all targets in marked areas)

Story Award: The pair of cybernetic zombies is not a significant threat to the PCs, even if they are unhooked from their control panels. Barring unusual circumstances, the PCs should receive no experience for defeating them.

A3. GRAVEL PIT (CR 11)
The double door leading into this room has an electronic lock. A PC can disable the lock with a successful DC 30 Engineering check, or fool the lock into thinking an authorized user has given it a command to open with a successful DC 35 Computers check. If the PCs fail these checks three times or a character fails one check by 5 or more, a silent alarm triggers in the security post (area **A8**). Malakar takes note of the alarm, but she still doesn't notify her superiors.

The floor of this chamber is covered in gravel, which stretches from wall to wall and is heaped in small hills and shallow hollows. The walls are scored and covered in small dents, and large sections are slightly discolored in what appear to be spray patterns, but they seem structurally sound. The area is thick with dust. To the left of the entrance is a metal cabinet with a large handle.

As the flagship of a major Corpse Fleet armada, the *Empire of Bones* sometimes has to mine planetoids and uninhabited worlds for the raw materials to make spare parts and munitions for itself and other ships in the armada, allowing it to perform long-range missions without needing to regularly return to a base to resupply. For this purpose, the crew maintains several of these gravel pits throughout the primary launch and recovery decks as holding pens for large, wormlike burrowing creatures called surnochs that function as living drills and can be loaded onto secure shuttles and transported to where they are needed. In addition, a surnoch's digestive system turns most types of rock into shimmering alloys that the officers use to decorate their quarters.

The apparent floor here is pulverized rock and is difficult terrain. The gravel is 30 feet deep, going down to the chamber's actual sunken metal floor.

Creatures: The two surnochs kept in this pit aren't well fed or cared for. Each has been fitted with a neural implant that helps the crew keep the creatures docile when they are being moved. This implant allows a crew member with an associated program in her comm unit to control a surnoch to a limited degree, similar to the effect of a *command* spell; this function is used primarily when forcing the creatures into shuttles to be transported to a planetoid's surface or returning after mining operations are complete. There are no crew members with this program currently in hangar country. Though the surnochs don't need to breathe, they are fitted with collars that provide them protection from the vacuum's lack of pressure (see Treasure below). The surnochs attack the PCs as soon as they enter the room.

SURNOCHS (2)   CR 9
XP 6,400 each
HP 145 each (*Starfinder Alien Archive* 108)

TACTICS
During Combat The surnochs are maddened by their long captivity and constant hunger. They attack immediately when a PC steps into the room, bursting up from the gravel. The surnochs follow the PCs into the corridor if possible, attacking any foe within reach of their bite attacks.
Morale The surnochs fight until killed.

Treasure: Since the surnochs are considered too valuable to kill unless absolutely necessary, the cabinet near the double door contains a *merciful venomous paragon semi-auto pistol* (with 16 small arm rounds), 3 doses of tier 3 sedatives (used to sedate a surnoch if it becomes unruly), and 3 doses of sprayflesh (in case a surnoch is injured in an accident). Each surnoch's atmosphere collar provides protection similar to the environmental protections of a suit of armor, lasting for 15 days when fully charged. A PC

can alter an atmosphere collar with a successful DC 32 Engineering check so that it functions as a gray force field armor upgrade (and can be sold as such).

A4. Slime Cell (CR 11)

The door leading into this room has an electronic lock. A PC can disable the lock with a successful DC 30 Engineering check, or fool the lock into thinking an authorized user has given it a command to open with a successful DC 35 Computers check. If the PCs fail these checks three times or a character fails one check by 5 or more, a silent alarm triggers in the security post (area **A8**). Malakar takes note of the alarm, but she still doesn't notify her superiors.

The ceiling, walls, and floor of this room are covered in heavy armored plates that show scratches and signs of scoring. Many of the plates seem newer and appear to have been bolted directly over damaged plates without removing the old coverings. Twisted, wrecked pieces of junk are piled up in the corners and where the walls meet the floor. Several pipes run through the room near the ceiling, with numerous valves along their lengths.

This cell is part of the *Empire of Bones*'s slime-patch system (*Starfinder Alien Archive* 101), an automated repair system designed to use material gathered from scavenger slimes to patch sections of the ship damaged in combat. The pipes and valves are used both to suck pieces of scavenger slime up to where the reservoir of slime patch material is kept and to dump useless junk into the room to "feed" the scavenger slimes.

Creatures: Two scavenger slimes are kept here. Over the years, they have cobbled together enough pieces of the broken technology dumped into this chamber to form workable weapons. Under normal operations, the door is kept secure, leaving the slimes to serve purely as a source of material for the ultranought's slime patch system. Once the door is opened, the scavenger slimes attack—not out of anger, but purely out of an instinctive desire to absorb and alter any technology the PCs might be wearing.

SCAVENGER SLIMES (2)   CR 9
XP 6,400 each

HP 145 each (*Starfinder Alien Archive* 100)

DEFENSE
Resistances cold 10

OFFENSE
Ranged LFD screamer +21 (2d10+9 So; critical deafen
    [DC 18]) or
    hailstorm-class zero rifle +21 (2d8+9 C; critical staggered
    [DC 16]) or
    snub scattergun +21 (1d12+9 B)

TACTICS
During Combat A scavenger slime attempts to target

multiple foes in the blast from its LFD screamer or its snub scattergun if possible. Otherwise it attacks the nearest target that doesn't have cover with its hailstorm-class zero rifle. The scavenger slimes do not consider each other targets when making these decisions, but neither do they make any effort to avoid catching one another in the area of their weapons if multiple other targets are in that area.
Morale The scavenger slimes fight until killed.

Treasure: The LFD screamer, hailstorm-class zero rifle, and snub scattergun from each scavenger slime can be removed and used normally with a successful DC 25 Engineering check for each weapon.

A5. Suffocation Chamber (CR 10)

The door leading into this room has an electronic lock. A PC can disable the lock with a successful DC 30 Engineering check, or fool the lock into thinking an authorized user has given it a command to open with a successful DC 35 Computers check. If the PCs fail these checks three times or a character fails one check by 5 or more, a silent alarm triggers in the security post (area **A8**). Malakar takes note of the alarm, but she still doesn't notify her superiors.

A metal podium with numerous controls on it stands in the center of this room. Padded, vertical beds with numerous straps and restraints fill the room, most with numerous stains and small tears in their padding. Each bed sits beneath a bright spotlight from the ceiling, which illuminates the room brightly. Four large vents are visible in the ceiling.

Unlike most of the rest of the *Empire of Bones*, this chamber is specifically designed to sustain an atmosphere when the door is closed. The podium in the center of the room controls the vents and tanks in the room's ceiling, which can create, maintain, and summarily remove nearly any atmosphere. The podium also allows for minute adjustments to the composition and density of an atmosphere once it's established. As a standard action, a character at the podium can begin the process of creating nearly any form of atmosphere (normal, thick, thin, or even toxic; *Core Rulebook* 395), return the room to a state of vacuum, or alter the gravity in the chamber (anywhere from zero gravity to strong gravity; *Starfinder Core Rulebook* 401). When atmosphere begins pumping into the room, the door automatically closes and locks. It takes 1d4 minutes for atmospheric conditions to be established, removed, or substantially changed.

The room's emergency security key (see the sidebar on page 15) is kept in a compartment within the control podium.

If the room contains a normal or thick atmosphere and the door is forced or hacked open (see above), the air within the chamber rushes out into the corridor. Characters in the

EMPIRE
OF
BONES

PART 1:
CLOSE TO
THE BONE

PART 2:
MASS GRAVES

PART 3:
IN THE MARROW

PART 4:
DEAD TO RIGHTS

CONTINUING THE
ADVENTURE

SHIPS OF
THE LINE

SHIPS OF THE
CORPSE FLEET

ALIEN
ARCHIVES

CODEX OF
WORLDS

corridor within 10 feet of the door must succeed at a DC 20 Reflex save or be knocked prone by this rush of air.

The room is generally used as an interrogation chamber for living captives, but it can also be used as part of a ritual to suffocate living prisoners and turn them into common nihilis.

Creature: Lieutenant Kreth, a powerful nihili who was once a drow, is an information-extraction expert and this chamber's primary user. He is skilled at using its ability to pump out air out of the chamber slowly both as a form of torture and as a way to create more nihilis loyal to the Corpse Fleet to bolster the crew's numbers.

KRETH	CR 10

XP 9,600
Male drow nihili (*Starfinder Alien Archive* 42, 82)
NE Medium undead
Init +5; **Senses** darkvision 60 ft.; **Perception** +19
Aura gravity well (5 ft., DC 19)

DEFENSE   **HP** 165
EAC 23; **KAC** 24
Fort +12; **Ref** +12; **Will** +11
Immunities undead immunities

OFFENSE
Speed 30 ft., climb 20 ft.
Melee comet hammer +22 (4d6+18 B)
Ranged elite semi-auto pistol +19 (3d6+13 P)
Offensive Abilities decompression gaze (15 ft., DC 19, 2d8+8 B)

TACTICS
Before Combat If the PCs set off the alarm as they try to enter the room, Kreth readies an action to activate the room's atmosphere controls to pump a toxic atmosphere (this functions as ungol dust poison; *Starfinder Core Rulebook* 419) into the chamber as soon as one or more characters enter.
During Combat Kreth does his best to remain within 15 feet of as many foes as possible in order to expose them to his decompression gaze. He resorts to using his pistol only if necessary, in which case he seeks to fire from cover (especially if doing so forces foes to move within range of his gaze in order to strike back at him).
Morale Kreth seeks to escape if reduced to 55 or fewer Hit Points, moving to area **A8** to inform Commander Malakar of the boarders and work with her to eliminate them. If escape seems impossible, Kreth fights until destroyed.

STATISTICS
Str +8; **Dex** +5; **Con** —; **Int** +3; **Wis** +0; **Cha** +1
Skills Athletics +24 (+32 to climb), Computers +19, Intimidate +19
Other Abilities unliving
Languages Common, Eoxian
Gear freebooter armor III, comet hammer with 2 batteries (20 charges each), elite semi-auto pistol with 16 small arm rounds, personal comm unit

Development: A PC who succeeds at a DC 25 Engineering check while examining the podium finds that it can be used as an environmental recharging station for armor (*Starfinder Core Rulebook* 198).

A6. BRIG (CR 12)

The double door leading into this room has an electronic lock. A PC can disable the lock with a successful DC 30 Engineering check, or fool the lock into thinking an authorized user has given it a command to open with a successful DC 35 Computers check. If the PCs fail these checks three times or a character fails one check by 5 or more, a silent alarm triggers in the security post (area **A8**). Malakar takes note of the alarm, but she still doesn't notify her superiors.

This room is brighter than most of the ship, with crisp white light flooding down from the entire ceiling. A series of four barred cells runs the length of the aft wall, each with a barred door with a keypad lock. A metal cabinet hangs on the fore wall, behind a small metal desk with a computer terminal and a metal chair built into it.

This is hangar country's brig, one of a few found throughout the *Empire of Bones*. They rarely see much use, as Corpse Fleet discipline runs toward execution more than imprisonment, but sometimes crew members are put in lockdown if a disagreement escalates to the level of a brawl or if a more serious offense requires investigation before a sentence is passed.

The four cells appear to just be barred cages, but invisible, airtight force fields extend between all of the bars, giving each cell door hardness 35 and 60 Hit Points. Each cell can

KRETH

be opened from the computer built into the desk (see below) or unlocked with a successful DC 32 Engineering check.

The cabinet behind the desk is currently unlocked. This is where the room's emergency security key is stored, but the small slot where it is normally kept is empty, as the marooned ones who have escaped from their cells (see Creatures below) have confiscated the key. If the PCs already have another security key in their possession, they can immediately tell that the empty slot is the exactly the size of a key. The cabinet also contains a makeshift distress beacon (which is emitting the signal the PCs might have picked up when they boarded the *Empire of Bones*; see page 9), as well as some other equipment (see Treasure below).

The secured tier 4 computer in this room is used exclusively to control the cell doors and maintain a list of prisoners (who they are, when they began their incarceration, and when they were removed). A PC who hacks the computer (Computers DC 29) not only can open and close the cell doors but also learns that the cells are supposed to contain "four dwarf-form corporeal undead: names unknown, loyalties unknown" who were imprisoned 6 months ago. There's no note of these prisoners ever being released, even though the cells appear to be empty.

Creatures: Four marooned ones have set up an ambush in this room. They were dwarven crew members of a mining vessel that was surveying asteroids for valuable materials in a system in Near Space. When they found a particularly large vein of adamantine in a large asteroid, their captain stole the metal they mined and then abandoned them to die rather than share the profits for finding such a rich deposit. The *Empire of Bones* later captured and killed the mining ship captain and went to retrieve the adamantine, only to discover the abandoned crew had risen as undead.

However, the marooned ones weren't yet ready to join the Corpse Fleet, and thus were locked in this brig. With their natural knack for engineering, they took advantage of the chaos of the battle and successfully escaped their cells, but they have yet to explore outside of the brig. Instead, acting largely on undead instinct, they fashioned a kind of distress beacon. After hiding it in the cabinet, they filched the security key and pried up some of the floor plates to conceal themselves. They assume their beacon will bring more victims, perhaps even some with access to a ship that will allow the undead to escape the *Empire of Bones*. When the PCs enter the room and discover the beacon, the marooned ones spring out to attack 1 round later. They can automatically detect the PCs' footfalls unless the PCs are attempting Stealth checks, in which case the marooned ones gain a +5 circumstance bonus to their opposed Perception checks to notice them. A PC who succeeds at a DC 31 Perception check can act during the surprise round.

Malakar is aware of this partial escape, but she is content to allow the PCs to handle this problem or let the marooned ones handle the problem of the PCs. Either way, she knows

EMERGENCY SECURITY KEYS

Hangar country's emergency security keys are digital storage devices the same size and general appearance of humanoid finger bones. Each key has, at one end, a micro plug that can be inserted into any of the computers onboard the *Empire of Bones*, datajack augmentations, or handheld computers such as datapads. While an emergency security key is essentially a tier 0 computer, it can't be directly hacked unless it is plugged in. When plugged in, a key attempts a handshake protocol with the device, looking for the receiving program that exists only in the *Empire of Bones*'s security terminals. If it connects, the key transmits encoded information to that receiving program, helping the user gain access to sensitive information on the terminal. The information can't be copied or altered, and any attempt to do so initiates a countermeasure that erases that information unless the user succeeds at a DC 32 Computers check.

she can sweep in with a contingent of marines to finish off any survivors, if necessary.

MAROONED ONES (4)   CR 8
XP 4,800 each

HP 115 each (*Starfinder Alien Archive* 76)

TACTICS
During Combat Each marooned one remains prone and either begins firing (benefiting from cover due to being in the floor) or attempts to grab an adjacent target. The marooned ones each make only a single attempt to grapple a foe, and if that fails, they then use their knives to stab adjacent foes or shoot their semi-auto pistols at those who are farther away.

Morale The marooned ones fight until destroyed.

STATISTICS
Languages Common, Dwarf

Treasure: The gear the marooned ones had on them when the *Empire of Bones* found them was taken and stored in the cabinet behind the desk, but other than retrieving their pistols and knives and grabbing the security key when they planted the phony distress beacon, the marooned ones have ignored it. The cabinet contains a *serum of enhancement* (commando), a grappler, 100 feet of adamantine cable, an advanced medkit, and a pouch of nine plasma sapphires (magic jewels worth 1,500 credits each, which all shine with the light equal to a beacon without using any power source). A tenth jewel appears to be a slightly brighter plasma sapphire, but it is actually a naturally occurring *standard photon crystal*.

A7. Sensor Suite (CR —)

This room is dark. Only a few lit buttons and displays pierce the blackness, illuminating no more than the rough shape of the area. Panels of computer screens, bundled data cables, and digital readout displays line the walls, with more than a dozen chairs arrayed in front of them. The constant chatter of beeps and clicks accompanies the data streaming across every readout.

This area contains the terminals and readouts of one of the *Empire of Bones*'s sensor suites, which are overseen by cybernetic zombies wired directly to the command center (see Creatures below). The monitors show the information about the space around the ship, including the details gathered by the ship's sensors about other vessels. All the terminals here are connected to a tier 7 computer with a security III upgrade module. It is possible to hack a terminal (so long as it is not occupied by a cybernetic zombie) with a successful DC 44 Computers check. This is likely too difficult for the PCs, but they gain the same access and information as if they took control of one of the cybernetic zombies (see Creatures below) if they manage to succeed.

A PC who succeeds at a DC 30 Perception check discovers a small hatch in the floor in the center of the chamber, which contains this room's emergency security key.

Creatures: In each of the 16 chairs sits a cybernetic zombie (*Starfinder Alien Archive* 114). They are wired into the control panels in a similar way as the cybernetic zombies in area **A2**, but unlike those undead, these zombies are active—constantly receiving commands through the cables from the consoles in the control panels, tapping on their displays, and sending information gained from the sensor array back through the same links. However, they don't attack the PCs or make any effort to defend themselves if attacked unless they are disconnected from their control panels. A zombie disconnects automatically if moved more than 5 feet from its original position, and there is a 25% chance that a kinetic attack damaging a zombie disconnects it. A disconnected cybernetic zombie attacks any non-undead in the room.

The PCs can hack into the flow of information between a single cybernetic zombie and the source of its commands with one successful DC 33 check in each of Computers, Engineering, and Mysticism (they can be attempted by a single character or by multiple characters working in tandem). If successful, the PCs learn that the cybernetic zombies are managed from cybercontrol (area **C2**) in the ship's command section, though this doesn't reveal the specific location of cybercontrol on the ship. Combined with access to the records in area **A8**, this information should be enough to deduce that cybernetic zombies function as interfaces for many of the ship's systems.

Once the PCs have taken over a cybernetic zombie, they can examine the specific orders it receives and the information it returns. This allows a PC trained in Computers to observe the space around the *Empire of Bones* with its sensors (the armada is still engaged in destroying defense systems on the Gate of Twelve Suns controller moons) and analyze how the ship's officers are using the cybernetic zombies. Even a cursory analysis is enough to understand the mindless cybernetic zombies are controlled by a command link used by someone in the ship's science officer role. This officer remotely controls the dozens of cybernetic zombies all across the ship in order to perform science officer actions in starship combat.

In addition, successfully hacking a cybernetic zombie reveals much about the way the computers aboard the *Empire of Bones* are organized, granting a +2 circumstance bonus to future Computer checks to hack the ultranought's computer systems.

Hacking into a single cybernetic zombie doesn't have much impact on the *Empire of Bones*, however. While it's possible to feed false information into the sensor control system, doing so creates a single outlier in the stream of reports from other cybernetic zombies here and those in other sensor suites in other sections of the ship. The system is designed to survive a failure of dozens of cybernetic zombies without creating a problem by comparing the majority of reports and weeding out those that don't match the majority. Even if this entire sensor suite was taken over (requiring a combination of successful Computers, Engineering, and Mysticism checks for each cybernetic zombie), the *Empire of Bones*'s crew are canny enough to simply write off the one set of clashing reports.

Development: A PC who succeeds at a DC 25 Engineering check realizes that one of the many power cables attached to each cybernetic zombies can also be used to recharge batteries and power cells, much in the same way as a recharging station (*Starfinder Core Rulebook* 234). The power cable must first be disconnected from the cybernetic zombie to be used in such a way; doing so disconnects the zombie from its control panel.

Story Award: If the PCs successfully hack an empty terminal or a cybernetic zombie and learn about the existence of cybercontrol (area **C2**) and the command link that controls the ship's cybernetic zombie crew, grant them 12,800 XP. However, the cybernetic zombies themselves aren't a significant threat to the PCs, even if they are unhooked from their control panels, so barring unusual circumstances, the PCs should receive no experience for defeating them. If you choose to award XP for defeating all the cybernetic zombies, omit the above story award.

A8. Security Post (CR 11)

The door leading into this room has an electronic lock. A PC can disable the lock with a successful DC 30 Engineering check, or fool the lock into thinking an authorized user has given it a command to open with a successful DC 35 Computers check. If a PC fails the Engineering check by 5 or more or the Computers check by any amount, a silent alarm

EMPIRE
OF
BONES

PART 1:
CLOSE TO
THE BONE

PART 2:
MASS GRAVES

PART 3:
IN THE MARROW

PART 4:
DEAD TO RIGHTS

CONTINUING THE
ADVENTURE

SHIPS OF
THE LINE

SHIPS OF THE
CORPSE FLEET

ALIEN
ARCHIVES

CODEX OF
WORLDS

triggers within the room. Commander Malakar then prepares as noted in her tactics (see Creature below).

This room has only a single door in the aft wall. A small dais in the center of the room is raised up a few feet, and pillars line the walls. Each pillar supports a display, all of which show collections of video streams of hallways, hangar bays, rooms, and other locations within this section of the *Empire of Bones*.

This is the security post for hangar country, designed to be a place from which the entire area can be monitored. It also serves as a remote backup for many of the functions of the brig (see area **A6**). It is staffed by the local section security officer (see Creature below), who is usually the highest-ranking Corpse Fleet officer assigned to the area. Unless the PCs come directly to this room from the hangar bay or have some way to avoid hangar country's security cameras, many of the monitors are replaying previous encounters they had in the area.

The central dais holds the main security console, from which all cameras and alarms in hangar country can be monitored and controlled. See Hacking the Security Console on page 18 for information on how the PCs can gain information from this terminal.

Creature: Commander Malakar is a truly ancient undead; her history stretches back to a time long before the Gap, when bullet-firing pistols were the cutting edge of military technology and Eox had no intention of allying itself with any other planet in what is now the Pact Worlds. She considers the current ruling bone sages of Eox to have betrayed their undead citizens and sees the Corpse Fleet as the true keepers of the destiny of the unliving. Yet while Eox's signing of the Absalom Pact angered her, she sees it as a temporary political aberration and still values the planet as the home world of the greatest undead in the galaxy. As a result, she mistrusts any creature that has ever been an enemy of Eox, including the captain of the *Empire of Bones*, Ghurd Nashal, who in life was a vesk warrior who fought against the Pact Worlds before and during the Silent War. By contrast, Malakar is loyal to Admiral Serovox (or at least sees the necrovite as a great and rising power who will lead the undead under their command to glory). Malakar has been working for some time to arrange for Nashal to be either destroyed or disgraced in a spectacular fashion that would cause Serovox to demote (and possibly execute) the captain.

Malakar has created two viruses and has laboriously inserted them into the ship's security systems (see Hacking the Security Console on page 18), but she has been waiting for the perfect opportunity to fully activate them. She sees the PCs' intrusion into hangar country as that opportunity and therefore has yet to alert her superiors to the party's presence. She hopes to either capture them alive and release them onto the section of the ship that would do the most

damage to Nashal's reputation, or kill them and turn them into undead loyal to her and Lieutenant Kreth (see page 14), who shares her disdain for Nashal, if not her drive to destroy the mohrg captain.

During the first few rounds of direct combat, Malakar quickly realizes that the PCs are the most worthy opponents she has faced in decades. In addition to her tactics presented below, she openly discusses the PCs' strengths and weaknesses as she sees them (especially if she has already observed them in combat via the security cameras). As she does her best to kill them, Malakar promises the PCs that she will hold places of honor for them aboard what she calls "her ship" as a reward for giving her quite a workout. A PC who succeeds at a DC 30 Perception check or a DC 22 check of an appropriate Profession skill (such as mercenary or soldier) can tell that the insignia of her uniform definitely aren't grand enough for her to be the captain of the *Empire of Bones*. If confronted about this, Malakar doesn't elaborate on her statements, noting only that "she has plans in motion" and that the PCs are a big part of them. However, Malakar isn't foolish enough to believe any claim by the PCs that they might be willing to work with her before she has a chance to finish them off.

MALAKAR   CR 11

XP 12,800

Female human pale stranger (see page 60)

HP 170

STATISTICS

Skills Acrobatics +25, Athletics +25, Computers +20, Engineering +20, Stealth +24

Gear elite semi-auto pistols (4), frag grenade IV, stickybomb grenade III, ultrathin longsword, detonators (2), emergency security key, system-wide comm unit

TACTICS

Before Combat Unless the PCs arrive at the security post directly after infiltrating the hangar, Malakar has been aware of their presence for some time. She sets up both her grenades to detonate in the area just inside the door to the security post. If the PCs attempt to sneak up to the door, Malakar can spot them through her cameras with a successful Perception check opposed by their Stealth check. If she knows exactly when they are coming (such as if the

silent alarm is triggered by their attempt to breach the security post's door), Malakar takes cover behind the security console.

During Combat If Malakar has set up her explosives, she triggers the stickybomb grenade by pushing the button on her remote detonator (no action) as soon as at least two targets are in the area or if a foe wielding a melee weapon moves towards her; she hopes to block the doorway with entangled foes. She triggers the frag grenade in the same way as soon as she can catch at least two PCs in the area. If a PC notices any explosives Malakar has not yet triggered, Malakar detonates them rather than allow anyone to attempt to disarm them. Otherwise, she fires at foes who seem to give their allies tactical advice or support, including envoys. If a foe gets adjacent to her, she takes a guarded step to move away and makes a stranger's shot as a standard action.

Morale Malakar knows if she loses the hangar country security post to living invaders, Serovox will have her destroyed. She fights to the end.

Treasure: The central pillar contains a sealed locker, which requires a successful DC 28 Engineering check to unlock. A PC who succeeds at a DC 22 Computers or Engineering check while examining the locker notices a touch-sensitive biometric sensor that is probably keyed to Malakar. Touching her hand to the sensor, even after she's become an inanimate corpse, opens the locker. The locker includes two batteries, two high-capacity batteries, two super-capacity batteries, one ultra-capacity battery, 90 small arm rounds, 100 longarm and sniper rounds, 60 heavy rounds, and 25 scattergun shells.

HACKING THE SECURITY CONSOLE

The security console is not a stand-alone computer, but is rather a keyboard and terminal designed to access the heavily secured tier 10 computer running the *Empire of Bones*'s security systems. A successful DC 53 Computers check is required to hack into it for any information. However, on the first failed check, a message on the display asks if this is a security emergency and prompts the user to insert an emergency security key (see the sidebar on page 15). Malakar has one emergency security key on her person (see the Gear entry of her stat block above), and there are additional emergency security

MALAKAR

keys in areas **A5**, **A6**, and **A7**. A PC who succeeds at a DC 22 Computers or Engineering check realizes these emergency security keys can all be used simultaneously, with each one granting a +4 circumstance bonus to Computers checks to hack the security console (these bonuses stack with each other). Additionally, any PC examining the terminal notices a touch-sensitive sensor on it. A PC who then succeeds at another DC 22 Computers or Engineering check determines that this is a biometric lock that must be keyed to Malakar. Placing her hand on the sensor, even after she has become an inanimate corpse, grants an additional +5 circumstance bonus to the Computers check to hack the security terminal.

So long as the PCs are using at least one emergency security key, a single successful Computers check grants access to all the information available from this terminal, and even a failed Computers check provides access to the terminal's basic functions with no negative consequences. However, if the PCs fail more than one Computers check without using at least one emergency security key, two countermeasures trigger. The first is a rank 4 shock grid, which requires each creature within 10 feet of the terminal to succeed at a DC 27 Fortitude save or be stunned for 1 round. The second time this countermeasure is triggered, it deals 14d6 electricity damage (Reflex DC 27 half) to each creature within 10 feet of the terminal. The second set of defenses is a feedback countermeasure, which triggers if a PC fails the Computers check by 5 or more, infecting every device used in the attempt with a virus that imposes a –5 penalty to all subsequent skill checks using that device. This virus can be removed from a device with a successful DC 30 Computers check. Both countermeasures are described on page 217 of the *Starfinder Core Rulebook*.

Once the PCs access to the security console, they can gain a great deal of information including basic information about the layout of the ship and Malakar's own plans. Answers to questions the PCs likely have are listed below. Activating any ship-wide security protocols requires an additional successful DC 53 Computers check to bypass the firewall protecting those protocols; neither the emergency security keys nor the biometric sensor grant their bonuses to this check. Any major changes (such as introducing a new virus into the system) made on this terminal don't affect the ship as a whole for a while, as it takes weeks for such changes to propagate through the ship's numerous computer systems. Malakar spent over a year subtly introducing her viruses to the system, and her efforts affect only the ship's security systems.

What can we learn about this ship? The *Empire of Bones* is a unique ultranought: a massive warship larger than battleships, carriers, and even dreadnoughts. It is one of the flagships of the Corpse Fleet and leads its own armada of vessels. You can show the players the ship's stat block (see the inside front cover), though they can't access any of the ship's systems from this terminal.

How can we take control of the *Empire of Bones*? Though crews throughout the ship are required for the vessel to function, all orders come from the command and control decks (see the *Empire of Bones* map on the inside back cover). While it might be possible to remotely hack some of those stations to control a single thruster or one sensor array, operating the entire ship requires taking control of the bridge (area **C4**) and cybercontrol (area **C2**) in the command section.

If the PCs haven't already learned how the cybernetic zombies in area **A7** are controlled, they can do so here. Additional information from the security terminal indicates that the command link from cybercontrol governs both the sensors and the engineering crews (functioning as the engineer and science officer roles). A different, related system on the bridge governs the gunnery and navigational crews (functioning as the pilot and gunnery roles). Controlling both the command link and the bridge systems allows an individual to act in the captain role.

How do we reach the command section? On a ship the size of the *Empire of Bones*, there are hundreds of ways to get from one section of the ship to another. However, the fastest and safest route from the primary launch and recovery decks to the command and control decks is travel via grav-train. There are grav-train stations near both hangar country and the command section. See Part 3 on page 20.

Who is in command of the ship? Admiral Serovox (see page 33) commands the entire armada for which the *Empire of Bones* is the flagship, and while they have the power to issue commands to any crew on board, they rarely get involved in the ship's day-to-day operations. Captain Ghurd Nashal (see page 31) is captain of the ship and Commander Malakar's direct superior. The records about both senior officers are limited but provide enough details to empower the PCs to attempt the appropriate skill checks to identify what kind of undead they are. In addition, Nashal's record includes a footnote mentioning something called Project Tombstone that appears to have been added by Malakar and is only on this particular security terminal.

What did Commander Malakar do with those security camera images of us? Searching through the logs of security video available on the terminal, it is clear that at some point, Malakar realized there were intruders in hangar country and periodically spotted them on hidden cameras in the ship's hallways. The log also notes that Malakar chose not to activate any alarms and didn't report the invasion to her superiors in the command section as part of something called Project Tombstone.

What is Project Tombstone? Nothing about Project Tombstone can be found in the main security logs, but if the PCs check Malakar's personal folders (a PC who succeeds at a DC 25 Computers check has this idea, if necessary), they find more information. A quick glance through the files reveals that the commander was working toward some kind of mutiny, and there are extensive notes on how a minor

threat to the *Empire of Bones* could potentially be used to eliminate, or at least embarrass, "inappropriate members of the command staff." The PCs can easily discover the members of the ship's command staff include Admiral Serovox, Captain Ghurd Nashal, and several other commanders on the same level as Commander Malakar.

Also in the Project Tombstone files are notes on a pair of computer viruses Command Malakar has introduced to the security computers across the entire *Empire of Bones*. One virus is named Wraith 2.0, and prevents the security cameras and security robots on the ship from seeing or recording any creature that is entered into the virus's memory. Malakar planned to use this to aid in her escape from the vessel in case her plans went south. With a successful DC 30 Computers check, the PCs can add their own images into Wraith 2.0's memory, causing the ship's security to ignore them. This doesn't allow them to access secure areas; it only causes the robots and cameras to not react to them.

The other virus is named TombRobber. This program is capable of creating false security alerts anywhere on the ship, and can include in these alerts false security footage of anything in Wraith 2.0's memory. With a successful DC 25 Computers check, the PCs can take control of TombRobber, allowing them to activate it from anywhere on the *Empire of Bones* (using any comm unit, datapad, or similar device). If the PCs need to get a night's sleep, using TombRobber draws enough attention away from their true location to allow them to confidently hole up in an unused room (such as a security closet or maintenance tunnel) long enough to do so, as long as they don't make a great deal of noise or otherwise draw attention to themselves. Each use of TombRobber requires a different emergency security key, giving the PCs a finite number of times they can take one of these breaks.

PART 3: IN THE MARROW

Given the size of the *Empire of Bones*, the main transport system to move from one deck to another (and sometimes from one section to another) involves grav-trains, small multiple-car trams that run throughout the ship on tracks that produce their own gravity. Massive shafts with grav-trains on every wall (each with its own local gravity field) traverse the central spine of the ship, while smaller routes branch off from the major corridors, sometimes even running along the ceilings of large foot-traffic thoroughfares. Grav-trains can change routes at switching points every few hundred feet on most tracks, and grav-train stations are scattered periodically through the ship to allow loading and unloading of cargo and

passengers, as well as adding or removing cars for routine maintenance. The grav-trains usually operate on autopilot along regular preset routes, but an override allows security personnel to take command of a grav-train and determine its route and speed when necessary.

It's a short trip of a few hundred feet from hangar country to the nearest grav-train station. With a map of the interior of the *Empire of Bones*, the PCs should have no difficulty reaching that area, and they can even reasonably find an unused cargo area or maintenance corridor if they need to take a quick break.

B. GRAV-TRAIN STATION

At the fore end of this massive chamber, two shallow channels run from port to starboard, disappearing at both ends into open tunnels. Glowing tracks run along the channels, and a four-car tram sits on the aft set of tracks. A hefty cargo crane can be seen on the fore side of the tracks near the port tunnels, with a pile of crates not far from it. Low walls demarcate a 25-foot-square area in the middle of the room, and five computerized workstations line the interior of the aft wall. A large column descends from the ceiling above the square, reaching to within 10 feet of the floor; it's covered in displays showing arrival and departure times along various routes within the ship. Three rows of hard benches line an area to the starboard of the walled-off area. Two large cargo doors, each 30 feet wide and 30 feet tall, occupy the port and starboard walls. A large metal trapdoor sits in the floor between the walled area and the portside cargo door. An observation post 50 feet from the floor and accessed by a metal ladder is in the port aft corner of the room. Three sets of 20-foot-wide bulkhead doors are evenly spaced along the aft wall; three large Xs have been painted on the floor in front of these doors.

A series of interconnected routes passes through major and minor transit corridors running the length and breadth of the *Empire of Bones*. Generally such corridors are used for priority transit between grav-train stations—usually for cargo, groups of troops, or repair crews—and officers often use them to move about more quickly than going by foot or wheeled cart. The grav-trains generally run on set routes and schedules, but officers and security personnel can override that system to specify a different path.

The crane in the corner operates in the same way as the crane in area **A1**, except it is controlled from a seat on the crane (which is too exposed to offer cover), and can attack only targets within 60 feet of its base. The trapdoor is a secured hatch that leads to a shaft that runs down 60 feet to a storage area (which is sealed off by another metal hatch) that contains currently unused flatbed grav-train cars and maintenance materials. The trapdoor is controlled by a tier 2 computer (Computers DC 21 to hack) built into the floor

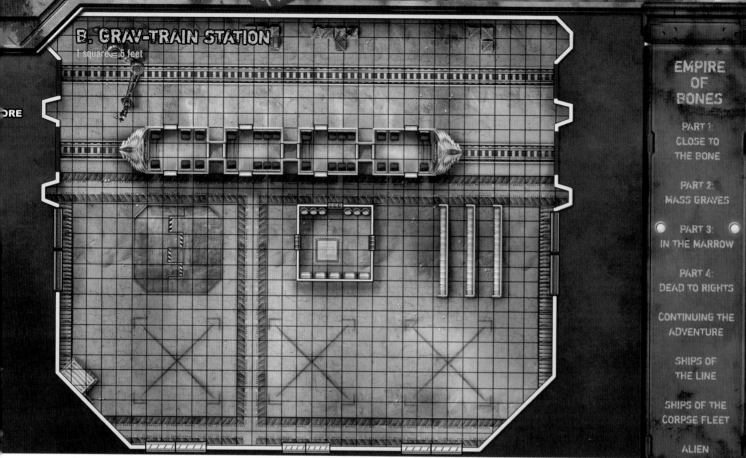

B. GRAV-TRAIN STATION
1 square = 5 feet

EMPIRE
OF
BONES

PART 1:
CLOSE TO
THE BONE

PART 2:
MASS GRAVES

PART 3:
IN THE MARROW

PART 4:
DEAD TO RIGHTS

CONTINUING THE
ADVENTURE

SHIPS OF
THE LINE

SHIPS OF THE
CORPSE FLEET

ALIEN
ARCHIVES

CODEX OF
WORLDS

adjacent to it. The door is simple enough that opening and closing it is a basic function of the computer, and it takes 2 rounds to fully open. The observation post is 50 feet up, is accessed by a ladder, and gives creatures in it improved cover against attacks from anything at ground level.

The following are standard traits of the grav-train stations and all major grav-train transit corridors. Use the Grav-Train Station map above for the encounters in areas **B1** and **B2**, since the design of such stations within the *Empire of Bones* is standardized.

Ceilings, Doors, and Walls: The ceilings are 60 feet high in the stations and most of the transit corridors, and the doors are thick steel doors (hardness 30, HP 125, break DC 35). The walls are standard starship interior walls (hardness 30, HP 1,440 per 10-foot-by-10-foot section, break DC 45).

Security: The *Empire of Bones*'s concealed security cameras are located every 100 feet along each transit corridor and inside every grav-train car. The grav-train stations are outside of Malakar's assigned area, so different section security officers monitor these feeds. Unless the party is being stealthy or using the Wraith 2.0 virus (see below), a section security officer immediately notices the PCs when they enter a station; use the statistics for Malakar on page 18 if you need that security officer's Perception skill bonus. Unlike Malakar, this security officer is completely loyal to the captain and triggers an alarm that blares throughout the entire *Empire of Bones*. This manifests as a strobing white light in all rooms and corridors and a ship-wide warning broadcast to all crew

comm units to be on alert for intruders. The PCs can listen in on this alert if they have taken a comm unit from a defeated crew member and understand Eoxian.

If the PCs have activated Wraith 2.0, no alarm is triggered until they steal a grav-train. When the security forces notice a grav-train making an unexpected departure, they suspect something is amiss and send a patrol to investigate the hangar country station. Unless the PCs took care to hide the bodies of the undead they encountered there, the patrol reports the apparent attack to their superiors, who eventually get back to the ship's mohrg captain. Nashal assumes the worst—a boarding party—and activates a ship-wide alarm as described above about 20 minutes after the PCs steal the grav-train. However, his broadcast to the crew (which the PCs can listen in on as described above) is given with more passion and contains more details. He explains that the intruders have destroyed valuable personnel, including the long-serving Commander Malakar (which is discovered during a quick sweep of the sections near the hangar country station), and should be considered hostile and extremely dangerous. Nashal gives the order to kill the PCs on sight, and he is able to describe them unless the PCs took steps to erase the footage of themselves found in area **A8**. He also warns all sections of the ship to be on high alert, noting the boarders have been spotted in a grav-train station and their ultimate destination is unknown. He orders extra security forces to all security posts, data centers, engineering decks, armories, and munitions decks. While he

also takes some steps to increase security in the command section (see page 28), he doesn't announce those measures over the comm units.

B1. Hangar Country Station (CR 13)

With the map of the ship they acquired in area **A8**, the PCs can make their way to this major grav-train station from hangar country without incident, entering through any of the doors in the aft wall. Trying to enter this room through the cargo doors or grav-train tunnels requires going much further afield on this deck, a process likely to involve multiple encounters with security robots and corpsefolk marines.

The grav-train in the station is currently held in place by a set of eight mooring clamps (one on each side of each car), which a PC can notice before entering the train with a successful DC 20 Perception check. If the PCs try to move the grav-train before removing the mooring clamps, the grav-train's computer issues an error message noting that the grav-train can't proceed until station control retracts the mooring clamps attached to it. Without the aid of this message, a PC who succeeds at a DC 20 Culture check identifies the station control area as the point where such mooring clamps would be controlled; releasing the clamps requires a successful DC 25 Computers check to hack the terminal in the station control area. Failing this, the clamps can be removed from one side of one grav-train car as a full action with a successful DC 30 Strength check, or they can be destroyed. Each clamp has hardness 20 and 45 HP, but any area attack or attack against the clamps that misses hits the grav-train car. The PCs must remove or destroy all eight sets of clamps to free the entire grav-train, or they can remove or destroy the clamps from one of the two end cars and then decouple that car from the others with a successful DC 32 Engineering check; doing so means the grav-train they are using in **Event 4** has only one-quarter its total Hit Points.

Once the mooring clamps have been removed or destroyed, the PCs can hack into the grav-train's tier 2 computer with a successful DC 21 Computers check.

Creatures: Normally each grav-train station is staffed with two bone trooper commandos—one in the security post and one wandering the area—and two cybernetic zombies operating the station control terminals. However, the captain prefers to have more security troops on duty when the *Empire of Bones* is engaged in major military operations, so he assigned an additional detachment of two baykoks and two more bone trooper commandos to the station and recalled the cybernetic zombies. One baykok stands on the raised observation post, while the other lounges across one of the benches. The four bone trooper commandos mingle with each other within the station control area.

The crew are on alert due to the battle with the Gate of Twelve Suns' defenses raging outside, and the staff here immediately attack anything that isn't clearly undead. Even if the PCs somehow manage to disguise themselves as undead, the commandos demand an explanation for their presence without a scheduled transfer while the ship's crew should be at combat stations. They open fire 1 round later unless the PCs somehow convince the undead they have legitimate business. As soon as any of the crew attack, one of bone trooper commandos rushes to one of the workstations and activates an alarm (a move action) that alerts the section security officer (see Development on page 23).

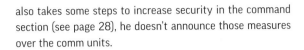

BAYKOKS (2) CR 9
XP 6,400 each
HP 144 each (see page 55)

TACTICS
During Combat One baykok is in the raised observation post when the PCs arrive, and it stays there to take advantage of the improved cover the position offers for as long as it can attack PCs from the position. This baykok focuses on shooting foes who are hanging back from the front line if possible, using its infused ammunition attacks in the hopes of paralyzing such targets. The other baykok moves to the station control area as soon as combat breaks out. It initially stays with the bone trooper commandos, but it moves to other locations if doing so allows it to hit multiple targets with its dread howl or gives it a chance to devour a soul.

Morale The baykok in the observation post is willing to allow the PCs to escape if leaving the post would be clearly suicidal, assuming (correctly) the captain would want a first-hand report of what the PCs are like and what they are capable of. The second baykok does everything in its power to stop the PCs and fights until it's destroyed.

BONE TROOPER COMMANDOS (4) CR 7
XP 3,200 each
NE Medium undead
Init +8; **Senses** darkvision 60 ft.; **Perception** +14

DEFENSE   HP 126 EACH
EAC 19; **KAC** 21
Fort +9; **Ref** +9; **Will** +11
DR 5/—; **Immunities** cold, undead immunities

OFFENSE
Speed 30 ft.
Melee standard taclash +17 (1d4+12 S)
Ranged tactical seeker rifle +16 (2d8+9 P) or
    flash grenade II +17 (explode [10 ft., blinded 1d4 rounds, DC 15])

TACTICS
During Combat These commandos are experienced combatants who take cover if possible, use flash grenades early in combat to blind foes, and use their taclashes to disarm foes who are using particularly effective weapons. They immediately take cover in the station control area, using its short wall to protect them

from enemy fire. If that position is overrun by PCs, they fall back to take cover behind the individual grav-train cars (shooting through the gaps between the cars). After that, they take cover behind the crates if necessary.

Morale These commandos fight until destroyed.

STATISTICS

Str +5; **Dex** +4; **Con** −; **Int** +0; **Wis** +0; **Cha** +2

Skills Acrobatics +14, Athletics +19, Stealth +14

Other Abilities unliving

Languages Common, Eoxian

Gear vesk overplate I, tactical seeker rifle with 32 longarm rounds, standard taclash, flash grenades II (2), personal comm unit

Development: If one of the bone troopers manages to alert the section security officer, a grav-train with four more baykoks arrives to investigate 10 minutes after the fight ends.

EVENT 4: RACE AGAINST DEATH (CR 12)

Once the PCs have control of a grav-train and leave the hangar country station, they need to get to the grav-train station closest to the command section. With Wraith 2.0 active, the PCs are invisible to security cameras, but the grav-train they are in isn't. Eventually, their presence aboard the *Empire of Bones* will be detected because of this, but they have enough time to take a 10-minute rest to regain Stamina Points first if they wish. Soon after, though, a corpsefolk marine and two baykoks in a security tram spot them. A chase ensues! This event uses the vehicle chase rules beginning on page 282 of the *Starfinder Core Rulebook*.

Creatures: One corpsefolk marine pilots the security train, focusing his full attention on keeping pace and, if possible, attacking the PCs' grav-train. The baykok security troops fire their combat rifles at the PCs whenever possible.

CORPSEFOLK MARINE	**CR 7**

XP 3,200

HP 126 each (see page 4)

TACTICS

Morale If the baykoks are destroyed and the security train becomes broken, the corpsefolk marine gives up pursuit to go report to his superiors.

BAYKOKS (2)	**CR 9**

XP 6,400 each

HP 144 each (see page 55)

TACTICS

During Combat The baykoks target those PCs making the most effective ranged attacks, or the PC piloting the grav-train if no PCs are successfully shooting at them. If the chase lasts more than 10 turns, the baykoks stop firing at the PCs and instead fire on the grav-train itself, seeking to disable it.

Morale The baykoks pursue the PCs as long as possible.

If their corpsefolk marine pilot is destroyed, one baykok activates the security train's autopilot as a swift action. After that, if their security train becomes broken, the baykoks try to board the PCs' grav-train. If that fails, the baykoks fly to the nearest grav-train station to report to their superiors.

Vehicle Chase: While the grav-trains can run only on the tracks, these tracks pass through nearly every section of the ship—there are miles of transit corridors dedicated to their use, with numerous corridors, intersections, junctions, and switchbacks, making it possible to race against another grav-train and eventually lose it in the maze of transit corridors. The PCs have just left the primary launch and

BONE TROOPER COMMANDO

EMPIRE OF BONES

PART 1: CLOSE TO THE BONE

PART 2: MASS GRAVES

PART 3: IN THE MARROW

PART 4: DEAD TO RIGHTS

CONTINUING THE ADVENTURE

SHIPS OF THE LINE

SHIPS OF THE CORPSE FLEET

ALIEN ARCHIVES

CODEX OF WORLDS

recovery decks (where hangar country is located) and should be attempting to reach the command and control decks (where the command section is located). The quickest route is to take the vertical major transit corridor in the aft section of the ship, but if they do so, they will need to fight the ellicoths they find at the command section station (area **B2**), as well as the two baykoks and corpsefolk marine chasing them (see Creatures on page 23), which is likely an overwhelming encounter for them.

However, the PCs can try to escape from the pursuing security train by driving through the smaller tunnels that pass through other sections (see the map on the inside back cover). Each section represents an area of the ship containing dozens of decks that provide for all the various functions of a starship the size of a small city. Each section is essentially adjacent to a few other sections, as well as to the major transit corridor, which offers an express route from any one section to another (except for the areas above the command and control decks, which have only limited grav-train access for security reasons). The sections are big enough that the PCs can stay within a single section for as many zones as they wish (essentially taking tracks in a huge loop within the section). They can move to any adjacent section whenever they advance a zone; if they do, the pilot gains a +2 circumstance bonus to her next Piloting check.

The grav-train the PCs have commandeered is a standard model used to carry small cargo and personnel throughout the *Empire of Bones*. It is durable (it was built for a ship of war, after all) but neither particularly fast nor designed for direct combat. The unarmored windows are large enough that characters within the train gain only partial cover. The security train is designed to maintain security in the transit corridors in case of a boarding action and to find and immobilize runaway grav-trains. It is smaller, faster, and more heavily armored than a typical grav-train, with protected gun ports to allow fire from within its cover, but it isn't able to switch tracks as rapidly. While both vehicles list a collision attack, they can normally collide only with things on the same track or on an intersecting track.

The areas detailed in Chase Environmental Zones on pages 26–27 include examples of active hazards, altered attacks, altered movement, new tricks, or split routes you can present during the chase. You can also use them to create your own chase environmental zones if your PCs want to travel to a section on the map that isn't listed on pages 26–27. You may find it helpful to give this information to your players so they have a sense of what new options they'll have in each section.

The chase begins in the major transit corridor. The security train begins in the same zone as the PCs' grav-train and does everything it can to remain in the same zone. If the PCs manage to escape, they lose their pursuers and can move with relative safety around the *Empire of Bones*. See area **B2** for more information on what happens when the PCs arrive at the command section station on the command and control decks.

If the PCs fail to escape and their train is destroyed or stopped in some manner, they have to confront the baykoks and the corpsefolk marine on foot, likely in one of the grav-train corridors, and then either commandeer the security train or travel by foot until they can obtain a new grav-train at another station.

GRAV-TRAIN	LEVEL 10

PRICE 38,000

Colossal land vehicle (15 ft. wide, 10 ft. tall, 100 ft. long)
Speed 60 ft., full 1,100 ft., 130 mph
EAC 23; **KAC** 24; **Cover** partial cover
HP 150 (75); **Hardness** 15
Attack (Collision) 12d10 B (DC 11)
Modifiers +2 Piloting, –2 attacks (–4 at full speed)
Systems autocontrol; **Passengers** 48

SECURITY TRAIN	LEVEL 8

PRICE 20,000

Huge land vehicle (15 ft. wide, 10 ft. tall, 20 ft. long)
Speed 60 ft., full 1,200 ft., 140 mph
EAC 25; **KAC** 25; **Cover** cover
HP 130 (65); **Hardness** 20
Attack (Collision) 8d10 (DC 14)
Attack grappler (see below)
Modifiers +2 Piloting (for keep pace pilot action only), –2 attacks (–4 at full speed)
Systems autocontrol, autopilot (Piloting +12)

SPECIAL ABILITIES

Grappler (Ex) The security train's grappler gun can be used only against vehicles the security train is engaged with during a vehicle chase. The grappler targets KAC, but the user doesn't take the security train's normal penalties to attacks. The pilot of a vehicle hit with the grappler takes a –5 penalty when using the break free action.

Story Award: If the PCs successfully evade the security train, award them 3,200 XP, in addition to the experience they gained from defeating the two baykoks and the corpsefolk marine.

B2. Command Section Station (CR 12)

For security reasons, the grav-train system has only a single transfer point into the command and control decks, where the command section is located. Nearly every route to the nerve center of the ship requires invaders to move through this grav-train station, creating a defensible choke point in the event the *Empire of Bones* is boarded. This also allows security forces from anywhere in the ship to use grav-trains to rapidly redeploy to protect the command and control decks. As the stations all have a standardized design, use the Grav-Train Station map on page 21 for this encounter.

The PCs can arrive by the grav-train they commandeered or exit the grav-train prior to reaching the station and enter

from either the port or starboard tunnel. The three aft doors lead to the command and control decks. Since the area is currently on lockdown following Nashal's order to increase ship security (see Security on page 21), all the doors and hatches in or out are sealed and locked (Engineering DC 35 to bypass the security seals).

Creatures: By the time the PCs arrive in this grav-train station, Nashal is certainly aware enemy troops are on board his ship, even though he may not know the details about them (depending on the outcome of their earlier encounters). The captain feels he needs extra security for the command and control decks but doesn't want to redirect troops that he can have scouring the rest of the ship for the intruders. Luckily for the captain, he keeps three ellicoths—massive creatures native to Eox—in a special menagerie on the officer and VIP quarters deck. He believes owning these creatures proves his loyalty to his undead masters and his desire to conquer Eox in the name of the Corpse Fleet. The ellicoths hate Nashal, as he doesn't feed them very often. Nashal has ordered the normal personnel of this station evacuated and has placed his ellicoths here. He (correctly) assumes the ellicoths will attack any living or undead creatures they encounter, making it difficult for the PCs to move through this choke point. While rounding up the ellicoths later will prove troublesome, the captain is willing to handle that inconvenience when the time comes, after the Stellar Degenerator has been secured by the Corpse Fleet. Similar to the surnochs in area **A3**, the ellicoths are fitted with electronic atmosphere collars.

If the PCs manage to subdue, incapacitate, or somehow befriend the ellicoths, they can hack the computer in the station control area (see area **B1**) and redirect a cargo grav-train to this station. Only special cargo grav-trains can transport the ellicoths, and only along the widest transit corridors; none of those regularly serve the command and control decks. The ellicoths have to squeeze to fit on a train (which they aren't too happy about). The PCs can send the ellicoths to the *Empire of Bones*'s largest shuttle bay on the cargo area deck, which has a dedicated grav-train station. How the PCs proceed from there to get the ellicoths off the ultranought is beyond the scope of this adventure. In any case, the ellicoths can't be cajoled or coerced into the ship's normal corridors in order to reach the command section or any other location.

ELLICOTHS (3)   CR 9
XP 6,400 each
HP 145 each (*Starfinder Alien Archive* 48)
TACTICS
During Combat The ellicoths are rarely fed and are currently starving. Each one tries to use its soul drain ability on a different PC. Once they have fed, each ellicoth focuses on a different PC and tries to impale that PC with its gore attacks. An ellicoth that is reduced to

fewer than half its Hit Points attempts to use its soul drain ability on any nearby target.

Morale The ellicoths are maddened by their long captivity, but not entirely senseless. If an ellicoth is reduced to 30 or fewer Hit Points, it attempts to retreat to a corner of the grav-train station. However, if it is damaged again after doing so (even via collateral damage, such as from a grenade), it becomes enraged and fights to the death.

Development: If the PCs stay in this grav-train station for more than a few minutes after the fight is over, a grav-train arrives with one baykok (see page 55) and five bone trooper commandos (see page 22). These defenders call for backup when they see the PCs, and another such train arrives a few minutes after that fight ends. This cycle repeats endlessly,

ELLICOTH

EMPIRE OF BONES

PART 1: CLOSE TO THE BONE

PART 2: MASS GRAVES

PART 3: IN THE MARROW

PART 4: DEAD TO RIGHTS

CONTINUING THE ADVENTURE

SHIPS OF THE LINE

SHIPS OF THE CORPSE FLEET

ALIEN ARCHIVES

CODEX OF WORLDS

CHASE ENVIRONMENTAL ZONES

The following chase environmental zones can be found throughout the Empire of Bones and are used in the **Event 4** vehicle chase.

BATTERIES AND RESERVE POWER CORE

Power Drain (Altered Movement): Corpse Fleet policy is to keep the ship's backup batteries and reserve power core fully charged at all times. This draws power from the grav-train tracks on this deck, imposing a –2 penalty to Piloting checks to speed up.

CARGO AREA

Dislodge Cargo (New Trick, Piloting DC 27): The pilot clips a pile of cargo in a way that causes it to fall on a train behind hers, imposing a –2 penalty on attack rolls and skill checks made by the creatures in the struck train for 1 round. A character can also perform this trick during the combat phase by succeeding at a ranged attack against AC 22 that deals at least 15 damage to the contents of the cargo area.

CREW QUARTERS

Security Troops (Active Hazard): Each round the PCs move through this section, a corpsefolk marine (either standing on a platform as the grav-train hurtles through a station or at a security post within the transit corridors) takes a shot (dual acid dart rifle +17 [2d8+9 A & P; critical corrode 2d4]) at a randomly determined PC.

DRIFT ENGINES

Warped Space-Time (Altered Attacks): Though the Empire of Bones's Drift engines aren't currently active, there is still enough reality-warping power coming off of them to make physical ranged attacks more difficult, as bullets and grenades don't travel in their normal trajectories. All ranged attack rolls against KAC take a –2 penalty.

ENGINEERING CONTROL

Fire Control Foam (Active Hazard): Each round the PCs move through this section, a bone trooper engineer (using fire control systems designed to ensure none of the passages through engineering control carry fires from elsewhere in the ship into this crucial area) attempts to cover the PCs' grav-train with fire-retardant foam (ranged attack +12; on a successful attack, for 1d4 rounds all characters within the grav-train treat everything outside the train as having concealment).

MAIN COMPUTER CORE

Fog (Altered Attacks): The massive amount of coolant used to keep the miles of computer banks operational causes fog to build up in the transit corridors through the main computer core, granting concealment to everyone. Since the grav-trains are on rails and are normally automated, this minor design flaw is not considered a serious issue.

MAIN ENGINES

Drive Through Fire (New Trick, Piloting DC 27): As the Empire of Bones takes damage from the Gate of Twelve Suns defenses, minor fires have broken out in the ship's massive engines. While the grav-trains are being automatically detoured around the fires, a pilot can force her grav-train onto a rail that goes through a burning section. All passengers gain concealment for 1 round, but the grav-train takes 10d10 fire damage. Each creature on board the train takes half that damage but can attempt a DC 21 Reflex saving throw to halve the damage again. Any train behind the grav-train performing this trick must also succeed at this trick (and face the same consequences) or allow the chased grav-train to escape.

MAIN POWER CORE

High-Energy Field (Altered Attacks): The high-energy field that reach out from the main power core cause all attacks against EAC to take a –2 penalty, but such attacks deal an additional 2d10 damage (of the same energy type).

MAINTENANCE BAYS

Dodge Between Moving Payloads (New Trick): Within the maintenance bays, large vehicles and chunks of machinery that have been brought in for repair are moved along the tracks, including tracks that cross those the PCs are on. A pilot can override the safety systems and get close enough to a large payload on another track that it might hit a grav-train following hers. The pilot chooses the DC of the Piloting check she wants to attempt (representing how close she pilots her grav-train to hitting a payload). If she succeeds, each train behind hers must succeed at a Piloting check with the same DC or be subjected to a single attack (melee attack +21, 10d10 B). If the piloting attempting this trick fails her check by 5 or more, her grav-train is subjected to the attack instead.

MAJOR TRANSIT CORRIDORS

Sudden Track Change (New Trick, Piloting DC 24): A pilot can cause her grav-train to suddenly change tracks to one of the dozens of other routes available. This disengages the grav-trains (if they were engaged), and the other grav-train can't engage the grav-train that switched tracks for 1 round. This otherwise functions as split routes that have no other modifications to them.

EMPIRE
OF
BONES

PART 1:
CLOSE TO
THE BONE

PART 2:
MASS GRAVES

PART 3:
IN THE MARROW

PART 4:
DEAD TO RIGHTS

CONTINUING THE
ADVENTURE

SHIPS OF
THE LINE

SHIPS OF THE
CORPSE FLEET

ALIEN
ARCHIVES

CODEX OF
WORLDS

MANEUVERING THRUSTERS

Constant Detours (Altered Movement): Normally grav-trains don't move through the banks of maneuvering thrusters when the *Empire of Bones* is in a combat situation. Because of the danger of superheated gases and exhaust, the grav-tracks through here are constantly being blocked off and the grav-trains rerouted. All Piloting checks to do anything but slow down take a –4 penalty.

PRIMARY, SECONDARY, AND TERTIARY GUN DECKS

Jump the Rails (New Trick, Piloting DC 31): While inertial dampeners reduce the recoil of the massive starship weapons currently firing at the Gate of Twelve Suns' defenses, the recoil is still much stronger on the gun deck than elsewhere on the vessel. By wildly accelerating on a tight turn just as the guns fire, a pilot can derail her grav-train from its tracks. If she succeeds at the Piloting check, the grav-train slides across a deck and reattaches to adjacent tracks, and the pursuing train takes a –4 penalty to Piloting checks for 2 rounds, as it has to seek a junction to follow the new route. If the pilot fails this check, she doesn't get the timing right and her vehicle stays on its current tracks, but if she fails by 5 or more, her grav-train leaps from the tracks at a spot where there are no other tracks to reattach to. Her vehicle then comes to a full stop and the chase ends, allowing any pursuers to catch up.

PRIMARY AND SECONDARY LAUNCH AND RECOVERY DECKS

Duplicate Tracks (Split Routes): All the decks dedicated to launching or recovering fighters and other starships have duplicate tracks on parallel routes behind different bulkheads, to ensure pilots and munitions can always reach the fighters, even if the area is damaged. One route is shorter, granting a +2 bonus to Piloting checks to keep pace or speed up. A second route's tracks are more twisty, granting a +2 bonus to Piloting checks to evade. A third route's lights are malfunctioning, and the constant flickering grants a +2 bonus to Piloting checks to perform a trick.

PRIMARY SENSOR DECKS

No Targeting Systems (Altered Attacks): Within this area, the feedback created by the *Empire of Bones*'s technological and magical sensor systems prevents items and augmentations (such as targeting computers or a mechanic's exocortex) from granting bonuses to attack rolls.

SCIENCE AND NECROMANCY LABS

Negative Energy (Altered Attacks): The years of necromantic research and rituals performed in this section of the ship cause all attacks in these zones that deal bludgeoning, slashing, or piercing damage to deal an additional 1d10 negative energy damage to living targets.

effectively preventing the PCs from resting to regain Stamina Points here.

Treasure: Each ellicoth's atmosphere collar provides protection similar to the environmental protections of a suit of armor, lasting for 15 days when fully charged. A PC can alter an atmosphere collar with a successful DC 32 Engineering check so that it functions as a gray force field armor upgrade (and can be sold as such).

EVENT 5: DEAD AIR

Captain Ghurd Nashal has been monitoring the command section station since he realized that intruders have gained access to his ship. Even if the PCs are hiding themselves from the security cameras using the Wraith 2.0 virus, Nashal can see the violence inflicted on his pet ellicoths. Shortly afterward, the fight in area **B2** concludes, Nashal attempts to communicate with the PCs. He sends a request to parley through the *Empire of Bones*'s specially calibrated comm units. If the PCs have taken any such devices from the undead they have defeated, they can answer easily. If they haven't, they spot a message across all the displays in the command section grav-train station that explains how the PCs can adjust their own comm units to be able to speak with the captain. The PCs don't have to stay in one place if they decide to talk to Nashal; they can begin the trek through the ship's corridors to the command section (area **C**).

Nashal is genuinely interested in talking to the warriors bold enough to attack his miles-long starship from within, and he hopes to trick them into revealing their ultimate goal (though he doesn't expect to succeed). He is also having his science officer, Lieutenant Renzar, attempt to track the PCs if they answer his communication (see below).

The captain begins by asking their names, honestly noting that he would rather know more about such interesting opponents before having them destroyed. If the PCs killed one of more of the ellicoths in area **B2**, Nashal specifically mentions that he would have been willing to allow them to escape with their lives if they simply fled, but now they have angered him by killing his favored pets, as grotesque as they are. This is not true, but Nashal wants to see how they react to the claim.

He goes on to ask what they hope to accomplish, since it's impossible for them to defeat the ship's crew of thousands. He assumes they are attempting sabotage of some kind, but assures them the *Empire of Bones* is now the greatest power in the galaxy and that even if they manage to destroy one cannon or one engine, it will have no significant impact on the ship's fighting power.

During this conversation, Renzar (see page 31) uses the ship's sensors to attempt to triangulate the PCs' position. A PC can detect this attempt with a successful DC 30 Computers check. Shutting off the comm units they are using isn't enough to completely deflect this triangulation. Instead, the PCs can throw Renzar off their trail by succeeding a

Computers check opposed by Renzar's Computers check (she has a total Computers skill bonus of +24). Activating the TombRobber virus gives the PCs a +4 circumstance bonus to this check.

If Renzar successfully locates the PCs (which happens automatically if the PCs don't detect her triangulation attempt), four baykoks (see page 55) arrive at their location within 5 minutes to deal with them. Ten minutes after that, a squad of two baykoks and eight corpsefolk marines (see page 4) travel to that same location. The PCs might not be aware of the approaching threat, unless one of them succeeds at a DC 30 Perception check to hear the first group of baykoks coming. Successful Stealth checks opposed by the baykoks' Perception checks allow the PCs to slip away from their location without a fight. Activating the TombRobber virus isn't enough to avoid this conflict; if the PCs use the program to create a false security report, Nashal sends security forces to both their real location and the false alert, just to be thorough.

Story Award: If the PCs have a conversation with Nashal and either avoid having their location discovered or manage to escape the area before security forces arrive, award them 19,200 XP.

PART 4: DEAD TO RIGHTS

From the command section grav-train station (area **B2**), the PCs have easy access to the command and control decks, which contain most of the central control rooms from which the officers' orders are sent out to the various areas of the gigantic vessel. The most important of these is the command section, which includes the ship's primary bridge and cybercontrol (from which commands are issued to the hordes of cybernetic zombies throughout the *Empire of Bones*). With a map of the interior of the ship, the PCs should have no difficulty reaching the command section, and they can reasonably find an unused cargo area or maintenance corridor if they need to rest (unless they are tracked down by the ghoul Renzar in **Event 5**). The exact distance from the grav-train station to area **C1** of the command section is irrelevant, though it should take the PCs less than 30 minutes to arrive if they hustle through the nondescript and dimly lit corridors.

C. COMMAND SECTION

By the time the PCs reach this area, the *Empire of Bones* has destroyed all the defenses of the Gate of Twelve Suns able to harm the armada. The small amount of damage dealt to the ultranought has been fixed, and most of the

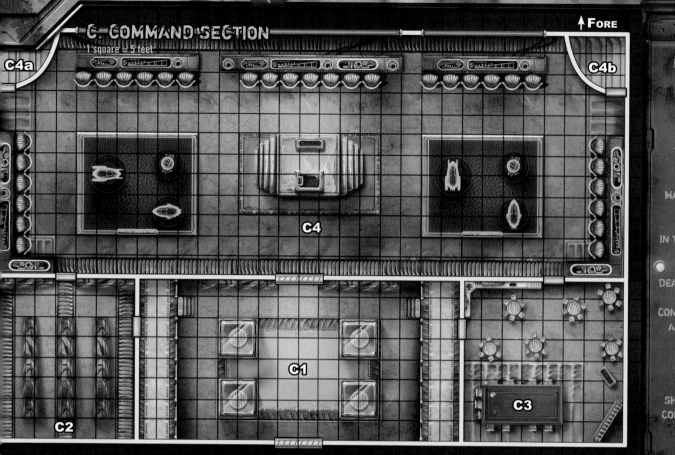

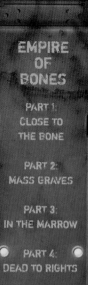

EMPIRE OF BONES

PART 1:
CLOSE TO
THE BONE

PART 2:
MASS GRAVES

PART 3:
IN THE MARROW

PART 4:
DEAD TO RIGHTS

CONTINUING THE
ADVENTURE

SHIPS OF
THE LINE

SHIPS OF THE
CORPSE FLEET

ALIEN
ARCHIVES

CODEX OF
WORLDS

armada's swifter ships have returned to their carriers for their own repairs. Admiral Serovox is focused on thoroughly scanning the system and the portal to ensure there are no traps or hidden defenses that would pose a major threat before approaching the Stellar Degenerator. While the admiral might be aware of the PCs' presence on the command and control decks, they trust Captain Nashal and his security forces to deal with the intruders. This gives the PCs the opportunity to strike, but they need to be quick, as Serovox is only a short amount of time away from realizing that nothing else is standing in the way of the Corpse Fleet gaining control over the ancient superweapon.

The following are standard traits of the command section.

Ceilings, Doors, and Walls: The ceilings are 20 feet high unless otherwise noted, and the doors are thick steel doors (hardness 30, HP 125, break DC 35). The walls are standard starship interior walls (hardness 30, HP 1,440 per 10-foot-by-10-foot section, break DC 45).

Security: The security camera feeds are monitored around the clock on monitors in area **C2** and can be called up on the display in area **C3** with a few simple commands. If the PCs have activated Wraith 2.0, the cameras show only the results of their actions rather than exposing them directly. Otherwise, Captain Ghurd Nashal knows the PCs are in the command section and prepares accordingly.

C1. TROPHY HALL (CR 12)

The double door to this room from the corridor is securely locked (Engineering DC 32 to disable). Any effort to open the door by force (or if a PC fails the Engineering check to disable the lock by 5 or more) sets off a silent alarm in the room, alerting its occupants.

This large room has double doors centered in the fore and aft walls. Two large computer consoles flank the fore door. Ten-foot-wide raised platforms with metal railings run along the port and starboard walls, each with an exit out of the room. Four large display cases made of a clear material stand evenly spaced in the center of the room. Each case contains a different item under a harsh white spotlight: a red-and-gold spear, a humanoid skull and spine, a desiccated severed hand with a gem embedded in the palm, and a spacesuit helmet with swirling red mist within it and blood spattered on the inside of the visor.

This is Serovox's trophy room, where they keep the most precious mementos of their greatest conquests and most noteworthy vanquished foes. Though Nashal is ostensibly in charge of the *Empire of Bones*, he acquiesced to this spectacle of Serovox's victories after the admiral threatened to add the captain's tongue to the collection. The cases are made of inch-thick transparent aluminum (hardness 10, HP 15), and each case's door is locked (Engineering DC 30

to disable). The cases' contents are described in Treasure below.

The double door leading to the bridge is under total lock down on Serovox's orders. A successful DC 40 Engineering check can bypass the lock. Nashal (area **C2**) holds a key card that also opens this door.

Creatures: There are three kurobozus guards in this room, all from a monastic order that has worked with the Corpse Fleet for centuries. These kurobozus were once living ascetics who believed that undeath will eventually consume the entire galaxy before spreading to take over all planes of existence. They underwent torturous rituals to gain their current undead existence and are honored to be guardians of powerful undead such as the captain and admiral. Normally, only one or two kurobozus are present in the command section, but Nashal called others from elsewhere on the ship to guard this area when he learned about the PCs' presence on the *Empire of Bones*.

KUROBOZUS (3) — CR 9

XP 6,400 each

HP 135 each (see page 58)

STATISTICS

Gear *spell ampoule of haste, spell ampoule of lesser resistant armor, spell ampoule of see invisibility*, personal comm unit

TACTICS

Before Combat If the PCs set off the door alarm (see above), one kurobozu uses a *spell ampoule of lesser resistant armor* (choosing to gain damage reduction), one uses a *spell ampoule of haste*, and the third uses a *spell ampoule of see invisibility* before the PCs can enter the room. The kurobozu with the damage reduction positions herself to one side of the aft door and readies her black apoxia ability, while the other two take cover behind trophy cases and wait to attack PCs who move farther into the room.

During Combat The kurobozus believe spellcasters are the most powerful creatures in the universe, and they first attack any creature they see casting spells. They switch to attacking anyone who moves to one of the port or starboard doors out of the room. If two of them are destroyed, the remaining kurobozu moves to a computer console near the door to the bridge and signals that the intruders are too powerful for them to stop.

Morale The kurobozus' entire existence is predicated on serving the Corpse Fleet. They fight until they are destroyed.

Development: The Corpse Fleet officers in the adjacent rooms ready themselves for battle if they hear fighting in this room or if a kurobozu sets off the alarm (see above). They prefer to let the PCs come to them.

Treasure: The trophy cases contain objects of significant power that were won by Serovox. The *eyes of Rhean* float serenely within the space helmet, the skull and spine are wired together with the *runeworm*, the spear is the *spear of fates*, and the desiccated hand has the *warlord stone* embedded in it.

RUNEWORM

EYES OF RHEAN — LEVEL 13

HYBRID ITEM	PRICE 55,000	BULK L

Serovox pried this pair of pale sapphire gems from the head of an inevitable they destroyed in a duel. When you hold one of the eyes in one hand, you can control the other as a spy drone that can't be upgraded. You see what the flying eye sees through the eye you hold. However, if you place the gems over your own eyes, they burrow into your skull and replace two of your eyes (destroying the optic nerves of any additional eyes if you have more than two eyes), functioning as a long-range darkvision capacitors augmentation. You can still send out one eye as a spy drone, during which time the eyes do not grant you darkvision. When the eyes aren't embedded in a skull and aren't in use, a reddish mist slowly coalesces around them.

RUNEWORM — LEVEL 12

HYBRID ITEM	PRICE 37,000	BULK –

Currently interlaced with the skull and spine of one of Serovox's defeated foes, this hybrid item appears to be a 24-inch-long metallic centipede covered in runes. When it is placed near your ear (or a similar orifice), it animates and enters your body. Once inside you, the *runeworm* intertwines with your internal anatomy and releases an arcane virus that rewrites and improves some part of your body's function. It functions as a *mk 2 synergizing symbiote*, which is able to increase an ability score by 4. However, it is so advanced that it can instead upgrade any mk 2 personal upgrade already in your system to a mk 3 personal upgrade, increasing the ability score bonus from +4 to +6.

SPEAR OF FATES — LEVEL 13

TECHNOLOGICAL ITEM	PRICE 102,300	BULK 2

This unique weapon belonged to a Knight of Golarion who attempted to kill Serovox a few years before the signing of the Absalom Pact and the creation of the Corpse Fleet. It is a golden spear with a ruby blade and functions as both an inferno flame doshko and a white star plasma caster. It holds one ultra-capacity battery, which powers all uses of the weapon. Switching the weapon from melee functionality to ranged functionality (or vice versa) is a swift action.

WARLORD STONE — LEVEL 14

MAGIC ITEM   **PRICE** 75,000   **BULK** –

This stone holds the collected memories, philosophies, and tactics of an ancient alien warlord, and is currently set in the palm of its original owner. This *mk 3 ability crystal* can increase any one ability score by 6 if you spend 1 hour communing with the item, as fragments of the ancient alien warlord's psyche flood your mind and body. Its magic is then forever spent.

C2. CYBERCONTROL (CR 14)

Three rows of computer displays take up the center of this room, with additional control panels lining the fore wall. Monitors line the port, starboard, and aft walls, showing various decks and grav-train corridors of the ship's interior and the Gate of Twelve Suns, as well as the position, direction, and possible firing arcs of dozens of armada ships in the system. Heavy doors are set into the fore and starboard walls.

This is the control room for the command link system that sends orders directly to the cybernetic zombies that run many of the systems throughout the ship (such as the ones the PCs encountered in area **A7**). The rows of terminals function as a tier 10 computer. When used in conjunction with experienced officers and the non-cybernetic zombie crew, this command link system allows the crew of the *Empire of Bones* to operate at an extremely high level of efficiency (represented by the skill checks listed for the starship on the inside front cover). However, even without the assistance of the free-willed crew in key positions, these computers allow a startlingly small number of creatures to operate the ship (as long as the cybernetic zombie crew are still functional).

An authorized user can command the thousands of cybernetic zombies running the various sections of the ship to perform the engineer and science officer roles of the *Empire of Bones*, and to use up to two of the four +10 bonuses available from the ship's computer. Hacking the computers here to gain basic access requires a successful DC 53 Computers check, and a PC must succeed at an additional DC 53 Computers check each time she wants to perform an engineer or science officer action during starship combat. However, with the cybercontrol command key (a small disc-shaped apparatus held by Nashal), the PCs can gain total access to the command link system and perform engineer

and science officer actions as they see fit (once they gain control of the bridge, of course). Access to both the command link system and the bridge's command throne (see area **C4**) also allows a character to fill the captain role in starship combat.

The fore door leads to the bridge and is currently under total lockdown. A PC can bypass the lock with a successful DC 40 Engineering check. Nashal holds a key card that also opens this door.

Creatures: Currently present is Ghurd Nashal, the ship's captain, who is overseeing the armada's repairs from here while Serovox is on the bridge working to secure the Stellar Degenerator. In life Nashal was a vesk who killed thousands in the war with the Pact Worlds and embraced undeath as a mohrg rather than peace with his former enemies. Lieutenant Renzar, a ghoul science officer and trusted ally of the captain, is also on duty here. As a security measure, two kurobozus are at the captain's side.

KUROBOZUS (2) — CR 9

XP 6,400 each

HP 135 each (see page 58)

TACTICS

Before Combat If given warning, the kurobozus flank the starboard door, ready to pummel any intruders who enter.

During Combat The kurobozus try to keep the PCs from entering this room. If possible, they focus their attacks on anyone who shoots past them to harm the captain.

Morale Loyal to the Corpse Fleet, the kurobozus fight until they are destroyed.

RENZAR — CR 10

XP 9,600

Female elebrian ghoul mechanic (*Starfinder Adventure Path #3: Splintered Worlds* 54)

NE Medium undead

Init +8; **Senses** darkvision 60 ft.; **Perception** +24

DEFENSE   HP 150
EAC 23; **KAC** 24

Fort +11; **Ref** +11; **Will** +11

Immunities undead immunities

OFFENSE
Speed 30 ft.

Melee buzzblade dueling sword +18 (2d6+10 S) or bite +18 (2d8+10 P plus ghoul fever [DC 15] and paralysis [DC 19])

Ranged yellow star plasma rifle +20 (2d10+10 E & F; critical burn 1d8)

Offensive Abilities override (DC 19), target tracking

TACTICS
Before Combat Lieutenant Renzar positions herself near

the fore door to get a possible shot at multiple PCs in a line through the starboard door with her plasma rifle.

During Combat Renzar stays out of melee combat as best she can, though she isn't afraid to bite a PC who gets too close to her.

Morale The lieutenant is both loyal to Nashal and fearful of punishment from Serovox if she were to flee from combat. She continues fighting until destroyed.

STATISTICS

Str +0; **Dex** +8; **Con** −; **Int** +5; **Wis** +3; **Cha** +0

Skills Acrobatics +19, Computers +24, Engineering +24, Stealth +19

Other Abilities artificial intelligence (exocortex), expert rig (accelerated datajack), mechanic tricks (improved overcharge), miracle worker 1/day, remote hack (DC 19), unliving

Languages Common, Eoxian

Gear freebooter armor III, buzzblade dueling sword with 1 battery (20 charges), yellow star plasma rifle with 2 high-capacity batteries (40 charges each), personal comm unit

GHURD NASHAL   CR 11

XP 12,800

Male vesk mohrg (see page 59)

CE Medium undead

Init +5; **Senses** darkvision 60 ft.; **Perception** +20

DEFENSE   HP 180

EAC 24; **KAC** 26

Fort +13; **Ref** +13; **Will** +12

Immunities undead immunities

OFFENSE

Speed 30 ft.

Melee slam +23 (2d8+19 B) or

clawed tongue +23 (2d6+19 S plus paralyzing touch [DC 20])

Multiattack clawed tongue +17 (2d6+19 S plus paralyzing touch [DC 20]), 2 slams +17 (2d8+19 B)

Ranged tactical autobeam rifle +20 (5d4+11 F; critical burn 2d4) or

shock grenade III +20 (explode [15 ft., 3d12 E, DC 18])

Offensive Abilities create spawn

TACTICS

Before Combat If Nashal is aware the PCs are hacking the door into cybercontrol, he activates his white force field and takes up a position in the aft end of the room.

During Combat Nashal fires his autobeam rifle at PCs who step through the door. If two or more PCs push past the kurobozus to get into the room, he activates the rifle's automatic fire, unconcerned about whether he catches his allies in the spray. He then drops the rifle to the ground, throws a shock grenade, and enters melee combat. He tries to paralyze as many foes as possible, moving from one enemy to the next.

Morale Nashal is a fearless warrior who would never flee or surrender to invaders on board his ship. He fights until he is destroyed.

STATISTICS

Str +8; **Dex** +5; **Con** −; **Int** +0; **Wis** +0; **Cha** +3

Skills Athletics +25, Engineering +20, Intimidate +20

Other Abilities unliving

Gear advanced iridishell (white force field [15 HP]), shock grenades III (2), tactical autobeam rifle with 1 high-capacity battery (40 charges), bridge key card, cybercontrol command key, system-wide comm unit

C3. Ready Room

This elegant room has smooth, bone-white walls and red-stained wooden floors. A large table apparently carved from

GHURD NASHAL

a single enormous slab of stone takes up much of the aft section of the room, with a blank computer display hanging from the ceiling nearby. Smaller stone pillars topped with black glass tabletops, each surrounded by several smaller chairs, are scattered throughout the rest of the room. A countertop that runs along the port wall and around the corner along the fore wall holds delicately formed crystal goblets and what appear to be food dispensers.

This is the ship's ready room, a multifunction conference room and lounge for senior officers, and (when desired) a private meditation chamber for the admiral. The chairs are well upholstered and comfortable, and the commissary station is able to produce anything from synthesized blood to foods for the living, in case important guests come on board who enjoy such things. As an area used by different officers and crew shifts, the chamber holds no valuables.

The fore door leads to the bridge and is currently under total lockdown. A PC can bypass the lock with a successful DC 40 Engineering check. Nashal also holds a key card that opens this door.

C4. BRIDGE (CR 15)

A dais in the center of this large room supports an imposing throne-like chair with a computer console just in reach. Five-foot-deep recesses are located to the port and starboard of the dais, and walls of holoprojectors that stretch down from the ceiling surround each. The projectors fill the pits with three-dimensional holograms of the local space, including the Gate of Twelve Suns, the ships of the Corpse Fleet armada, and a massive cone-shaped megastructure sitting in a section of nonstandard space beyond the Gate. Three floor-to-ceiling windows show the stretch of space in front the vessel. Rows of chains sit in front of bank of controls adjacent to the windows and most of the port and starboard walls. Curved walls cut off the port and starboard corners of the fore walls; each has a door set in it. Three more doors are spaced along the aft wall.

This is the main bridge, used to command the *Empire of Bones* and communicate with other Corpse Fleet ships in the armada. The control panels across the front of the room are the primary navigational and gunnery controls (all currently manned by cybernetic zombies), and those on the aft and on the port and starboard walls can be configured to transmit orders to or from any section of the ship.

The impressive chair on the dais is the *Empire of Bones's* command throne, which was designed to be used by the ship's captain to give orders and receive information. Serovox recently claimed it as their personal post. It is also a console for the tier 10 computer that handles tactical and navigational duties. Hacking this system to gain basic access requires a successful DC 53 Computers check, and a PC must succeed at an additional DC 53 Computers check each time she wants to perform a gunner or pilot action during starship combat. Since the armada reached the Gate of Twelve Suns, Serovox has tightened security so that only they can designate someone as an authorized user (using their own electroencephalon as a command key similar to Nashal's cybercontrol command key), and such designation must be renewed every 24 hours. Both Nashal and Serovox are permanently authorized users. Gaining access to both the bridge's command throne and the command link system in area **C2** allows a character to fill the captain role in starship combat. Furthermore, once the PCs have gained access to the command throne, an authorized user can direct the cybernetic zombies on the bridge to fill the gunner and pilot roles of the *Empire of Bones* and use up to two of the four +10 bonuses to computer checks available from the ship's computer (see the ship's statistics on the inside front cover).

Areas **C4a** and **C4b** are emergency elevator shafts that lead to escape pods, allowing the bridge crew to quickly flee to the secondary launch decks (see the map on the inside back cover).

Creatures: Since arriving at the Gate of Twelve Suns, Serovox has spent nearly all their time on the bridge. They communicated with officers elsewhere in the ship as needed and occasionally withdrew to the ready room (area **C3**) to meditate, but that all ended when it became clear the PCs were aboard. The admiral is in the command throne when the PCs enter the bridge. There are also two kurobozus here, stationed near the emergency evacuation shaft doors, as well as a hulking mass of undead flesh and metal known as a gatecrasher.

Sixteen cybernetic zombies (*Starfinder Alien Archive* 114) are spaced evenly at the seats in the computer controls around the outside of the room. They have all been wired into the starship for so many years they are no longer capable of any independent action. Even if detached from the consoles or attacked, the cybernetic zombies take no actions other than to continue to operate the controls to the best of their abilities. They are not a threat to the PCs, and the PCs should gain no experience for destroying them.

Serovox is impressed the PCs have made it this far and is happy to tell them so, declaring it proof the heroes are "worthy to join the Corpse Fleet" once their mortal forms

have been slain. The admiral will gladly banter with the PCs for a bit before a fight begins, and might continue to converse during combat. Serovox is generally very calm and collected, no matter the situation. The following are some questions the PCs might have for Serovox, along with the admiral's responses.

Commander Malakar was planning some kind of mutiny! "Oh, I know all about her plot. Honestly, I was looking forward to the struggle between her and Captain Nashal. A senior officer does need to encourage ambition in subordinates, after all. She was making real progress, too. Ironically, I was going to offer her command of her own ship at the completion of this mission. But I suppose you put an end to all that."

What is your mission? "To eliminate life, of course. Life is the source of all foibles, all weaknesses, and ultimately all conflict. Only the whispered perfection of undeath can be allowed to exist."

How did you find us? "I had a tracker placed on your ship and on the ship of those Devourer buffoons. Though I imagine we would have found you sooner or later, given that you all make so much noise."

Why run the entire ship by direct control from the bridge? Doesn't it make your ship vulnerable to have everything controlled by these cybernetic zombies instead of real crew members? "Would you trust ordinary ghouls to make crucial military decisions? No, of course not! This is the greatest ship in the entire Corpse Fleet, and I prefer having it as close to being under my direct command as possible. Besides, the only way to control this ship is to destroy me and Captain Nashal, and at that point, what do I care what happens?"

Why do you talk so much during a fight? "In the end, the brief abnormality of your lives will end, and I'll see to it that such fine specimens as yourselves are converted into potent agents of the Corpse Fleet. Under my command, of course. I find it useful to have a quick word with the fleeting flicker of life a body hasn't released yet in order to determine what form of undeath will best suit it in the eons that follow its last breath."

We will defeat you! "It doesn't matter if you win or lose here. Even if you manage to defeat us, the Corpse Fleet has more ships. More armadas. And all the time in the universe. As long as the Stellar Degenerator exists, the Corpse Fleet will seek to control it. Sooner or later, we will succeed. And then, everything dies once and for all."

KUROBOZUS (2) CR 9
XP 6,400 each
HP 135 each (see page 58)

TACTICS
Before Combat If Serovox seems to be ramping down their discussion with the PCs, the kurobozus move in from their posts in front of the emergency shaft doors.

During Combat Each kurobozu chooses a different PC to focus its attacks on, moving in to make as many unarmed strikes as possible.
Morale Loyal to the Corpse Fleet, the kurobozus fight until they are destroyed.

GATECRASHER CR 10
XP 9,600
HP 198 (see page 57)

TACTICS
Before Combat When it seems like Serovox is finished speaking with the PCs or that the PCs are about to attack, the gatecrasher activates its *haste circuit*. If it doesn't manage this before combat, it takes the time to activate the upgrade only if it needs to do so to reach a PC in a single move action.
During Combat The gatecrasher is willing to get between the admiral and the PCs, especially if that gives it a good line of sight to attack multiple foes with its shock caster. The gatecrasher moves without concern for whether it stays behind cover or exposes itself to enemy fire. If a foe is successfully attacking it from beyond its ability to attack back, it uses its *forcepack* to fly to that foe, even if doing so provokes attacks of opportunity.
Morale The gatecrasher loves combat above all else. It fights until it is destroyed.

SEROVOX CR 13
XP 25,600
Nonbinary elebrian necrovite (*Starfinder Alien Archive* 80)
NE Medium undead
Init +8; **Senses** blindsense (life) 60 ft., darkvision 60 ft.; **Perception** +23
Aura fatigue (30 ft., DC 21)

DEFENSE HP 190 RP 5
EAC 29; **KAC** 30
Fort +12; **Ref** +16; **Will** +14
Defensive Abilities fast healing 10, rejuvenation (1d8 days); DR 5/—; **Immunities** cold, electricity, undead immunities

OFFENSE
Speed 30 ft., fly 60 ft. (Su, average)
Melee red star plasma sword +20 (4d8+13 E & F; critical severe wound [DC 21])
Ranged aurora arc pistol +22 (3d6+13 E; critical arc 2d6)
Offensive Abilities undead mastery
Spells Known (CL 13th)
  5th (3/day)—*greater dispel magic, wall of force*
  4th (4/day)—*corrosive haze* (DC 23), *greater invisibility, resistant armor, rewire flesh* (DC 23)
  3rd (at will)—*displacement, explosive blast* (DC 22)

TACTICS
Before Combat If the heroes set off alarms or resort to blasting their way through the doors to the bridge, Serovox casts *displacement* on themself.

During Combat Serovox casts *greater invisibility* on themselves as soon as combat begins. They then attempt to cut one foe off from her allies with *wall of force*, preferably enclosing that foe with another undead to attack her. They try to dispel ongoing enemy spells that prove troublesome. Whenever invisible, they prefer to fly near the ceiling of the bridge, moving after every attack so their position is impossible to pin down. When reduced to 40 or fewer Hit Points, Serovox becomes irked and begins attacking with their plasma sword.

Morale Serovox is an admiral commanding a whole armada, and the heroes are all that stand between them and a weapon that could mean the end of all life and galaxy-wide ascendancy of all undead. Besides, they hope that the heroes either don't understand the electroencephalon or will find its ability to command the rank-and-file crew of the *Empire of Bones* too useful to destroy it, enabling the admiral to rejuvenate in a few days. The admiral fights until destroyed.

STATISTICS

Str +0; **Dex** +8; **Con** –; **Int** +6; **Wis** +0; **Cha** +4

Skills Bluff +28, Computers +28, Diplomacy +28, Mysticism +28, Sense Motive +28

Other Abilities magic hacks (mental mark, tech countermeasures), unliving

Gear estex suit IV (deflective reinforcement, *mk I spell reflector*), aurora arc pistol with 1 high-capacity battery (40 charges), red star plasma sword with 1 high-capacity battery (40 charges), *electroencephalon command key* (see below), system-wide comm unit

Treasure: The key to Serovox's undead power is their electroencephalon command key, which also functions as a way for the PCs to take control of the *Empire of Bones*. Though no other necrovite can use it as an electroencephalon, the PCs can still sell it to the right buyer as an curiosity of powerful necromantic magic or as an example of Corpse Fleet security measures. However, if the item isn't destroyed, Serovox will rejuvenate 1d8 days after being defeated. The PCs can decide to leave the command key on the bridge to be obliterated when the Empire of Bones crashes into the Stellar Degenerator, or they can take it with them to destroy on their own. The item has the normal amount of hardness and Hit Points as an item of its level, so the PCs can destroy it however they see fit.

ELECTROENCEPHALON COMMAND KEY		LEVEL 14
HYBRID ITEM	PRICE 75,000	BULK 1

This is Serovox's electroencephalon (*Starfinder Alien Archive* 81), as well as the command key for the primary computers of the *Empire of Bones*. It grants the wielder authorized access to any computer on the ship and can grant another creature authorized for 24 hours. Additionally, the electroencephalon is tied directly to the engines, sensors, and weapons of the ship, allowing anyone holding it to feel the ship as an extension of her own body. A creature holding it gains a +10 circumstance bonus to all skill checks attempted as part of starship combat.

EVENT 6: BAD OMENS (CR 15)

Once the PCs have defeated Admiral Serovox and taken control of the command section, they have several hours during which they are in control of the ship. This window of opportunity is their best chance to fly the ship through the Thirteenth Gate and into the Stellar Degenerator. With access to the ship's core computers, the PCs can easily determine that the colossal ultranought will suffer a massive engine failure upon hitting the superweapon, creating an explosion powerful enough to destroy both juggernauts forever (though not powerful enough to destroy the Gate of Twelve Suns itself).

While it isn't a long flight to the Thirteenth Gate from the *Empire of Bones*'s current location, if the PCs leave the ship's bridge too early, the ultranought might be destroyed or knocked off course before impacting with the Stellar Degenerator. Indeed, the two next-largest ships in the Corpse Fleet armada—a pair of Thaumtech Omenbringers (named the *Dusk Blade* and *Orphanmaker*)—move to intercept the *Empire of Bones* as soon as it begins flying toward the portal to the demiplane holding the ancient weapon. The captains of those ships are aware that Serovox was being cautious about approaching the ancient superweapon, and know the admiral would have contacted them if the situation had changed. No amount of diplomacy or trickery can convince them to take any course of action other than attacking the ultranought once it deviates from the admiral's plan. In truth, the captains don't care whether the admiral is still alive or not—if the two Omenbringers destroy the *Empire of Bones*, their captains can take control of the superweapon themselves, to much acclaim.

Starship Combat: The *Empire of Bones* is a tier 20 starship, and with the *electroencephalon command key* and access to cybercontrol, the PCs can control it, but they don't have the skill ranks and bonuses of a typical tier 20 starship crew. At this point, the PCs should be 12th level and have 12 ranks in many of the applicable skills needed for starship combat, but that's still a far cry from the 20 ranks assumed in the *Empire of Bones* stat block on the inside front cover. Even with the massive shields and firepower of the ultranought, with the PCs in charge, it's only as effective as a tier 16 starship. That means the two Omenbringers, each a tier 14 starship, constitute a hard encounter for the PCs. Add to that the lack of familiarity the players have with the *Empire of Bones* and the lack of time to form tactics or plan ahead, and the encounter becomes an epic one.

However, the PCs don't have to destroy the two Omenbringers, just get the *Empire of Bones* past them. The *Empire of Bones* is 36 hexes from the portal to the demiplane containing the Stellar Degenerator (you can use *Starfinder Flip-Mat Basic Starfield* to track this distance). Once the

EMPIRE OF BONES

PART 1: CLOSE TO THE BONE

PART 2: MASS GRAVES

PART 3: IN THE MARROW

PART 4: DEAD TO RIGHTS

CONTINUING THE ADVENTURE

SHIPS OF THE LINE

SHIPS OF THE CORPSE FLEET

ALIEN ARCHIVES

CODEX OF WORLDS

ultranought reaches the portal, it is impossible to prevent the vessel's impact with the superweapon. The Omenbringers are between the *Empire of Bones* and the demiplane entrance, with the *Dusk Blade* 10 hexes from the ultranought and the *Orphanmaker* 20 hexes away. If either battleship is destroyed, has critical damage to three systems at once, or loses half its Hull Points, the two vessels flee rather than risk destruction at the hands of the mighty *Empire of Bones*.

DUSK BLADE AND ORPHANMAKER	TIER 14

Thaumtech Omenbringers (*Starfinder Core Rulebook* 307)
HP 400 each

EMPIRE OF BONES	TIER 20

Blackwind Annihilator (see inside front cover)
HP 1,050

EVENT 7: ABANDON SHIP! (CR 12)

With the Omenbringers destroyed or driven off, there is nothing the remaining ships of the Corpse Fleet armada can do to prevent the *Empire of Bones* from crashing into the Stellar Degenerator, assuring the destruction of both.

Chances are the PCs don't want front row seats to the impact.

Getting far enough away from the *Empire of Bones* to survive the coming explosion requires the PCs to exit in a starship, or at least an escape capsule. They could take the emergency escape elevators from the bridge down to escape pods on the secondary launch decks (located in a hangar close enough in design to the one the PCs entered through that you can use the map of area **A** on page 10 to represent it), or they could rush to take a grav-train back down to the hangar where they left whatever ship they used to get to the *Empire of Bones*.

The PCs should feel like they have only a limited amount of time before it becomes impossible for them to escape alive, but unless they do something foolish like take an hours-long rest, they can make it off the *Empire of Bones* in time. However, the players don't have to know this! You can heighten the sense of danger by describing events in the background as they rush through the ultranought's corridors. Some of these elements could include strobing white lights, displays flashing messages in Eoxian warning of an imminent collision, and subtle changes in gravity as the *Empire of Bones* begins to pass through the portal. Ramp up the intensity of these details as time passes, especially during the few rounds of combat with the security baykoks that try to stop the PCs (see Creatures and Hazard below).

Creatures: Regardless of what route they choose, the PCs are destined to run into one last line of defenders. While most of the officers and self-willed crew on the ship are too busy looking for their own way off the *Empire of Bones*, nearly all the baykoks from the security force are so dedicated to hunting the PCs that they are willing to die to have a chance to track down the invaders. Since the PCs are most likely hidden

from the security cameras (thanks to the Wraith 2.0 virus), the baykoks have divided up in teams of three to try to cover every likely escape route off the ship. Whether it's in a hangar (use the map for area **A1** on page 10), a grav-train station (use the map for area **B** on page 21), or a random corridor (use *Pathfinder Map Pack: Starship Corridors* to represent such areas), the PCs will run into one team of three before they can make it to their escape method of choice.

BAYKOKS (3)	CR 9

XP 6,400 each
HP 144 each (see page 55)

Hazard: As the *Empire of Bones* approaches the threshold of the portal to the demiplane containing the Stellar Degenerator, gravitational anomalies begin engulfing the ultranought. These irregularities counteract the artificial gravity in large swaths of the ship, plunging them into zero-gravity, increasing the gravity to extreme levels, or even reversing the gravity entirely. At the end of each round of combat with the baykoks, roll 1d20. On a result of 11 or higher, the local gravity is altered drastically; roll on the table below to determine how the gravity changes. This new level of gravity remains until another roll changes it. On a result of 10 or higher, add 1 to the next end-of-the-round d20 roll; this increase is cumulative, but resets when gravity next changes.

d%	Gravity
1–20	**Extreme Gravity:** Each character takes 2d6 nonlethal damage at the beginning of its turn. If the character has 0 Hit Points, this is lethal damage. The effects of high gravity also apply.
21–40	**High Gravity:** Each character moves at half speed, can jump only half as high or far, and can lift only half as much. The ranges of thrown weapons are halved. A flying creature has its maneuverability worsened by one step (minimum clumsy) and plummets to the ground unless it succeeds at a DC 25 Acrobatics check.
41–60	**Low Gravity:** Each character can jump three times as high or far and can life three times as much. The ranges of thrown weapons are tripled.
61–80	**Zero Gravity:** Characters and unattached objects begin to float slightly off the ground. See page 402 of the *Starfinder Core Rulebook* for the full rules of zero gravity.
81–100	**Reverse Gravity:** The gravity reverts to standard level but its direction reverses. Characters and unattached objects fall toward the ceiling (or back down to the floor if gravity reverses a second time). Each non-flying character takes an amount of damage from the fall that depends on the height of the ceiling in the area (1d6 per 10 feet fallen).

EMPIRE
OF
BONES

PART 1:
CLOSE TO
THE BONE

PART 2:
MASS GRAVES

PART 3:
IN THE MARROW

PART 4:
DEAD TO RIGHTS

CONTINUING THE
ADVENTURE

SHIPS OF
THE LINE

SHIPS OF THE
CORPSE FLEET

ALIEN
ARCHIVES

CODEX OF
WORLDS

CONCLUDING THE ADVENTURE

Whether they return to their own ship, steal another Corpse Fleet ship, or trust in escape pods to get them away from the *Empire of Bones*, the PCs get barely far enough away to avoid being badly damaged when the ultranought impacts the Stellar Degenerator. The armada ignores them as it rushes to try to either stop the *Empire of Bones* (uselessly, since the two Omenbringers have been destroyed or fled already) or dock with the ultranought in the hopes of regaining command (which might have worked if the undead attempting it had more time).

When the *Empire of Bones* collides with the much larger Stellar Degenerator, for a split second, it appears nothing will happen. Then the ultranought deforms in shape, with rays of black and red energy shooting out of it. The Stellar Degenerator cracks at the point of impact, and then explodes in a prismatic fireball of incandescent plasma. The shock wave of the explosion warps the space around the portal, and then the demiplane tears itself apart, destroying its contents. Those Corpse Fleet ships close to the portal are ripped to pieces as ripples in reality emanate from the catastrophe. Those ships from the armada that survive flee into the Drift over the next few minutes.

How the PCs return to the Pact Worlds depends upon their method of escape. Their own vessel (and most Corpse Fleet starships) have Drift engines, meaning the PCs can get home at their leisure; however, anyone entering Pact Worlds space in a Corpse Fleet ship will have a lot of quick explaining to do to patrolling Steward vessels. If the PCs took an escape pod, they can land it on Gate 1's controller moon. Luckily, the pod has a Drift-capable distress beacon that the heroes can send back to the Pact Worlds with their current coordinates in order to request a rescue. The Starfinder Society sends a vessel to pick them up, which arrives in 5d6 days. Biding their time on the controller moon, the PCs can easily find enough food and water to sustain them, though for the first few days, pieces of debris from the epic space battle above them occasionally rain down. On the plus side, the fallout from the collapse of the demiplane causes shimmering multihued lights to play across the planet's night sky.

Once they make it back to Absalom Station, the PCs are met with praise and relief from anyone who knew the seriousness of their mission. Chiskisk, their contact within Starfinder Society, is particularly interested in hearing the tales of their exploits, and recommends that they write up accounts of their adventures or take their story to the vid-lecture circuit. How much the PCs tell to the galaxy is up to them, but if they are completely forthcoming, they soon find fame as saviors. After all, they put the threat of the Stellar Degenerator to rest once and for all.

CONTINUING THE CAMPAIGN

"THE KISHALEE RULED OVER THE GALAXY MILLENNIA AGO. FEW RUINS COULD SURVIVE FOR SO LONG. OUR OWN CIVILIZATION TOO SHALL FALL, LEAVING BEHIND ONLY CRUMBLING REMAINS. YET, THERE IS ONE GREAT PRESERVER OF HISTORY: SPACE. THE LIGHT WE SEE FROM DISTANT REALMS IS BUT AN ECHO OF DEAD SUNS THAT HAS TRAVELED TRILLIONS OF MILES TO REACH OUR EYES. EVEN IF A SECOND GAP OVERTOOK US AND WIPED AWAY OUR COLLECTIVE KNOWLEDGE, I KNOW THAT CENTURIES FROM NOW, ANOTHER BLAZING FLASH WOULD SHINE IN THE NIGHT SKY, CHRONICLING THE DEEDS OF A BRAVE FEW STARFINDERS WHO DARED TO REDISCOVER OUR GALAXY'S FORGOTTEN PAST AND INSPIRED US TO LOOK TO THE FUTURE."

—LUWAZI ELSEBO, FIRST SEEKER OF THE STARFINDER SOCIETY

The Dead Suns Adventure Path might conclude with the destruction of the Stellar Degenerator and the PCs' escape from the collapsing demiplane, yet the action need not end there. Not only do the PCs' discoveries open up countless new avenues for adventure, but the heroes have also made numerous allies and enemies over the course of the campaign who could easily become ongoing patrons— or antagonists.

Ancient Superweapons: In their generations-long conflict with the sivvs, the kishalee built dozens of laboratories and factories to test new weapons hitherto unknown in the Pact Worlds. When they defeated their rivals, the kishalee gradually decommissioned these sites, moved operations to more resource-rich planets, or even lost control of them in conflicts with other species. Although none of these weapons represent the raw destructive power of the Stellar Degenerator, agents who recover any surviving engineering data are only a few steps away from re-creating another devastating superweapon. To the Corpse Fleet or the Cult of the Devourer, recovering such schematics might represent a worthy consolation prize. Seeking revenge against the PCs, or their patrons or allies, might be the first order of business for these villains thereafter.

In Search of Survivors: As the kishalee civilization declined, far-flung settlements ceased communication with their home system and became physically isolated. The kish of Istamak represent only one of potentially hundreds of surviving lineages, and in partially deteriorated consoles hidden within that floating city, the PCs can piece together the locations of other kishalee colonies. No doubt some of these populations have died out, leaving behind unspoiled caches of kishalee technology that the party might recover. In other places, the kishalee could have adapted to new climates, regressed technologically, or even continued their research to honor the collapsing empire they left behind. Tracking down disparate kishalee sites could keep the PCs busy for decades, particularly if some of these lost societies failed not from attrition but due to the dangerous beings already inhabiting their newfound homes. In addition, as suggested in the Ancient Superweapons section, the PCs might not be the only ones looking for lost kishalee sites. Competitors and enemies might have the same idea.

The Oatia Exodus: The elves who built the Temple of the Twelve left their city of Loskialua behind millennia ago using a ritual they called the Celestial Voyage. Without the benefits of Drift travel, the elves spent untold centuries in transit before arriving in a system less than a light-year from the sacred Gate of Twelve Stars and still live there to this day. After the Thirteenth Gate opens and is destroyed, the Oatia elves send armed researchers to investigate. Signs of the gate's desecration might set these fervent Ibra worshipers on the party's trail. However, if the PCs can appease the militant astronomers, they could work together to explore countless wonders throughout the galaxy.

Starfinder Heroes: After discovering evidence of the ancient kishalee species, exploring the misunderstood ruins of Ukulam on Castrovel, and averting a cosmic catastrophe threatened by an ancient superweapon, the PCs return to the Pact Worlds as heroes. Their accomplishments gain even greater praise within the Starfinder Society, where Chiskisk helps them to become venture-captains in the organization and to publish their findings. With the Society's resources, the group can readily recruit teams of archaeologists and xenobiologists to help them with future exploits, particularly when they receive invitations to delve deeper into mysteries such as Aballon's First Ones, the origins of Orikolai (*Starfinder Core Rulebook* 466), or the gradual collapse of kishalee society. Alternatively, those who learn of the PCs' past exploits might try to recruit them to solve other problems throughout the galaxy.

What If the PCs Lose? Without the party's intervention, the Corpse Fleet and the Cult of the Devourer inevitably clash for control of the Stellar Degenerator. Whichever group prevails spells potential calamity for the Pact Worlds. The Corpse Fleet's enmity toward the "traitorous" pact brokers of Eox makes that planet and the Pact Worlds as a whole a likely target, although the complex superweapon likely requires considerable repairs and calibration before it could wither the Pact Worlds' sun. The Cult of the Devourer, on the other hand, is a reckless foe, and Pact Worlds astronomers might learn of the PCs' failure when the zealous cultists begin attacking uncharted systems, destroying stars in various systems out of a chaotic desire to spread destruction.

Failure also likely means the PCs' deaths, with their bodies at the Corpse Fleet's mercy. Any second team sent to stop the Stellar Degenerator could find itself clashing with the undead Starfinders now serving Admiral Vurannka (*Starfinder Adventure Path #3: Splintered Worlds* 46)! Even if many of the original party members survived, if they had to retreat while leaving any comrades behind, the necromancers of the Corpse Fleet reanimate the forsaken as ongoing antagonists who know their former comrades' every strategy and weakness.

What If the Stellar Degenerator Survives? Although the campaign assumes the PCs destroy the Stellar Degenerator, they might choose to recover it instead. Such a device quickly attracts the attention of ambitious treasure hunters, doomsday cults, and independent warlords. Even leaders of the Pact Worlds fail to agree on whether to destroy the weapon or keep it as a deterrent against the Swarm or other enemies yet unknown. This indecisiveness sorely tempts the Veskarium's more hawkish high despots to swoop in and capture the superweapon to forward their own goals. Before long, the PCs might have to face numerous factions vying for the device. Those who want the Stellar Degenerator destroyed for the greater good might take matters into their own hands to prevent the Pact Worlds from tearing themselves apart.

AGENT OF APOCALYPSE

Scholars who are familiar with atrocites (*Starfinder Adventure Path #4: The Ruined Clouds* 56), the Devourer's destructive apostles, speculate that the creatures were once mortal before performing a devastating act and earning their god's transformative blessing. If this theory is true, then the much more powerful apocalypse atrocites must arise from mortals who engineer world-shattering cataclysms. Much like other atrocites, the apocalypse atrocite known as Twinned Echo borrows the form of a member of a living species—in its case that of a sarcesian, a species supposedly descended from the inhabitants of Damiar and Iovo, the two planets whose destruction long ago formed the Diaspora. Cultists of the Devourer speak its name in hushed whispers and oral legends passed from cell to cell suggest this atrocite's blasphemous evangelism founded the Devourer's worship in what would become the Pact Worlds, though the faith rose to prominence sometime during the Gap.

Few know that when word of the *Acreon* and Drift Rock first circulated, it was Twinned Echo who goaded the Cult of the Devourer to investigate further. Soon after hearing of the cult's initial successes, the apocalypse atrocite departed to incite destruction in other solar systems, expecting that it would sense the cultists' victory when they at last activated whatever superweapon was hidden within the Gate of Twelve Stars. When the PCs destroyed the Stellar Degenerator, Twinned Echo assumed the destructive ripples indicated the weapon's activation and use. When the atrocite arrived in the system, using the destructive event as a beacon, it instead found the shattered remains of the Corpse Fleet and the scattered survivors of the Devourer's disciples. However, where the defeated cult saw a lost opportunity, the atrocite perceived untapped potential. The real weapon wasn't the Stellar Degenerator—it was the star system.

Twinned Echo has sent out a call to Devourer cultists across multiple star systems, calling upon them to reconfigure the Gate of Twelve Stars into a new superweapon. The system has numerous destructive possibilities, depending on what best suits your campaign. The stars maintain their configuration only due to powerful gravitational phenomena that the kishalee created—a network of impossibly dense cosmic strings within the stars' controller moons—and Twinned Echo might harness these to remotely manipulate a distant system's gravity and cause rampant tidal forces to tear planets to pieces. While the Thirteenth Gate opened onto a demiplane, canny engineers could reconfigure the mechanisms of the system to create wormholes that abduct populous planets and catapult them into hostile space (or into blazing stars). Alternatively, the extradimensional framework might require only modest alteration to simulate Drift engine technology, allowing the entire star system to shift into the Drift and reappear atop other worlds, ravaging entire civilizations with the heat of a dozen suns. As a third possibility, parts of the Stellar Degenerator could be reverse-engineered from the debris of the destroyed superweapon and other instances of kishalee technology found across the galaxy to create a device that causes a sun to quickly go supernova—absorbing its closest planets and obliterating the rest with a combination of heat and radiation. Any of these strategies require time and resources, though carrying out these plans would attract unwelcome attention.

That attention comes in the form of Gevalarsk Nor, the Eoxian ambassador on Absalom Station. Noticing that the Pact Worlds' Devourer cultists are rallying rather than retreating and regrouping, he begins investigating the cult's activities and sends reconnaissance expeditions to the Gate of Twelve Suns. Those few who report back send news of Twinned Echo and its new project. Unfortunately, Nor's influence is somewhat diminished from the Corpse Fleet's involvement in recent events, and he has expended considerable political capital distancing himself and Eox from the rogue armada. Unable to mobilize the Knights of Golarion, the Stewards, or any other force, Ambassador Nor looks to the PCs. His exact approach varies based on the PCs' existing relationship with him; he might approach them directly if he is on good terms with the heroes, or he might lure them into meeting with him under false pretenses if their past is less amicable. As much as the two parties might dislike each other, Nor is ready to cut a deal. After all, Nor's intelligence identifies Eox as the atrocite's primary target. However, the incomplete weapon ultimately promises to be utterly indiscriminate, and any attack capable of destroying Eox would likely also devastate some or all of the other Pact Worlds.

The growing number of cultists convening around the Gate of Twelve Suns makes a direct assault outright suicidal, even at higher levels. Instead, the PCs can intercept the cult's scavengers as they pick over kishalee ruins in search of the necessary technology to harness the system's power. Such missions might take them to the three moons of Iktrios, where radioactive pulses from the nearby dying star killed most life but left behind immense vermin, or Rendratt-5, where kishalee scientists designed biotech innovations so sophisticated that these augmentations eventually developed sapience and parasitized their creators. No matter where the PCs go, they can count on Gevalarsk Nor's support, which might include undead agents or even exclusive access to Eox's necrograft technology.

If the PCs can cause enough trouble for Twinned Echo, they might lure it away from the Gate of Twelve Stars to fight on more even terms. Otherwise, the PCs might have to capture

a Devourer starship and return to that star system under the guise of cultists carrying the essential technology. Once on the leading controller moon, the PCs can infiltrate the atrocite's operation, which has attracted cultists of numerous unfamiliar alien species. Before long, though, the PCs must corner Twinned Echo and end its schemes once and for all. If they can't prevent the atrocite from escaping, the PCs may have to chase the evil outsider across numerous worlds, all while it raises new Devourer armies.

TWINNED ECHO   CR 17

XP 102,400

Unique atrocite (*Starfinder Adventure Path #4: The Ruined Clouds* 56)

CE Large outsider (chaotic, evil, native)

Init +3; **Senses** blindsense (life) 60 ft., darkvision 60 ft.; **Perception** +29

DEFENSE   **HP** 290

EAC 31; **KAC** 30

Fort +17; **Ref** +15; **Will** +20

Immunities poison, vacuum

OFFENSE

Speed 40 ft., fly 60 ft. (Su, average)

Melee slam +26 (8d6+25 B)

Ranged void bolt +28 (4d8+17 force; critical severe wound [DC 24])

Spell-Like Abilities (CL 17th; melee +27, ranged +28)

  1/week–*interplanetary teleport* (self only), *plane shift*

  1/day–*disintegrate* (DC 26), *gravitational singularity*

  3/day–*bestow curse* (DC 24), *greater dispel magic*, *greater synaptic pulse* (DC 25), *heat leech* (DC 25)

  At will–*enervation*, *mirror image*, *see invisibility*

Space 10 ft.; **Reach** 10 ft.

Offensive Abilities rending maelstrom, words of disintegration

STATISTICS

Str +8; **Dex** +3; **Con** +3; **Int** +1; **Wis** +5; **Cha** +11

Skills Intimidate +34, Mysticism +34, Sense Motive +29

Languages Abyssal, Common; telepathy 100 ft.

Other Abilities no breath

SPECIAL ABILITIES

Rending Maelstrom (Su) When Twinned Echo strikes the same creature twice in the same turn with its slam or void bolt attack, as a reaction, it can create a *cosmic eddy* centered on the target creature (Reflex DC 24). Twinned Echo is immune to this effect. Once Twinned Echo has used rending maelstrom, it must wait 1d4 rounds before it can do so again.

Void Bolt (Su) Twinned Echo can fire bolts of energy from the menacing haze that swirls above it. The bolt has a range increment of 50 feet.

Words of Devastation (Su) Once per day as a swift action, Twinned Echo's many mouths can speak words of total devastation. For the next 3 rounds, any chaotic evil worshiper of the Devourer within 120 feet of Twinned Echo adds the severe wound critical hit effect to its attacks, in addition to any existing critical hit effects. If an attack already has the severe wound critical hit effect, increase the save DC of that effect by 2 instead. If Twinned Echo takes damage during this 3-round period, the effects of its words of devastation end.

TWINNED ECHO

EMPIRE OF BONES

PART 1: CLOSE TO THE BONE

PART 2: MASS GRAVES

PART 3: IN THE MARROW

PART 4: DEAD TO RIGHTS

CONTINUING THE CAMPAIGN

SHIPS OF THE LINE

SHIPS OF THE CORPSE FLEET

ALIEN ARCHIVES

CODEX OF WORLDS

INVASIVE SPECIES

As the PCs race to escape the Stellar Degenerator's demiplane as the superweapon and the *Empire of Bones* collide, it seems the heroes are ready to return to the Pact Worlds and the adulation of its citizens, but this might not be the case. The physics of a collapsing demiplane may defy even the *Sunrise Maiden*'s engines, leaving the PCs in a dangerous maelstrom of debris. As they dodge fragments of the Corpse Fleet's flagship, they can glimpse holes in the dying demiplane that reveal dozens of other realities. At last, their traumatized starship spins out into an unfamiliar star system with a habitable planet nearby. Thankfully, the PCs find an outpost of the Halfblood Frontier Company, a half-orc colonization firm that specialized in laying the groundwork for future settlements on otherwise uninhabited planets. With the firm's help, the PCs can perform the essential repairs and blast off toward the Pact Worlds, soon to receive their hero's welcome—or so they think.

The demiplane's destruction tore into several other extraplanar spaces, releasing their contents. Most dangerous of these ejecta was a creature of Stygian spores from Abaddon. Known as Naxikriot, this outsider restlessly travels the cosmos, infecting living creatures with spores that cause the victims to seek out populous areas and infect more hosts, much like a fiendish cordyceps fungus. In small numbers, these deaths are tragic, but Naxikriot can bind the souls from larger groups into the surrounding terrain, using the quintessence to reshape the landscape in Abaddon's image. When a world is suitably infected to sustain the transformation, Naxikriot stows away on or hijacks a starship that it can crash into a another world ripe for infection and, ultimately, destruction.

Naxikriot has already brought more than one ancient starfaring society to its knees, but its latest conquest should have been its last. Although the fiend's spores eventually consumed their civilization, a group of surviving mystics tracked down the fiend, bound it within an extradimensional prison, and used the last of their magic to catapult their infected world into their sun, destroying all of the outsider's spores—and themselves—in the process.

Naxikriot had lingered in maddening solitary confinement within its sterile cell for uncounted centuries when the nearby collapsing demiplane shredded its prison. Discorporated, Naxikriot surreptitiously hitched a ride on the *Sunrise Maiden* to the Halfblood Frontier Company's outpost. Although it is likely to escape the PCs' notice at first, the party might eventually notice its accumulating spoor or the symptoms of the fiend's attempts to infect them one at a time. Realizing they've been carrying a lethal contagion on board is only half the problem. The PCs discover they have acted as the vector

for Naxikriot, which jumped ship at a promising port before the PCs knew what was happening.

Reports begin rolling in from population centers the PCs visited after their triumph. The half-orc frontier settlement stops responding, and rescue ventures find only a blasted hellscape of fungal rot in the middle of an otherwise fertile forest. Spores might reach Castrovel, where they take root in the aggressive ksariks (*Starfinder Alien Archive* 70), which spontaneously evolve to act as unharmed carriers for the fungal contagion. Infectious filaments could blow through the streets of Absalom Station, where a week before the PCs enjoyed a ticker-tape parade. The extent of the devastation depends largely on how widely the PCs traveled and the scale of story you want to tell. Naxikriot could lurk somewhere nearby, or it might have moved on, hitching a ride on some other starfaring vessel.

The fiend need not be so single-minded, though. Centuries of imprisonment might have addled Naxikriot's mind, leaving it confused and longing to create something akin to home. Perhaps instead it seeks answers in the vile gardens it creates, finding insights in each one about the Gap and the collective amnesia everyone experienced, almost as though they had drunk from the River Styx. As the PCs chase after the fiend, homing in on increasingly fresh sites of infection, they might obtain similar insights from the growths. Perhaps the fungus-covered hosts speak of forgotten events, and the extraplanar wastelands left behind might resemble familiar ruins leftover from the Gap. Whether these situations capture previously missing truths or are the fiend's fictitious inventions is up to you.

Ultimately, the PCs must corner Naxikriot if they are to end its destructive rampage. When fighting against a being that can slip into the smallest vents, though, the PCs have to pick or shape their battleground carefully. Fighting the outsider might be as simple as tricking it into a carefully sealed lab or quarantined warehouse, but it could take more complicated and cunning plans to ultimately force the fiend to stand and fight. Only then can the PCs eliminate the creature once and for all. Alternatively, the PCs can banish Naxikriot to the Great Beyond, which is a simpler but temporary solution.

NAXIKRIOT   CR 16
XP 76,800
NE Large outsider (evil, extraplanar, plantlike)
Init +2; **Senses** darkvision 60 ft.; **Perception** +28

DEFENSE   HP 268
EAC 30, **KAC** 31
Fort +14; **Ref** +16; **Will** +19

Defensive Abilities fast healing 10; **Immunities** acid, disease, poison; **Resistances** cold 10, electricity 10, fire 10

OFFENSE

Speed 40 ft., climb 40 ft.

Melee gore +27 (4d8+23 P) or tendril +29 (3d8+23 B plus soul spores)

Multiattack gore +21 (4d8+23 P), 2 tendrils +23 (3d8+23 B plus soul spores)

Ranged spit +27 (5d4+16 A plus soul spores)

Space 10 ft.; **Reach** 10 ft. (20 ft. with tendril)

Offensive Abilities infestation

STATISTICS

Str +7; **Dex** +2; **Con** +4; **Int** +10; **Wis** +5; **Cha** +3

Skills Athletics +28, Bluff +33, Life Science +33, Mysticism +33, Stealth +28

Languages Abyssal, Common; infected telepathy 300 ft.

Other Abilities discorporation, plantlike

SPECIAL ABILITIES

Discorporation (Ex) As a standard action, Naxikriot can dissolve into a cloud of spores, functioning as a swarm of Fine creatures. This transformation grants Naxikriot the swarm defense, swarm immunities, distraction (DC 24), and swarm attack (3d8+23 A plus soul spores) traits as well as a fly speed of 40 feet (Ex, average). While the transformation lasts, Naxikriot is unable to make other attacks. Naxikriot returns to its natural form if it falls unconscious or dies. It can otherwise return to its natural form as a move action.

Infected Telepathy (Su) This ability functions as telepathy except that Naxikriot can communicate only with creatures that have the sporulated template graft.

Spit (Ex) Naxikriot's spit attack has a range increment of 30 feet.

SOUL SPORES

Type disease (contact); **Save** Fortitude DC 24

Track mental; **Frequency** 1/hour for 6 hours

Effect progression track is Healthy–Weakened–Impaired–Befuddled–Controlled; a controlled victim gains the sporulated simple template graft (see below) and follows the instructions of Naxikriot as per *charm monster*; controlled is the end state.

Cure 2 consecutive saves

SPORULATED TEMPLATE GRAFT

Sporulated creatures are infested with the consciousness-altering spores of Naxikriot. Unless otherwise instructed, these creatures seek out populous areas to infect. A PC who gains the sporulated simple template graft typically becomes an NPC under the GM's control (assume the PC has the array an NPC would need to take the class graft of that PC's class).

Traits: Gains the plantlike subtype; infected telepathy (see Special Abilities in Naxikriot's stat block above).

Abilities: The creature gains a spit attack that deals acid damage as appropriate for a creature of its array and CR (*Alien Archive* 129–132). When killed, the creature releases soul spores in a 10-foot-radius burst, with a save DC appropriate for a creature of its array and CR.

EMPIRE OF BONES

PART 1: CLOSE TO THE BONE

PART 2: MASS GRAVES

PART 3: IN THE MARROW

PART 4: DEAD TO RIGHTS

CONTINUING THE CAMPAIGN

SHIPS OF THE LINE

SHIPS OF THE CORPSE FLEET

ALIEN ARCHIVES

CODEX OF WORLDS

NAXIKRIOT

SHIPS OF THE LINE

"THE *MERCILESS BLADE* IS AS MUCH A CITY AS IT IS A STARSHIP, AND YOU'VE GOT TO UNDERSTAND HOW BOTH FUNCTION TO KEEP IT FLYING. SURE, YOU MIGHT BE A WHIZ-BANG ENGINEER, ABLE TO STRIP AND REASSEMBLE A REACTOR COIL BLINDFOLDED, BUT THAT DOESN'T MEAN SQUAT WHEN IT'S TIME TO CONVINCE THE BURSAR THAT YOU NEED A COUPLE HUNDRED THOUSAND CREDITS TO BUY THE POLYCARBON PLATE NECESSARY TO REPAIR A FEW DINGS IN THE HULL. YOU'LL FIND YOU NEED A DEFT HAND AT BOTH POLITICS AND MECHANICS, AND A WELL-TIMED FAVOR OR A CONVINCING ARGUMENT SHOULD BE FOUND RIGHT NEXT TO YOUR WRENCHES AND BLOW TORCHES IN YOUR TOOLBOXES. OTHERWISE, WE'RE ALL SUCKING SPACE."

—ENGINEERING GUILD CHIEF MOZMURAN GRIMHELM

Modern shipyards can regularly construct starships of various sizes ranging from Tiny to Colossal. Although a few starships, such as the *Idari*, are much larger than typical Colossal ships, most are ancient vessels built for extraordinary events and lack the engines necessary for travel through the Drift. However, so-called ships of the line—massive starships equipped with Drift engines—do exist. These rare ships are of such extraordinary dimensions and powers that they form the centers of the fighting lines of the largest and most fearsome navies. Groups that have at least planetary reaches and resources are the only ones capable of funding these vessels, which include the Corpse Fleet flagship *Empire of Bones*, the Veskarian *Conqueror of Worlds* and *Merciless Blade*, and the largest few of the Drift engine–equipped dwarven Star Citadels.

Most ships of the line act either as mobile bases of operations or as flagships, but some act as both. Base ships perform well for colonization or long-range exploration, and some act as autonomous armadas, carrying myriad smaller vessels inside hangars. Some base ships are independent political entities that function as itinerant city-states in space. Flagships are the most powerful vessels their respective militaries can field, supported by cruisers, escorts, scouts, supply tenders, and other ships. Military dictatorships that can afford to do so keep a Supercolossal flagship as a symbol of the state's power and a mobile command base for top military leaders. Any navy keeps close watch over its ships of the line, since losing those craft would be a devastating blow.

Even among factions that have the resources to construct a Supercolossal starship, most prefer to operate and maintain multiple dreadnoughts and carriers for the same cost and crew needs. Rumors claim that some factions have secret ships of the line, or that other Supercolossal vessels exist that serve the interests of long-collapsed empires. Little convincing evidence exists of such secret titans of the stars, but the vastness of space makes it impossible to rule out these possibilities.

This article introduces ships of the line as starships with a new size category, Supercolossal. Supercolossal vessels are over 6 miles long, weigh more than 2,000 megatons, and take a –8 penalty to AC and TL. Except as detailed in the following sections, these starships use the normal rules presented in Chapter 9 of the *Starfinder Core Rulebook*.

BASE FRAME

Each base frame determines a starship's size, maneuverability, hull strength, starting weapon mounts, number of expansion bays, and other capacities.

BASE SHIP

Size Supercolossal
Maneuverability clumsy (–2 Piloting, turn 4)
HP 450 (increment 75); **DT** 15; **CT** 90
Mounts forward arc (4 heavy), port arc (4 heavy), starboard arc (4 heavy), turret (2 capital)

Expansion Bays unlimited; a base ship with increased width or length can support more expansion bays
Minimum Crew 150; **Maximum Crew** 100,000
Cost 250

ULTRANOUGHT

Size Supercolossal
Maneuverability clumsy (–2 Piloting, turn 4)
HP 550 (increment 100); **DT** 20; **CT** 110
Mounts forward arc (2 capital, 2 heavy, 1 spinal mount), port arc (2 capital, 3 heavy), starboard arc (2 capital, 3 heavy), turret (1 capital, 2 heavy)
Expansion Bays unlimited; an ultranought with increased width or length can support more expansion bays
Minimum Crew 250; **Maximum Crew** 5,000
Cost 350

POWER CORE

Supercolossal ships have massive power needs. They also have enormous space dedicated to power systems, allowing them to use power cores that won't fit in other vessels. A Supercolossal ship can mount one of the power cores of Supercolossal size shown in the following table. If a Supercolossal starship has a Supercolossal power core, the vessel can have up to four backup cores; those cores must be designed for Huge or Gargantuan starships. If a Supercolossal starship does not have a Supercolossal power core, the vessel can instead mount up to five power cores designed for Colossal ships.

CORE	SIZE	PCU	COST (IN BP)
Titan Light	Sc	700	50
Titan Heavy	Sc	950	60
Titan Ultra	Sc	1,200	70

THRUSTERS

Supercolossal ships depend on enormous thrusters that focus on speed, since the maneuverability of ships of this size is hard to improve.

THRUSTER	SIZE	SPEED (IN HEXES)	PILOTING MODIFIER	PCU	COST (IN BP)
SC4 thrusters	Sc	4	+1	300	16
SC6 thrusters	Sc	6	+0	400	20
SC8 thrusters	Sc	8	–1	500	24

ARMOR

A Supercolossal ship has a size multiplier of 8 for determining its armor's Build Point cost.

COMPUTERS

Supercolossal starships use the computer systems normally available to other starships. This main computer system must be mk 4 or higher. Unlike typical starships, however, a

EMPIRE
OF
BONES

PART 1:
CLOSE TO
THE BONE

PART 2:
MASS GRAVES

PART 3:
IN THE MARROW

PART 4:
DEAD TO RIGHTS

CONTINUING THE
CAMPAIGN

SHIPS OF
THE LINE

SHIPS OF THE
CORPSE FLEET

ALIEN
ARCHIVES

CODEX OF
WORLDS

Supercolossal ship can have a second computer system of a lower mark than the main system.

A Supercolossal vessel also has enough space to augment a mk 4 or better mononode computer with subordinate systems called network nodes; these nodes increase the computing power of the augmented mononode computer. A node might be a dedicated technological system, a hardwired cybernetic undead creature, a biotech calculating organism, a magitech information crystal, or one of a myriad of other devices that increase computer processing power and accessibility.

Regardless of their appearances, network nodes cost significantly fewer Build Points than computers that offer the same bonuses. The cost of a network node is equal to the mark of the mononode computer the network node augments, and the network node provides one bonus as if it were one node of the augmented computer. Network nodes consume a lot of power, so a computer can have a maximum number of connected network nodes no higher than half its mark. The following table summarizes these network node parameters.

NAME	BONUS	NODE MAXIMUM	PCU	COST (IN BP)
Mk 4 network node	+4	2	8	4
Mk 5 network node	+5	2	10	5
Mk 6 network node	+6	3	11	6
Mk 7 network node	+7	3	13	7
Mk 8 network node	+8	4	15	8
Mk 9 network node	+9	4	17	9
Mk 10 network node	+10	5	19	10

CREW QUARTERS

On a Supercolossal ship with common crew quarters, the sheer size of the vessel allows 10% of the crew to have good quarters and 1% to have luxurious quarters at no additional cost. On a Supercolossal ship with good quarters for the majority of the crew, 10% have luxurious quarters at no additional cost.

TACTICAL SENSOR TANK

DEFENSIVE COUNTERMEASURES

Supercolossal ships take a −8 penalty to the TL they gain from defensive countermeasures.

DRIFT ENGINE

A Supercolossal starship can mount only a Signal Basic Drift engine, at a cost of 16 BP.

EXPANSION BAYS

A Supercolossal ship uses the same expansion bays as other starships do. A Supercolossal ship can hold an unlimited number of expansion bays, none of which ever go unused. Any expansion bay in a Supercolossal ship represents numerous chambers grouped together over a wide area or many decks and augmented with reserve systems and retaskable configurations. Therefore, a bay such as an arcane laboratory on a Supercolossal ship indicates not a single lab, but the ship's facilities that allow the crew to perform tasks requiring an arcane lab. Enough of these spaces exist on a ship of the line to accommodate any number of crew members who might need access the ship's specific expansion bays.

MODIFIED EXPANSION BAYS

The following expansion bays work differently for ships of the line.

Cargo Holds: Supercolossal ship frames have one cargo hold for every 10 Build Points of the frame's cost. Additional cargo holds cost 5 BP per cargo hold.

Hangar Bay: A Supercolossal ship's hangar bay can accommodate up to eight Medium ships, with two Small ships or four Tiny ships taking the same space as one Medium ship. Expanding an existing hangar bay to accommodate eight more Medium ships adds only 1 BP to the hangar bay's cost.

EXCLUSIVE EXPANSION BAYS

A few expansion bays are available only to Supercolossal ships.

EXPANSION BAY	PCU	COST (IN BP)
Drift booster	40	20
Recycling system	2	1
Tactical sensor tank	2	1

Drift Booster: A Drift booster is a rail for launching smaller ships into the Drift from within a Supercolossal vessel's hangar bay. A smaller ship that launches from within the Supercolossal vessel's hangar bay using the Drift booster can temporarily raise its Drift engine rating by 1. This increase lasts only as long as the smaller ship stays in the Drift and on the same course after launching using the Drift booster. If the boosted

ship changes course or leaves the Drift, this temporary increase ends.

Recycling System: A recycling system enables a Supercolossal starship to be nearly self-sustaining, operating independently for decades or even centuries. A combination of smelters, biomass processors, manufacturing, and UPB converters allows the ship to convert almost all its waste into goods and materials.

Tactical Sensor Tank: A tactical sensor tank (TST) allows a Supercolossal ship to coordinate the sensor readings of multiple escort craft into a unified picture of surrounding space and then share this information with each starship. Science officers can use a TST to link the sensors of any number of allied vessels in range of the TST-equipped ship's sensors. The sensor range for all linked ships extends as far as the farthest-reaching range among them, since the TST system collects data from linked vessels, correlates possible sensor targets, and sends that information to all linked ships.

SECURITY, SENSORS, AND SHIELDS

In many cases, a ship of the line has weaker security, sensors and shields than the most powerful of its escort ships. Supercolossal vessels depend on their massive Hull Point totals to carry them through combat, and they instead focus their BP and PCU on massive weapons few other vessels can compete against.

SPINAL-MOUNT WEAPONS

Any Supercolossal ship can mount multiple capital weapons, but the dreaded ultranought can have an even larger weapon, known as a spinal-mount weapon. These immense devices of destruction are built along the vessel's core spine, and they can channel the power of the ship's engines and reactors directly into massive, direct-fire attacks that can obliterate most targets. No ship of the line can mount more than one spinal-mount weapon, although spinal-mount weapons have multiple apertures or focusing lenses that are part of a single weapon. A spinal-mount weapon must be mounted in the front arc of a ship.

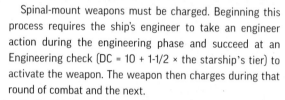

PICKETS

When starships move in groups, they sometimes use pickets—escort craft whose crews remain on watch to prevent surprise attacks and spot enemies far enough away to allow time for favorable reactions. Supercolossal ships regularly use such escort vessels to scan for enemy targets. At the beginning of starship combat, if a higher-tier ship of any size uses escorts in this way, the highest-tier escort is considered to be the highest-tier ship in a flotilla when randomly determining the distance between opposing sides (see Beginning Starship Combat on pages 316–317 of the *Starfinder Core Rulebook*).

Spinal-mount weapons must be charged. Beginning this process requires the ship's engineer to take an engineer action during the engineering phase and succeed at an Engineering check (DC = 10 + 1-1/2 × the starship's tier) to activate the weapon. The weapon then charges during that round of combat and the next.

On the third round, during the gunnery phase, the spinal-mount weapon can be fired with the shoot gunner action. Because aiming the weapon requires moving the ship, the gunner gains a +2 bonus to gunner checks when using her ranks in Piloting instead of her base attack bonus. If the gunner wants to use her base attack bonus, she gains a +1 bonus to her gunner checks if she is trained in Piloting. Additionally, if the gunner fires no other weapons during the same round as the spinal-mount weapon, it deals an additional 1 damage per die. Once a spinal-mount weapon is fired, it cannot be activated again for 2d4 rounds.

If the gunner doesn't fire a spinal-mount weapon on the first round that it is fully charged, a member of the crew must take an engineer or gunner action each round (requiring no skill check) to keep it on standby. If no member of the crew takes this action, the weapon functions as if it had been fired and cannot be activated again for 2d4 rounds.

SPINAL-MOUNT WEAPONS

SPINAL-MOUNT WEAPONS	RANGE	DAMAGE	PCU	COST (IN BP)	SPECIAL PROPERTIES
Gravity annihilator	Long	8d6 × 10	50	60	Tractor beam
Hypermass cannon	Long	6d6 × 10	40	30	Line
Particle acceleration gun	Long	9d4 × 10	50	30	Line
Nova ram	Long	6d10 × 10	75	45	Line
Ultra plasma cannon	Medium	9d6 × 10	80	35	Line
Ultra X-laser cannon	Long	6d8 × 10	90	60	Line
Ultragraser	Medium	6d8 × 10	75	70	Irradiate (high), line
Ultralaser	Long	6d4 × 10	30	25	Line
Ultramaser	Long	6d8 × 10	60	40	Line
Vortex devourer	Medium	6d12 × 10	80	80	Vortex

EMPIRE OF BONES

PART 1: CLOSE TO THE BONE

PART 2: MASS GRAVES

PART 3: IN THE MARROW

PART 4: DEAD TO RIGHTS

CONTINUING THE CAMPAIGN

SHIPS OF THE LINE

SHIPS OF THE CORPSE FLEET

ALIEN ARCHIVES

CODEX OF WORLDS

SHIPS OF THE CORPSE FLEET

"ATTENTION CREW, THIS IS YOUR CAPTAIN SPEAKING. I KNOW THE LAST FEW WEEKS HAVE BEEN DULL FOR YOU, PICKING THROUGH THE REMAINS OF COLONIES FOOLISH ENOUGH TO THINK THEY'D SURVIVE OUT HERE IN THE VAST. I HEAR YOUR COMPLAINTS IN THE CORRIDORS. YOU THINK US NO BETTER THAN SCAVENGERS. YOU WONDER IF WE'LL SEE ANY ACTION. BUT REMEMBER, THIS IS OUR DUTY TO THE CORPSE FLEET! WE PROVIDE BODIES TO FILL OUR BARRACKS SO WE CAN ONE DAY ERASE THE LIVING FROM THIS GALAXY. NOW, OUR SENSORS ARE PICKING UP A DISTRESS BEACON FROM A PACT WORLDS SHIP WITH A DISABLED ENGINE AND AN UNCONSCIOUS ENGINEER. WE SHALL COME TO THEIR AID... AND MAKE SOME FRESH CORPSES!"

—CAPTAIN KOVLOV AMALAN OF *THE LAST BREATH*

The scientists and engineers of the exiled undead navy known as the Corpse Fleet regularly invent new and deadly ways to upgrade their starships for the fleet's unending war. The following systems can be purchased using starship Build Points, but these expansions and weapons are available only on the black market or directly from Corpse Fleet agents.

EXPANSION BAYS

The following expansion bays aid the undead of the Corpse Fleet in their battle against the living.

EXPANSION BAY	PCU	COST (IN BP)
Arcane mortuary	1	2
Corpse recycler	2	2
Ghost drive	10	5

ARCANE MORTUARY

An arcane mortuary contains equipment that aids spellcasters in creating undead. A spellcaster using this mortuary must still provide any special materials that undead creation requires. The benefit of using the arcane mortuary is that undead created there have 10% more Hit Points than a typical undead creature of the same CR. An arcane mortuary can also store up to five Medium or smaller corpses without them deteriorating due to time. One Large corpse can be stored in place of two Medium ones.

CORPSE RECYCLER

A corpse recycler allows a starship crew to render bodies into parts for necrografts (*Starfinder Adventure Path #3: Splintered Worlds* 42). In a process that takes 1 hour, a carcass fed into the recycler produces a number of necrograft UPBs equal to 10 × the CR of the creature from which the corpse originated. These UPBs can be used only to create necrografts.

GHOST DRIVE

A ghost drive can be installed only on a Large or smaller starship. During the helm phase, as a science officer action, you can attempt a Computers check (DC = 10 + 1-1/2 × the starship's tier) to activate the ghost drive. If the check is successful, the ghost drive becomes active and the vessel in which it is equipped becomes insubstantial.

An active ghost drive has several effects in starship combat. The drive pulls power from the thrusters, so the insubstantial starship's speed is 2 lower, and its distance between turns is 1 higher. An insubstantial starship can move through hexes containing enemy starships without allowing those foes to make free attacks. Additionally, if other starships move through the hex containing the insubstantial starship, that does not allow it to make free attacks.

WEAPONS

The following weapon special properties are results of the Corpse Fleet's ghastly innovations. New weapons using these properties can be found in the table below.

NUMBING

A weapon with the numbing special property fires concentrated negative energy. Living creatures on a starship that takes Hull Point damage from a numbing weapon must succeed at a Fortitude saving throw (DC = 10 + 1-1/2 × the firing starship's tier) or take a –2 penalty to all starship combat actions for 1d3 rounds.

VOLATILE

Only tracking weapons can have the volatile special property. Such a weapon breaks apart when destroyed before its intended impact. When a volatile projectile hits a starship but a gunner succeeds at destroying the projectile with a point weapon, the volatile weapon still deals half its damage.

STARSHIP WEAPONS

LIGHT WEAPONS	RANGE	SPEED (IN HEXES)	DAMAGE	PCU	COST (IN BP)	SPECIAL PROPERTIES
DIRECT-FIRE WEAPONS						
Negative-energy gun	Medium	–	2d6	10	7	Numbing
TRACKING WEAPONS						
Light carrion-missile launcher	Long	12	3d8	10	5	Limited fire 5, volatile

HEAVY WEAPONS	RANGE	SPEED (IN HEXES)	DAMAGE	PCU	COST (IN BP)	SPECIAL PROPERTIES
DIRECT-FIRE WEAPONS						
Negative-energy cannon	Medium	–	5d6	15	15	Numbing
TRACKING WEAPONS						
Heavy carrion-missile launcher	Long	10	6d10	15	15	Limited fire 5, volatile

CAPITAL WEAPONS	RANGE	SPEED (IN HEXES)	DAMAGE	PCU	COST (IN BP)	SPECIAL PROPERTIES
DIRECT-FIRE WEAPONS						
Super negative-energy cannon	Long	–	2d10 × 10	40	60	Numbing
TRACKING WEAPONS						
Mega carrion-missile launcher	Long	8	3d8 × 10	15	25	Limited fire 5, volatile

CORPSE FLEET STARSHIPS

When it defected from Eox upon the signing of the Absalom Pact, the Corpse Fleet took with it a great number of Eoxian military starships. These vessels had been outfitted for war against the other worlds of the system in previous centuries, and the Corpse Fleet has taken great pride in maintaining and upgrading them. However, as the years have passed, many Pact Worlds starship manufacturers have made great strides in the field of engineering. In order to keep up with the improvements made by their enemies and to replace the ships they have lost in various skirmishes, the Corpse Fleet has designed many unique vessels.

In addition to the Eoxian ships on pages 306–307 of the *Starfinder Core Rulebook* and the Corpse Fleet vanguard described on pages 50–51 of *Starfinder Adventure Path #3: Splintered Worlds*, the following vessels are mainly manufactured on the roving planetoid named Barrow (*Starfinder Adventure Path #3: Splintered Worlds* 61).

BARROW BONESHARD

The Corpse Fleet launches waves of Barrow Boneshards to harry its foes. Typically, each Barrow Boneshard is piloted by one heavily damaged undead creature, perhaps missing its lower half or most of its limbs. Such pilots are wired directly into the controls and considered to be prime candidates for suicide missions.

BARROW BONESHARD — TIER 1/3

Tiny racer
Speed 14; **Maneuverability** perfect (turn 0)
AC 16; **TL** 13
HP 20; **DT** –; **CT** 4
Shields none
Attack (Forward) flak thrower (3d4)
Attack (Aft) flak thrower (3d4)
Power Core Micron Heavy (70 PCU); **Drift Engine** none; **Systems** basic computer, budget short-range sensors, mk 3 armor; **Expansion Bays** none
Complement 1

CREW
Pilot gunnery +4, Piloting +10 (1 rank)

BARROW DIRGESINGER

Dirgesingers form the backbone of the Corpse Fleet's corpse collection efforts. Their crews search the galaxy for derelict vessels, fresh battlefields, and unlucky colonies where corpses can be found. These bodies are either turned into undead creatures or fashioned into necrografts. Every so often, a bloodthirsty Barrow Dirgesinger crew engages in battle to create the cadavers they seek.

BARROW DIRGESINGER — TIER 2

Small light freighter
Speed 8; **Maneuverability** good (turn 1); **Drift** 1
AC 16; **TL** 15
HP 40; **DT** –; **CT** 8
Shields basic 40 (forward 10, port 10, starboard 10, aft 10)
Attack (Forward) coilgun (4d4), light EMP cannon (special)
Attack (Port) gyrolaser (1d8)
Attack (Starboard) gyrolaser (1d8)
Power Core Pulse Black (120 PCU); **Drift Engine** Signal Basic; **Systems** advanced medium-range sensors, basic computer, crew quarters (common), mk 3 armor, mk 2 defenses; **Expansion Bays** cargo bays (2), corpse recycler
Modifiers +4 Computers, +1 Piloting; **Complement** 5

CREW
Captain gunnery +4, Intimidate +7 (2 ranks), Piloting +8 (2 ranks)
Engineer Engineering +8 (2 ranks)
Gunner gunnery +5
Pilot gunnery+5, Piloting +13 (2 ranks)
Science Officer Computers +11 (2 ranks)

BARROW RELIQUARY

The crews of Barrow Reliquaries are among the most diplomatic and educated of all Corpse Fleet soldiers. Although the navy fields only a handful of these vessels, their crews are tasked with exploring the Vast in search of necromantic objects and alien undead creatures whose goals align with those of the Corpse Fleet. Some of these new allies are transported back to Corpse Fleet holdings in order to coordinate plans with the navy's high-ranking officials.

BARROW RELIQUARY — TIER 5

Medium explorer
Speed 8; **Maneuverability** good (turn 1); **Drift** 2
AC 19; **TL** 18
HP 65; **DT** –; **CT** 13
Shields light 60 (forward 15, port 15, starboard 15, aft 15)
Attack (Forward) light plasma torpedo launcher (3d8)
Attack (Port) light particle beam (3d6)
Attack (Starboard) light particle beam (3d6)
Attack (Turret) light plasma cannon (5d10)
Power Core Pulse Green (150 PCU); **Drift Engine** Signal Booster; **Systems** basic medium-range sensors, crew quarters (common), mk 4 armor, mk 3 defenses, mk 2 trinode computer; **Expansion Bays** arcane laboratory, cargo holds (2), guest quarters (good)
Modifiers +2 to any 3 checks per round, +2 Computers, +1 Piloting; **Complement** 6

BARROW SPECTRE

BARROW RELIQUARY

BARROW BONESHARD

BARROW DIRGESINGER

EMPIRE
OF
BONES

PART 1:
CLOSE TO
THE BONE

PART 2:
MASS GRAVES

PART 3:
IN THE MARROW

PART 4:
DEAD TO RIGHTS

CONTINUING THE
CAMPAIGN

SHIPS OF
THE LINE

SHIPS OF THE
CORPSE FLEET

ALIEN
ARCHIVES

CODEX OF
WORLDS

CREW

Captain Computers +13 (5 ranks), Diplomacy +11 (5 ranks), Intimidate +11 (5 ranks)

Engineer Engineering +11 (5 ranks)

Gunners (2) gunnery +9

Pilot gunnery +9, Piloting +12 (5 ranks)

Science Officer Computers +18 (5 ranks)

BARROW SPECTRE

A Barrow Spectre is a silent assassin of space, quickly moving into engagements, tearing through foes, and disappearing into the void. Due to the frequent use of ghost drives by Barrow Spectre crews, those who have survived encounters with these vessels often babble about ethereal starships that can't be shot.

BARROW SPECTRE	TIER 7

Large destroyer

Speed 8; **Maneuverability** average (turn 2); **Drift** 1

AC 19; **TL** 20

HP 170; **DT** –; **CT** 34

Shields light 80 (forward 20, port 20, starboard 20, aft 20)

Attack (Forward) heavy torpedo launcher (5d8), negative-energy cannon (5d8)

Attack (Port) coilgun (4d4)

Attack (Starboard) coilgun (4d4)

Attack (Aft) coilgun (4d4)

Attack (Turret) negative-energy gun (2d6)

Power Core Pulse Orange (250 PCU); **Drift Engine** Signal Basic; **Systems** basic medium-range sensors, crew quarters (common), mk 3 armor, mk 4 defenses, mk 2 trinode computer; **Expansion Bays** arcane mortuary, cargo holds (2), ghost drive

Modifiers +2 any 3 checks per round, +2 Computers; **Complement** 9

CREW

Captain Computers +16 (7 ranks), gunnery +11, Intimidate +14 (7 ranks)

Engineers (2) Engineering +19 (7 ranks)

Gunners (3) gunnery +11

Pilot gunnery +11, Piloting +14 (7 ranks)
Science Officers (2) Computers +16 (7 ranks)

BARROW CATACOMB

Each Barrow Catacomb can hold two Grave Casket shuttles (*Starfinder Adventure Path #3: Splintered Worlds* 50) and a couple land vehicles that can survive atmospheric entry to launch planetside assaults on targets Corpse Fleet command wants destroyed.

BARROW CATACOMB   TIER 8

Huge bulk freighter
Speed 6; **Maneuverability** poor (turn 3); **Drift** 1
AC 21; **TL** 20
HP 200; **DT** 5; **CT** 40
Shields medium 100 (forward 25, port 25, starboard 25, aft 25)
Attack (Forward) heavy laser cannon (4d8)
Attack (Aft) heavy laser cannon (4d8)
Attack (Turret) light carrion-missile launcher (3d6), light EMP cannon (special)
Power Core Nova Ultra (300 PCU); **Drift Engine** Signal Basic; **Systems** basic medium-range sensors, crew quarters (basic), mk 5 armor, mk 5 defenses, mk 2 duonode computer; **Expansion Bays** cargo holds (4), passenger seating (4), shuttle bay
Modifiers +2 to any 2 checks per round, +2 Computers; **Complement** 40

CREW

Captain (1 officer, 2 crew) Diplomacy +16 (8 ranks), gunnery +12, Intimidate +16 (8 ranks), Piloting +16 (8 ranks)
Engineers (2 officers, 7 crew each) Engineering +16 (8 ranks)
Gunners (2 officers, 5 crew each) gunnery +12
Pilot (1 officer, 2 crew) gunnery +12, Piloting +21 (8 ranks)
Science Officers (2 officers, 2 crew each) Computers +18 (8 ranks)

BARROW REAPER

Barrow Reapers, while massive, are also surprisingly fast and maneuverable for their size. Barrow Reapers often act as escorts for Corpse Fleet capital ships, but their hardy crews make effective boarding parties or ground troops, as well.

BARROW REAPER   TIER 10

Huge cruiser
Speed 8; **Maneuverability** average (turn 2); **Drift** 1
AC 24; **TL** 23
HP 230; **DT** 5; **CT** 46
Shields medium 140 (forward 35, port 35, starboard 35, aft 35)
Attack (Forward) mass driver (2d6×10)
Attack (Port) light plasma cannon (2d12)
Attack (Starboard) light plasma cannon (2d12)

Attack (Turret) negative-energy cannon (5d8)
Power Core Gateway Light (300 PCU); **Drift Engine** Signal Basic; **Systems** basic medium-range sensors, crew quarters (common), mk 6 armor, mk 6 defenses, mk 2 duonode computer; **Expansion Bays** cargo holds (4), synthesis bay, tech workshop
Modifiers +2 to any 2 checks per round, +2 Computers; **Complement** 80

CREW

Captain (1 officer, 4 crew) Diplomacy +19 (10 ranks), gunnery +12, Intimidate +19 (10 ranks), Piloting +19 (10 ranks)
Engineers (3 officers, 10 crew each) Engineering +19 (10 ranks)
Gunners (3 officers, 6 crew each) gunnery +14
Pilot (1 officer, 4 crew) gunnery +14, Piloting +24 (10 ranks)
Science Officers (2 officers, 7 crew each) Computers +21 (10 ranks)

BARROW EULOGY

A Barrow Eulogy can bring eight Necrofighters (*Starfinder Adventure Path #3: Splintered Worlds* 50) into battle, but it has enough firepower to defend itself if enemies threaten. Its port and starboard heavy laser arrays keep smaller craft from attacking its flanks while it launches its fighters.

BARROW EULOGY   TIER 12

Gargantuan carrier
Speed 4; **Maneuverability** poor (turn 3); **Drift** 1
AC 24; **TL** 22
HP 330; **DT** 10; **CT** 66
Shields medium 160 (forward 40, port 40, starboard 40, aft 40)
Attack (Forward) supermaser (2d8×10)
Attack (Port) heavy laser array (6d4)
Attack (Starboard) heavy laser array (6d4)
Attack (Turret) linked light particle beams (6d6)
Power Core Gateway Light (300 PCU); **Drift Engine** Signal Basic; **Systems** basic medium-range sensors, crew quarters (common), mk 6 armor, mk 5 defenses, mk 1 trinode computer; **Expansion Bays** cargo holds (6), hangar bay
Modifiers +1 to any 3 checks per round, +2 Computers, +1 Piloting; **Complement** 144

CREW

Captain (1 officer, 5 crew) Diplomacy +22 (12 ranks), gunnery +14, Intimidate +27 (12 ranks), Piloting +23 (12 ranks)
Engineers (2 officers, 30 crew each) Engineering +22 (12 ranks)
Gunners (3 officers, 15 crew each) gunnery +16
Pilot (1 officer, 5 crew) gunnery +16, Piloting +23 (12 ranks)
Science Officers (2 officers, 10 crew each) Computers +24 (12 ranks)

PART 1:
CLOSE TO
THE BONE

PART 2:
MASS GRAVES

PART 3:
IN THE MARROW

PART 4:
DEAD TO RIGHTS

CONTINUING THE
CAMPAIGN

SHIPS OF
THE LINE

SHIPS OF THE
CORPSE FLEET

ALIEN
ARCHIVES

CODEX OF
WORLDS

BARROW EULOGY

BARROW CATACOMB

BARROW REAPER

BARROW CENOTAPH

BARROW CENOTAPH

An impressive feat of necro-engineering, the Barrow Cenotaph is a machine of destruction, inside and out. Featuring bays for two sets of other vessels plus room to hold dozens of troops, this dreadnought sports some of the Corpse Fleet's most devastating weaponry. It is a lumbering vessel, but it can take more punishment than most starships manufactured in the Pact Worlds and beyond.

BARROW CENOTAPH	TIER 16

Colossal dreadnought

Speed 4; **Maneuverability** clumsy (turn 4); **Drift** 1
AC 25; **TL** 24
HP 600; **DT** 15; **CT** 120
Shields heavy 240 (forward 60, port 60, starboard 60, aft 60)
Attack (Forward) particle beam (8d6), super negative-energy cannon (2d10×10)
Attack (Port) heavy laser cannon (4d8), super plasma cannon (3d6×10)
Attack (Starboard) heavy laser cannon (4d8), super plasma cannon (3d6×10)
Attack (Turret) micromissile battery (2d6), micromissile battery (2d6)
Power Core Gateway Ultra (500 PCU); **Drift Engine** Signal Basic; **Systems** basic computer, advanced long-range sensors, crew quarters (common), mk 7 armor, mk 7 defenses; **Expansion Bays** cargo holds (8), hangar bay, passenger seating (6), shuttle bay
Modifiers +4 Computers; **Complement** 260

CREW

Captain (1 officer, 9 crew) Diplomacy +28 (16 ranks), gunnery +18, Intimidate +33 (16 ranks), Piloting +28 (16 ranks)

Engineers (3 officers, 35 crew each) Engineering +28 (16 ranks)

Gunners (4 officers, 20 crew each) gunnery +20

Pilot (1 officer, 9 crew) gunnery +20, Piloting +28 (16 ranks)

Science Officers (3 officers, 15 crew each) Computers +32 (16 ranks)

ALIEN ARCHIVES

VETERAN WARRIOR-CASTE SOLDIER PARTHAEL FINDS HERSELF THE
SOLE SURVIVOR OF A STORM BARGE CRASH MILES FROM THE NEAREST
DOME DURING THE MOST VIOLENT SERIES OF STORMS SHIMRINSARA
HAS EVER SEEN. RELYING ONLY ON HER WITS, HER TRAINING, AND A
FEW PIECES OF GEAR SHE SCAVENGED FROM THE WRECKAGE, OUR
INTREPID HERO FIGHTS FOR HER LIFE TO MAKE IT BACK TO CIVILIZATION
AND HER ARTISAN HUSBAND. IN A SERIES OF FLASHBACKS, WE GET
GLIMPSES OF HER LIFE THAT HINT AT THE TRUE CAUSES BEHIND HER
ACCIDENT. AS LIGHTNING, FIRE, AND SLEET RAGE ALL AROUND HER,
PARTHAEL MUST COME TO TERMS WITH HER OWN MORTALITY AND THE
MANY CHOICES THAT HAVE LED HER TO THIS POINT.

—EXCERPT FROM A REVIEW OF THE HOLOVID *SURVIVE THE TEMPEST*

EMPIRE
OF
BONES

PART 1:
CLOSE TO
THE BONE

PART 2:
MASS GRAVES

PART 3:
IN THE MARROW

PART 4:
DEAD TO RIGHTS

CONTINUING THE
CAMPAIGN

SHIPS OF
THE LINE

SHIPS OF THE
CORPSE FLEET

ALIEN
ARCHIVES

CODEX OF
WORLDS

BAYKOK

CR 9 **XP 6,400**

NE Medium undead

Init +6; **Senses** darkvision 60 ft.; **Perception** +17

DEFENSE
HP 144

EAC 23; **KAC** 23

Fort +11; **Ref** +11; **Will** +10

Immunities undead immunities

OFFENSE

Speed 30 ft., fly 60 ft. (Su, perfect)

Melee claw +18 (2d8+13 S)

Ranged combat rifle +21 (3d8+9 P)

Offensive Abilities devour soul, dread howl, infused ammunition

STATISTICS

Str +4; **Dex** +6; **Con** —; **Int** +0; **Wis** +0; **Cha** +3

Skills Acrobatics +17, Stealth +22, Survival +17

Other Abilities unliving

Gear d-suit III, combat rifle

ECOLOGY

Environment any

Organization solitary, gang (2–5), or flight (6–12)

SPECIAL ABILITIES

Devour Soul (Su) A baykok can take a standard action to devour the soul of an adjacent dead or dying creature. A dying creature can resist this attack with a successful DC 18 Fortitude save. If it fails, the target is instantly slain. If the creature is already dead, it can't attempt the saving throw, although the target can't have been dead for more than 1 hour. A creature subjected to this attack can't be brought back to life via *mystic cure* cast as a 4th-level or higher spell (though *raise dead* and more powerful effects work normally). When a baykok devours a soul in this way, it recovers a number of Hit Points equal to 2d10 + its CR and becomes hasted for 4 rounds (as if affected by *haste*). This is a death effect.

Dread Howl (Su) Once per day as a standard action, a baykok can let out a howl. Each living creature within a 30-foot-radius burst must succeed at a DC 16 Fortitude save or become paralyzed with fear for 1 round. A creature that succeeds at this saving throw is instead shaken for 1 round. This is a sense-dependent fear effect.

Infused Ammunition (Su) As part of making an attack or full attack with a projectile weapon, a baykok can create a round or rounds of ammunition made from bone and infused with negative energy. This ammunition appears loaded into the projectile weapon the baykok is wielding. The baykok can't create ammunition quickly enough to use when making an attack in automatic mode. Half the damage from attacks made with this ammunition is negative energy damage, and a creature struck by such an attack must succeed at a DC 16 Fortitude save or

be paralyzed for 1d3 rounds. A baykok can fire normal ammunition from its projectile weapon if it wishes, though such ammunition doesn't gain the extra benefits.

Those who revel too much in the thrill of chasing and killing living creatures might arise as baykoks after death.

BAYKOK TEMPLATE GRAFT (CR 4+)

Baykoks are flying undead devoted to the hunt.

Required Creature Type: Undead.

Suggested Array: Combatant or expert.

Traits: +1 EAC, –1 KAC.

Abilities: Devour soul (see above), dread howl (see above), infused ammunition (see above).

Suggested Ability Score Modifiers: Dexterity, Strength.

CORPSEFOLK

Elebrian corpsefolk operative
NE Medium undead
Init +6; **Senses** darkvision 60 ft.; **Perception** +14

DEFENSE   HP 42
EAC 14; **KAC** 15
Fort +3; **Ref** +6; **Will** +7
Defensive Abilities evasion; **DR** 5/magic; **Immunities** undead immunities

OFFENSE
Speed 40 ft.
Melee survival knife +7 (1d4+4 S)
Ranged static arc pistol +9 (1d6+3 E; critical arc 2) or tactical shirren-eye rifle +9 (1d10+3 P)
Offensive Abilities trick attack +1d8

STATISTICS
Str +1; **Dex** +4; **Con** —; **Int** +1; **Wis** +2; **Cha** +0
Skills Acrobatics +8, Intimidate +9, Sleight of Hand +13, Stealth +13
Other Abilities operative exploits (uncanny mobility), specialization (thief), unliving
Languages Common, Eoxian
Gear graphite carbon skin, static arc pistol with 2 batteries (20 charges each), survival knife, tactical shirren-eye rifle with 25 sniper rounds

ECOLOGY
Environment any (Eox)
Organization solitary, pair, or association (3–20)

Corpsefolk rise from the dead bodies of beings infused with necromantic energies. Though they often have an appearance similar to various forms of zombies, unlike those common undead minions, corpsefolk retain the memories of their previous lives, the skills and abilities gained through living experience, and the will to make decisions on their own. Undead creatures of this type were called "zombie masters" in ancient days, but as a common class of rank-and-file citizens of Eox and soldiers in the Corpse Fleet, they have become known as "corpsefolk" to reflect their independent mentalities.

Corpsefolk can be found in all roles in societies that accept undead citizens, often serving as assistants to powerful spellcasters, guards, marines, menial managers, and technicians. They are able to use any armor, equipment, and weapons they mastered in life and can even gain new skills. Though no less motivated than living creatures, and still able to experience both positive and negative emotions, corpsefolk generally take patient, long-term views of their existences. Even when enduring menial tasks, most corpsefolk assume their current positions are temporary, and as centuries or eons pass, they will come into positions of power and influence, freed as they are from the constraints of age, breath, food, and sleep.

Initially, a corpsefolk appears much as she did when she was alive, though with paler skin due to a lack of blood pumping through her veins. Some corpsefolk are a bit more sunken and emaciated, depending on how long their bodies were left to rot before rising as undead. However, as a corpsefolk progresses through the years, her body grows increasingly torn and tattered. Some corpsefolk resort to surgery and magic in an effort to maintain more wholesome appearances, but after a few decades, most cease to care what they look like and focus only on what they can do to gain wealth and power.

CORPSEFOLK TEMPLATE GRAFT (CR 2+)

The animated corpse of a dead sentient creature, a corpsefolk keeps the abilities, intelligence, and skills it had when it was alive. Most corpsefolk are far more cunning and dangerous foes than are common, mindless undead. They often have ambitions and aspirations to increase their station in whatever society they exist in.

Required Creature Type: Undead.

Traits: DR 5/magic; increase Hit Points by 20%.

Suggested Ability Modifiers: *Combatant*—Dexterity, Strength; *expert*—Dexterity, Intelligence; *spellcaster*—Wisdom, Dexterity.

GATECRASHER

CR 10 **XP 9,600**

LE Large undead

Init +5; **Senses** darkvision 60 ft.; **Perception** +19

DEFENSE

HP 198

EAC 24; **KAC** 25

Fort +12; **Ref** +12; **Will** +11

Immunities undead immunities

OFFENSE

Speed 20 ft.

Melee advanced swoop hammer +22 (3d10+18 B; critical knockdown)

Ranged aurora shock caster +19 (2d12+10 E, explode [15 ft., DC 19])

Offensive Abilities juggernaut of destruction

STATISTICS

Str +8; **Dex** +5; **Con** —; **Int** +0; **Wis** +3; **Cha** +1

Skills Athletics +19, Engineering +19, Intimidate +24

Other Abilities integral upgrades (*forcepack*, *haste circuit*, *targeting computer*), unliving

Languages Common, Eoxian

Gear advanced swoop hammer, aurora shock caster with 3 high-capacity batteries (40 charges each)

ECOLOGY

Environment any

Organization solitary, pair, or squad (3–6)

SPECIAL ABILITIES

Integral Upgrades (Su) A gatecrasher can install up to three armor upgrades (each with an item level no greater than the gatecrasher's CR) into its heavily armored frame. It is treated as wearing heavy or powered armor for this purpose. Its armor upgrades cannot be damaged or removed unless the gatecrasher is destroyed and leaves intact physical remains.

Juggernaut of Destruction (Ex) A gatecrasher can use a two-handed weapon in one hand without taking a penalty, and, when wielding two such weapons, as a full action can attack with each weapon once (taking a –6 penalty to each attack roll and to the saving throw DCs of any special properties or critical hit effects the weapons have), even if either of the weapons has the unwieldy weapon special property. A gatecrasher can use any

weapons designed for creatures within one size category of its size without penalty.

Gatecrashers are undead abominations, horrific blends of powered armor and necromancy-infused flesh. These undead monstrosities revel in combat, seeking it out wherever possible.

GATECRASHER TEMPLATE GRAFT (CR 5+)

Any living creature able to use heavy or powered armor in combat may become a gatecrasher after death.

Required Creature Type: Undead.

Required Array: Combatant.

Traits: +1 EAC.

Abilities: Internal upgrades (see above), juggernaut of destruction (see above).

Suggested Ability Score Modifiers: Strength, Constitution.

EMPIRE
OF
BONES

PART 1:
CLOSE TO
THE BONE

PART 2:
MASS GRAVES

PART 3:
IN THE MARROW

PART 4:
DEAD TO RIGHTS

CONTINUING THE
CAMPAIGN

SHIPS OF
THE LINE

SHIPS OF THE
CORPSE FLEET

ALIEN
ARCHIVES

CODEX OF
WORLDS

KUROBOZU

Human kurobozu solarian
CE Medium undead
Init +6; **Senses** darkvision 60 ft.; **Perception** +17

DEFENSE   HP 135
EAC 23; **KAC** 24
Fort +8; **Ref** +10; **Will** +12
Defensive Abilities evasion; **Immunities** undead immunities; **Resistances** cold or fire 5

OFFENSE
Speed 50 ft.
Melee unarmed strike +19 (1d6+13 B; critical stunned)
Multiattack 4 unarmed strikes +14 (1d6+13 B; critical stunned)
Offensive Abilities black apoxia (30-ft. cone, DC 18), flashing strikes, sage's bane (DC 18), stellar revelations (black hole [30-ft.-radius, pull 20 ft., DC 16], crush [DC 16], gravity surge [+7], starquake [1d8 B, DC 16])

STATISTICS
Str +4; **Dex** +6; **Con** −; **Int** +0; **Wis** +0; **Cha** +3

Skills Acrobatics +22, Athletics +22, Mysticism +22, Stealth +17
Other Abilities solar manifestation (armor), stellar alignment (graviton), unliving
Languages Common, Eoxian

ECOLOGY
Environment any
Organization solitary, pair, or guard (3–5)

SPECIAL ABILITIES
Black Apoxia (Su) As a standard action, a kurobozu can create a 30-foot cone of breathlessness, making it hard for creatures to breathe properly even if they are wearing environmental protection, such as a sealed suit of armor. Each creature within the area must succeed at a DC 18 Fortitude saving throw or be fatigued for 1d4 minutes. Creatures that do not breathe are immune to this effect.

Sage's Bane (Su) Once per day, as a reaction when a kurobozu successfully damages a foe with a melee attack, the kurobozu can cloud that foe's mind. The target must succeed at a DC 18 Fortitude saving throw or gain the flat-footed and off-target conditions, as well as be rendered unable to use any Wisdom-based skills or communicate through any means for 1d4 minutes.

Kurobozus, also known as black monks, are the vengeful undead remains of members of highly structured groups, such as ascetics, priesthoods, and solarian orders. They have empty, black eye sockets and often seem to be little more than leathery husks of skin, despite their significant physical power.

Some kurobozus arise when they violate the tenets of their orders in ways that create great suffering. Others are the result of living creatures following a rigid path designed specifically to lead to this undead state. Their entire lives are spent preparing themselves for a vile ceremony in which they are ritualistically choked to death.

KUROBOZU TEMPLATE GRAFT (CR 4+)
Disciplined and deadly, kurobozus are skilled undead fighters.

Required Creature Type: Undead.

Required Array: Expert.

Traits: Kurobozus can take the mystic, soldier, or solarian class graft despite using the expert array; swap base Reflex and Will saving throw bonuses before adjustments; +20 ft. land speed; gains unarmed strike attack that deals standard melee damage for CR and has the stunned critical hit effect.

Abilities: Black apoxia (see above), evasion, multiattack (4 attacks at −5 to melee attack bonus), sage's bane (see above).

Suggested Ability Score Modifiers: Dexterity, Strength.

MOHRG

CE Medium undead
Init +4; **Senses** darkvision 60 ft.; **Perception** +16

DEFENSE
HP 125

EAC 20; **KAC** 22
Fort +10; **Ref** +10; **Will** +9
Immunities undead immunities

OFFENSE
Speed 30 ft.
Melee clawed tongue +19 (1d6+14 S plus paralyzing touch [DC 19]) or
slam +19 (1d10+14 B)
Multiattack 2 slams +13 (1d10+14 B) and clawed tongue +13 (1d6+14 S plus paralyzing touch [DC 19])
Offensive Abilities create spawn, paralyzing touch (DC 18)

STATISTICS
Str +6; **Dex** +4; **Con** —; **Int** +0; **Wis** +0; **Cha** +2
Skills Acrobatics +16, Athletics +21, Stealth +16
Other Abilities unliving
Languages Common, Eoxian

ECOLOGY
Environment any
Organization solitary, gang (2–4), or mob (3–5 plus 4–12 occult zombies)

SPECIAL ABILITIES
Create Spawn (Su) A living humanoid creature slain by a mohrg's slam attack rises immediately as an occult zombie (*Starfinder Alien Archive* 115) of a CR equal to the victim's CR or level. This zombie is permanently under the mohrg's control. The mohrg recovers 1d8+4 Hit Points from the surge of negative energy created by the spawning process.

Paralyzing Touch (Su) A mohrg uses its clawed tongue to make its first melee attack each round. If a target is struck and damaged by this attack, it must succeed at a DC 18 Fortitude save or be paralyzed for 1d4 minutes.

A mohrg is a horrific undead that appears to be an ambulatory skeleton with a writhing, rotting mass of intestines held within its ribcage (or the creature's anatomical equivalent). A tendril of these intestines winds up into the mohrg's mouth, with a clawed tongue at the end. Though mohrgs can wear clothing and armor, they usually don't (or they wear clothes that expose their torsos), ensuring that their horrific appearances are maintained and their clawed tongues remain free to make attacks.

Mohrgs are created from the souls of those who revel in killing sentient victims, preferably in ways that bring considerable pain and suffering. In life, most mohrgs were executioners, murderers, torturers, or warmongering soldiers who dedicated themselves to spilling blood and eliciting tortured cries. So strong are these urges that even death can't stop them, and while the rest of their bodies rot away, a vile core of their bones and guts remains.

Early in a mohrg's existence, its need to kill often overrides its desire for self-preservation, leading many to take extreme risks to reach more victims, which sometimes leads to their own destruction. But as they age and grow more powerful, mohrgs become more cunning about fulfilling their urges. They often become part of larger groups, ranging from packs of undead roaming the dark places near civilization to organized military groups such as the Corpse Fleet, and use their positions within such groups to ensure their bloodlust can be slaked consistently for centuries to come.

MOHRG TEMPLATE GRAFT (CR 6+)
Hideous to behold and extremely deadly, mohrgs exist only to kill.

Required Creature Type: Undead.

Required Array: Combatant.

Abilities: Create spawn (see above), multiattack, paralyzing touch (see above).

Suggested Ability Score Modifiers: Strength, Dexterity.

EMPIRE OF BONES

PART 1:
CLOSE TO THE BONE

PART 2:
MASS GRAVES

PART 3:
IN THE MARROW

PART 4:
DEAD TO RIGHTS

CONTINUING THE CAMPAIGN

SHIPS OF THE LINE

SHIPS OF THE CORPSE FLEET

ALIEN ARCHIVES

CODEX OF WORLDS

PALE STRANGER

CR 11 **XP 12,800**

NE Medium undead

Init +12; **Senses** darkvision 60 ft.; **Perception** +20

Aura frightful presence (30 ft., DC 20)

DEFENSE   HP 170

EAC 24; **KAC** 25

Fort +10; **Ref** +10; **Will** +16

Immunities undead immunities; **DR** 11/magic; **SR** 21

OFFENSE

Speed 30 ft.

Melee ultrathin longsword +19 (4d8+14 S)

Ranged elite semi-auto pistol +21 (3d6+10 E or F or P)

Offensive Abilities stranger's shot

STATISTICS

Str +3; **Dex** +8; **Con** —; **Int** +0; **Wis** +0; **Cha** +5

Skills Acrobatics +25, Athletics +25, Computers +20, Piloting +20, Stealth +25

Feats Quick Draw

Other Abilities unliving

Languages Common, Eoxian

Gear elite semi-auto pistols (4), ultrathin longsword

ECOLOGY

Environment any

Organization solitary

SPECIAL ABILITIES

Stranger's Shot (Su) As long as a pale stranger is using a small arm (even a broken or archaic one), he can make ranged attacks without provoking attacks of opportunity and without consuming ammunition. With each attack, the pale strange can choose to fire bullets (dealing piercing damage), electrical bolts (dealing electricity damage) or laser beams (dealing fire damage), regardless of the type of small arm used or the type of damage the weapon normally deals. These attacks never count as attacks from archaic weapons. Such attacks always target a foe's KAC, even when dealing energy damage. Additionally, if the pale stranger aims as a swift action, the next ranged attack he makes during that round ignores all concealment and cover (even total cover) and deals an additional 1d6 damage.

Pale strangers are wasted-looking undead that wear dry, dusty garb, usually a uniform or clothing with similar significance. They always carry one or more small arms, with many ancient pale strangers favoring the weapons of bygone eras.

A pale stranger arises from the corpse of a small arms expert who was killed through betrayal, was slain by a hated enemy, or died while seeking vengeance for an act committed against him or his family. The first act of an arisen pale stranger is to kill the person or entities responsible for his death.

PALE STRANGER TEMPLATE GRAFT (CR 4+)

Wielding mystical firearms, a pale stranger is an implacable foe.

Required Creature Type: Undead.

Required Array: Combatant or expert.

Traits: DR equal to CR, bypassed by magic; spell resistance equal to CR + 11.

Abilities: Stranger's shot (see above).

Feats: Quick Draw.

Suggested Ability Score Modifiers: Dexterity, Strength.

SHIMREEN

Shimreen soldier
LN Medium humanoid (shimreen)
Init +7; **Perception** +11

DEFENSE   HP 84
EAC 17; **KAC** 20
Fort +7; **Ref** +5; **Will** +6
Resistances electricity 5

OFFENSE
Speed 35 ft.
Melee crystal lance +14 (1d3+12 P)
Ranged thunderstrike sonic rifle +11 (1d10+5 So;
     critical deafen [DC 13]) or
     frag grenade II +11 (explode [15 ft., 2d6 P, DC 13])
Offensive Abilities amplify (1d4), charge attack,
     fighting styles (blitz)

STATISTICS
Str +5; **Dex** +3; **Con** +0; **Int** +2; **Wis** +0; **Cha** +0
Skills Acrobatics +11, Athletics +16,
     Engineering +11
Languages Shimreeni, Terran
Other Abilities radiant
Gear shimreen crystal extracarapace II
     (functions as lashunta ringwear II),
     thunderstrike sonic rifle with 1
     high-capacity batteries (20
     charge), frag grenades II (2)

ECOLOGY
Environment any
     (Shimrinsara)
Organization solitary, pair,
     or cluster (3–8)

SPECIAL ABILITIES
Amplify (Ex) Whenever
     a shimreen takes energy
     damage, she can
     voluntarily take
     an additional
     1d4 damage
     of the
     same type
     by amplifying
     the energy within her
     crystalline form. This
     empowers her next
     melee attack. The
     next melee attack
     the shimreen
     makes
     releases
     this
     energy,

RACIAL TRAITS
Ability Adjustments: +2 Dex, +2 Int, –2 Wis
Hit Points: 4

Size and Type: Shimreens are Medium humanoids with the shimreen subtype.
Amplify: See the stat block, using level instead of CR.
Electricity Resistance: Shimreens have electricity resistance 5, thanks to their crystalline structure.
Radiant: See the stat block.
Shift Limb: A shimreen can transform one of her arms into a weapon as a swift action. This crystal lance is a natural weapon that deals 1d3 lethal piercing damage with unarmed strikes; this attack doesn't count as archaic. A shimreen gain a unique version of the Weapon Specialization feat with her natural weapon at 3rd level, allowing her to add 1-1/2 × her character level to her damage rolls with her natural weapon (instead of just adding her character level, as usual).

dealing an additional amount of damage equal to the extra damage the shimreen took (and of the same type). The shimreen can't take additional damage again until she releases the energy she is storing. If unused, this stored energy dissipates after 10 minutes. The amount of extra damage the shimreen takes (and deals) increases to 2d4 at CR 8 and 3d4 at CR 16.

Radiant (Ex) Shimreens constantly emit light (dim, normal, or bright) in a 5-foot radius and are immune to the dazzled condition. Shimreens can adjust their current level of light as a move action, but they can never extinguish it.

Shimreens hail from the storm-ravaged planet of Shimrinsara (see page 62), and are humanoids formed of glowing, jagged crystal.

SHIMRINSARA

Storm-Torn World of Master Artisans

Diameter: ×1; **Mass:** ×2
Gravity: ×2
Location: The Vast
Atmosphere: Normal
Day: 32 hours; **Year:** 540 days

Shimrinsara is a storm-battered world whose inhabitants, called shimreens, dwell within dazzling metropolises under the protective confines of sparkling domes. However, rather than fear the planet's fierce squalls, the shimreens harness the energy produced to power their industries, and have done so for as long as they remember—even before the Gap, according to their surviving records. As elemental tempests (most often electrical, but cold-, fire-, and sonic-based storms are not unheard of) bombard the domes, their crystalline lattices absorb and store this energy within colossal batteries located deep underground. This results in brilliant cascades of pulsating light that dance along the domes' surfaces in constant kaleidoscopes of shifting hues. The structures also deflect the violent gales that rage outside, keeping the inhabitants inside dry and serene.

This abundant supply of energy frees the cities' inhabitants to engage in ways of life that focus on culture rather than the pursuit of resources. However, inhabitants of neighboring systems are aware of these assets, and some have periodically tried to conquer Shimrinsara from. This constant threat has led shimreens to develop a dual-caste society. The majority of shimreens belong to the worker caste: artisans, barristers, engineers, entertainers, and scientists. A second caste, the warrior caste, includes those of more militaristic personalities. However, over time, these soldiers' tactics have become an art form unto themselves, treating battle as an elegant dance. The most famous of shimreen warriors perform spectacles of artful martial displays in staged and broadcasted fights that draw sizable crowds from all across Shimrinsara.

There are seven domed metropolises on Shimrinsara. These cities, known as the Jewels of Shimreen, are connected via a sophisticated system of energized tethers. Storm barges with giant crystalline sails traverse the blinding squalls along these tethers, bringing trade between the seven Jewels. The brightest of these Jewels is the capital city of Kaniqlu, where a council of seven governs the planet, with each of the cities represented equally by an elected representative.

Thanks to the constant storms, the environments outside of the domes are hostile to living creatures that lack energy resistance. Numerous types of fauna thrive within this strange weather, however, and many scholars believe that these species must have connections to the Elemental Planes somewhere in their ancestry. Studies to prove these connections are ongoing.

Shimreens are humanoids with multihued, glowing crystal carapaces that they prune and manicure to delineate between the genders. Female shimreens exaggerate the crystals atop their jagged heads to form stylized crowns. Males, on the other hand, let their carapaces grow wild around their entire heads, calling these clusters their "manes." Regardless of gender, shimreens are tall and lanky, with full-grown adults cresting 7 feet. More about shimreens can be discovered on page 61.

NEXT MONTH

THE REACH OF EMPIRE

By Ron Lundeen

The Against the Aeon Throne Adventure Path begins! Hired to transport supplies to a new Pact Worlds colony in the Vast, the heroes discover that the sinister Azlanti Star Empire has invaded, occupied the colony with a small military force, and placed the colony's residents under its iron fist. With the help of a few brave rebels, the heroes can liberate the colony from its merciless oppressors, only to learn that the Azlanti are on this world to investigate a crashed starship from before the Gap. By confronting the Aeon Guard lieutenant within the ruin, the characters can learn that the Azlanti have taken both an experimental starship drive and one of the colonists—an old friend of the heroes—back to the Star Empire!

NAKONDIS COLONY

By Ron Lundeen

Bankrolled by AbadarCorp a little over a year ago, the colony on the misty, forested world of Nakondis might be considered by some to be the perfect place to start a new life. Despite the constant fog, the weather is temperate and the foliage abundant. The mountains contain a unique type of conductive tin that makes an excellent material for constructing electronics. Though small, the main settlement of Maledon's Landing is home to a group of good, law-abiding people. Come for a visit and you might just want to stay!

SHIPS OF THE IMPERIAL FLEET

By Lyz Liddell

The Imperial Fleet has aided the Azlanti Star Empire in conquering a dozen star systems in the past few hundred years. This article presents new systems and weapons for Imperial starships, as well as examples of the types of deadly vessels the Imperial Fleet can bring to bear.

SUBSCRIBE TO STARFINDER ADVENTURE PATH

The Against the Aeon Throne Adventure Path begins! Don't miss out on a single exciting volume—head over to **paizo.com/starfinder** and subscribe today to have Starfinder Roleplaying Game, Starfinder Adventure Path, and Starfinder Accessories products delivered to your door!

EMPIRE
OF
BONES

PART 1:
CLOSE TO
THE BONE

PART 2:
MASS GRAVES

PART 3:
IN THE MARROW

PART 4:
DEAD TO RIGHTS

CONTINUING THE
CAMPAIGN

SHIPS OF
THE LINE

SHIPS OF THE
CORPSE FLEET

ALIEN
ARCHIVES

CODEX OF
WORLDS

BRAVE NEW WORLDS!

STARFINDER®

PACT WORLDS

Experience the wonders of the Pact Worlds in this definitive, 216-page hardcover campaign setting for the Starfinder Roleplaying Game! The book contains detailed gazetteers for all worlds of the Absalom Pact, as well as a new character theme for each Pact World. Travel the galaxy with the starships of Aballon, Verces, the Hellknights, the Iomedaeans, or the Xenowardens, or play as a member of one of six new alien races: shapechanging astrazoans, rolling bantrids, undead borais, plantlike khizars, robotic SROs, or winged strix. With tons of new archetypes, feats, spells, equipment, and NPC stat blocks, *Starfinder Pact Worlds* reveals the secrets and mysteries of the solar system and its inhabitants in all their science fantasy glory!

AVAILABLE NOW!